Systematic Analogue Computer Programming

Systematic Analogue Computer Programming

An introduction for students of science and engineering

Second Edition

A S CHARLESWORTH

Senior Hybrid Programmer
School of Mathematics, University of Bath

J R FLETCHER

Lecturer in Engineering Mathematics and Analogue Computing
School of Mathematics, University of Bath

Pitman Publishing

PITMAN PUBLISHING LIMITED
39 Parker Street, London WC2B 5PB

Associated Companies
Copp Clark Ltd, Toronto
Fearon Pitman Publishers Inc, Belmont, California
Pitman Publishing New Zealand Ltd, Wellington
Pitman Publishing Pty Ltd, Melbourne

First published in Great Britain 1967
Second Edition 1974
Reprinted 1974, 1976, 1978

Reproduced and printed by photolithography and bound in
Great Britain at The Pitman Press, Bath

Camera copy prepared by Morgan-Westley **/W**

ISBN 0 273 00375 5

PREFACE TO SECOND EDITION

The first edition of this book grew from six years of practical
experience in teaching analogue computing to mathematics and
engineering students; the second edition is the result of a further
six years of such experience, and with students from a continually
broadening spectrum of studies (including chemists, chemical
engineers, physicists, building technologists, and post-graduate
short-course students from many different disciplines). We have
received invaluable help in the form of constructive criticism from
many students, and from colleagues in this and other Universities
and Polytechnics who have made use of the book in its original form;
we hope that this "feedback" will have improved the book both from
the point of view of the class-teacher and from that of the student
who uses the book as a self-teaching aid.

    Much of the original material has stood the test of time and
usage and remains unchanged. One of the more important changes is
the inclusion of the new Chapter 5, to assist the *beginner* in the
matter of writing analogue laboratory reports. Time-scaling is now
introduced at an earlier stage. The chapter on Transfer Functions
has been extensively revised, and we particularly wish to thank
Dr. J. E. Marshall of the University of Bath for his advice and
criticism on this chapter. The chapter on diode circuits has been
brought up to date by the inclusion of patching as well as circuit
diagrams, and additional circuits needed for use primarily on 10 V
DC reference machines; we offer also an improved simulation of the
effect of semi-elastic end-stops.

    One deliberate omission must be mentioned; there are some
problems involving some types of non-linearity which are better
tackled by using hybrid techniques than by pure analogue methods
alone - but we have decided against introducing detailed discussion
of such techniques in this book, feeling - rightly or wrongly -
that the book should confine itself to basic analogue methods.

    Additional examples for laboratory use have been included where
experience has shown the need for them, and the Miscellaneous
Examples for Programming at the end of the book have been augmented
by several examples taken from examination papers and assessed
laboratory projects set by the University of Bath over the past few
years; we are indebted to the University for permission to use
such questions. The majority of the Miscellaneous Examples for
Programming are now given in S.I. units where appropriate.

Finally, we hope that in its "new look" the book will confirm old friendships and make many new ones. We shall continue to be sincerely grateful for all comments and criticisms, and for the detection of any remaining errors - the latter are, of course, entirely the responsibility of each author's collaborator.

A. S. Charlesworth
J. R. Fletcher

PREFACE TO FIRST EDITION

Universities, technical colleges and similar institutions are
rapidly expanding their computing services generally, and there is
a growing demand for basic training in analogue computing techniques
in many courses at both undergraduate and postgraduate levels. Such
training calls for suitable textbooks, including at least a few
which are elementary enough to be suitable for use by undergraduate
students meeting the subject for the first time. In the case of
digital computing there are several good elementary textbooks already
available, in addition to those at a more advanced level; in the
case of analogue computing, however, the majority of books available
are of the more advanced kind. It must be said at once that many of
the books dealing with analogue computing and analogue computers
(both subjects often occurring between the same pair of covers) are
excellent works, being both thorough in their coverage and well
presented. Many of these books are American in origin, and due
partly to this and partly to their extensive treatment, they are
sometimes expensive - perhaps prohibitively so from the standpoint
of many students, for whom the topic of analogue computing may form
only a small proportion of the total content of their studies. The
authors of this present book believe that there is a need for a
relatively cheap and relatively elementary textbook on the subject,
and have attempted to do little more than to lay some firm foundations upon which the reader may build an edifice of more advanced
work.

    In the field of digital computation there is, nowadays, a clear
distinction between the designer of the computer itself and the
operator or programmer who does the computing; the programmer, in
effect, treats the machine as a collection of "black boxes" which
solves problems, and the preparation of programmes in various computer languages can be learned without the need for detailed knowledge of how the black boxes work. In the field of analogue computation the distinction between the designer and the programmer has
been less clear; the electric analogue computer had its birth and
childhood in the electronics laboratory, and has often been designed,
built and operated by the same person or team. This process has
obscured the division between design and programming, as is evident
from those of the books on the subject in which analogue programming
is inextricably interwoven with circuit theory; the authors of the
present book, however, feel that (as in digital computing) efficient
programming need not require detailed knowledge of how the black
boxes work - in other words, there is a case for making some distinction between analogue computers and analogue computing, and this

book is primarily concerned with the latter. Nevertheless, the
authors will admit that the analogue computer programmer does need
to know a little of what goes on inside, and the reader of this
book will require a little knowledge of electrical theory - but not
much more than an acquaintance with the laws of Ohm and Kirchhoff.
In addition, the reader should have some familiarity with the kind
of differential equations which figure in the majority of first and
second year courses in mathematics, physics or engineering.

The authors hope that the reader of this book can come to look
upon the analogue computer as a usable tool (like the slide-rule,
the desk calculator and the digital computer), and that he (or she)
will acquire confidence in the handling of that tool in solving
problems which arise from the reader's own technological discipline.
Such confidence can come only from a certain amount of practical
experience, and the time available for such experience is necessarily
very limited in most college courses. The authors have found that,
in such circumstances, the quickest way to gain confidence is for
the student to adopt a formal framework of simple rules - rules
which can either obviate troubles before they arise or detect them
if and when they do, and rules which provide a computer solution
which can be properly interpreted in terms of the problem being
solved. This book is about such a framework of rules. In the early
chapters, the formulation of the rules is gone into in detail, and
the basic concepts of programming are reduced to a set routine; all
the major points are illustrated by working examples, the programming
for which is set out in full, and exercises suitable for laboratory
practice follow each section. As the student progresses further
through the book, detailed working of the examples occurs less and
less, and in the later chapters the authors do not presume to do
more than merely introduce some of the more advanced topics of the
subject. The student who needs to study these topics in more depth
should go on to read one or more of the books referred to in the
bibliography.

From amongst many colleagues on the staff of the Bath University
of Technology to whom the authors owe their sincere gratitude, two
persons in particular must be mentioned. One is Dr. J. R. Barker,
without whose unfailing interest and encouragement the draft of
the book might never have reached completion; the other is Mrs.
R.H.M. Westley, who in her own time typed the draft and re-typed
the final manuscript - and for whose care, expertise and quite
exemplary patience (in the teeth of all that the authors could do
in the way of making successive modifications), no praise is high
enough.

A. S. Charlesworth
J. R. Fletcher

CONTENTS

x

INTRODUCTION

An analogue computer is a piece of equipment whose component parts can be arranged to satisfy a given set of equations, usually simultaneous ordinary differential equations. If a physical system whose properties are to be studied can be described by such a set of equations, the study may often conveniently be carried out on the analogue computer.

In the electronic analogue computer variables are represented by continuously variable voltages, and integration is performed by a physical process involving the accumulation of electric charge on a capacitor. In the digital computer, integration is performed by a step-by-step incremental process involving counting. The comparison between balance-wheel (or pendulum) clocks and electric induction motor clocks illustrates the difference between the two types of computer: in balance-wheel or pendulum controlled clocks, the hands are advanced in discrete steps, one for each oscillation of the balance or pendulum. Such clocks are digital devices, integrating by adding angular displacements over a sequence of discrete small time intervals. In the electric induction motor clocks, the position of the hands changes continuously - such clocks are analogue devices, integrating the angular velocity of the motor shaft continuously with respect to time.

Numbers are supplied to a digital computer as sets of pulses, and the machine then carries out arithmetic or logical processes on the numbers in sequential fashion, following the instructions given to it in the 'programme' employed. On an analogue computer, the basic computing elements are able to add, subtract, multiply and integrate continuously varying voltages; hence a problem is solved by arranging these basic computing elements in such a way that the resulting electrical system satisfies the mathematical equations which describe the problem.

An analogue computer is used to solve problems about a physical system when it is inconvenient, dangerous or economically impossible to experiment with the system itself. For example, the design of an aircraft autopilot can be tested safely on the ground by connecting it to an analogue computer which obeys the dynamics of the aircraft to which the autopilot will ultimately be connected. To go further, parts of the autopilot itself might initially have been simulated and studied on the analogue computer because this is easier and cheaper than building an unsatisfactory autopilot in the first place.

A second example is the design of a motor-car suspension system. The differential equations obeyed by the masses and stiffnesses of the suspension can be simulated on the analogue computer and the parameters can be changed rapidly (by adjusting potentiometers) until a satisfactorily smooth ride is simulated. At that stage, the expensive process of fabricating a real suspension system is usually worth carrying out.

Analogue computers are much used by engineers who can use their engineering knowledge and intuition in adjusting the analogue to give a desired performance; the analogue gives a virtually instant-aneous response to such adjustments which makes it a very convenient tool. At the present time, this is quicker than solving the system equations on a digital computer for various values of the parameters. Of course, no computer, analogue or digital, will give an analytic or general solution to a set of equations.

The analogue computer, by its ability to solve equations which can be expressed in terms of addition, multiplication, integration etc., and so simulate different physical systems on different occa-sions, is a development of the much older idea of using scale models such as model ships in a water tank in the design of ocean-going vessels, or model aircraft in wind-tunnels when designing full-scale aircraft. With models, the two systems are similar physically; with analogues, they are only similar in that they both obey the same equations. However, the analogue computer is more flexible than a direct model for it can represent quite different physical systems on different occasions.

Sometimes analogue and digital computers are used together, connections being made via units which convert analogue signals into their digital equivalents, and vice versa. It is then possible to use the analogue computer to solve differential equations, which it does more quickly than the digital computer, and to use the digital computer to carry out algebraic operations to generate and store functions, and possibly to carry out any integrations which are required to be particularly accurate without needing to be high-speed. Such computing is one form of what is known as 'hybrid computing'.

CHAPTER 1

BASIC COMPUTING ELEMENTS

This book will be restricted to discussion of general purpose electronic analogue computers only.

There are three basic computing units which perform mathematical operations on the machine variables:

(1) Coefficient multiplier
(2) Summer
(3) Integrator.

In addition, +1 and -1 are available on the computer.

The symbols we shall use for the three basic units have not been internationally agreed, but are generally accepted. These symbols are as follows.

1.1 Coefficient multiplier

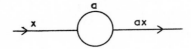

Figure 1

If x is the input variable, ax is the output variable where a is the constant setting of the multiplier. The only restriction on the coefficient multiplier is that $0 \leqslant a \leqslant 1$

1.2 Summer

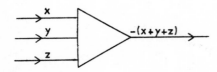

Figure 2

If x, y and z are input variables the output variable is $-(x + y + z)$.
Note that summers have an inherent sign reversal.

1.3 Integrator

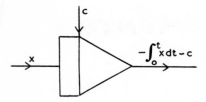

Figure 3

If x is the input variable the output variable is the integral of x
with respect to time. The integrator also has an inherent sign
reversal between input and output.

The initial condition (I.C.) is the value of the *integrator
output* when t = 0; the input required to obtain it acts as any
other input does as far as this sign reversal is concerned. Thus
in Figure 3, the integrator output when t = 0 is

$$-\int_{0}^{t=0} x \, dt \;-\; c = -c$$

(since the I.C. input is $+c$).

In addition to the above basic units, there are other computing
units among which are various forms of multiplier and function generator. These will be covered in more detail in chapters 12 and 14.

CHAPTER 2
LINEAR ORDINARY DIFFERENTIAL EQUATIONS

2.1 First order differential equations

Example 1

$$3\dot{x} + 2x = 0 \quad \text{given that } x = \frac{1}{2} \text{ at } t = 0$$

The first step to the solution is to arrange the equation so that the highest derivative alone is on the left-hand side:

$$\dot{x} = -\frac{2}{3}x \tag{i}$$

Suppose that we have the highest derivative dx/dt available; if we pass this into an integrator we shall obtain (ignoring, for the moment, the I.C.) $-x$ at the output:

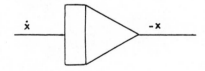

Figure 4

If this integrator is followed by a coefficient multiplier set to $\frac{2}{3}$ we shall obtain $-\frac{2}{3}x$:

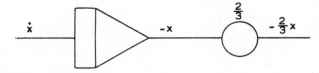

Figure 5

Now $-\frac{2}{3}x$ is the right-hand side of equation (i); the latter states that $-\frac{2}{3}x$ is equal to $\dot{x}$; if, therefore, we connect the right-hand side of Figure 5 to the left-hand side we are, in effect, equating

3

the two quantities concerned and thus satisfying the equation:

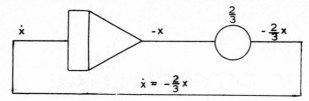

$$\dot{x} = -\frac{2}{3}x$$

Figure 6

This is the CLOSED LOOP diagram for this problem and it only remains for us to incorporate the initial condition that $x = \frac{1}{2}$ at $t = 0$. Thus the complete closed loop flow diagram will be

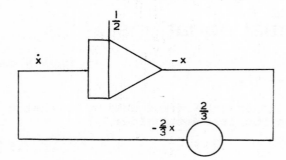

Figure 7

Note: Since the integrator output is $-x$, and when $t = 0$, $- x = - \frac{1}{2}$ it follows that the I.C. input must be $+ \frac{1}{2}$.

Example 2

$$4\dot{x} + 3x = 4 \quad \text{given } x = 0 \text{ at } t = 0$$

Rearrange: $\dot{x} = 1 - \frac{3}{4}x$

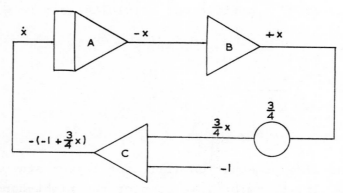

Figure 8

4

Summer B is used only to change the sign of x and is often termed an inverter.

Figure 8 is the closed loop diagram. Some computer operators prefer an OPEN LOOP diagram:

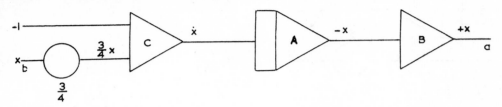

Figure 9

Inspection will show that Figure 9 and Figure 8 are identical except for the completion of the feedback loop between a and b.

Each system has its merits: the open loop diagram is simpler to draw for first considerations especially in complicated problems; the closed loop diagram is to be favoured however as a final working diagram since it is less likely to lead to omissions when making use of the flow diagram on the actual computer.

Exercise 1

Draw the open and closed loop diagrams for the following equations:

(1) $4\dot{x} + 3x = 0$ given $x = \frac{1}{4}$ at $t = 0$

(2) $8\dot{x} = 2 - 6x$ given $x = 0$ at $t = 0$

(3) $5\dot{x} + 2x + 4 = 0$ given $x = \frac{1}{3}$ at $t = 0$

(4) $3\dot{x} + x - 6 = 0$ given $x = \frac{1}{4}$ at $t = 0$

An integrator unit may be used as a dual purpose unit, for integration and summation simultaneously:

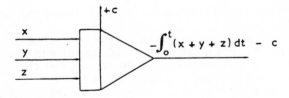

Figure 10

Returning to Example 2:

$4\dot{x} + 3x = 4$ given $x = 0$ at $t = 0$

i.e. $\dot{x} = 1 - \frac{3}{4}x$ (ii)

5

If $\dot{x}$ is not required as a solution, the functions of summer C and integrator A (Figure 8) may be performed by a single integrator:

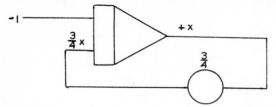

Figure 11

It can be seen that by not generating $\dot{x}$ we save two units and greatly simplify the diagram. For this reason the highest derivative is usually not computed unless it is expressly required. The inputs to the integrator are -1 and $+\frac{3}{4}x$; these taken together are equivalent to $-\dot{x}$ from equation (ii) and thus when integrated will give $+x$ as an output.
Note: Although the integrator then performs two functions, it is still only a single computer unit, and *only one* change of sign takes place.
     If we change the -1 input to $+1$, observe that this changes the signs of the variables *all the way round the loop* i.e. $-x$ will be generated.

Exercise 2

Repeat Exercise 1 giving closed loop diagrams so that the highest derivatives are not generated and $+x$ is produced as the final output in each case.

Example 3

$$4\dot{x} + 5x = 6 \qquad \text{given } x = 0 \text{ at } t = 0$$

Rearrange: $\dot{x} = \frac{6}{4} - \frac{5}{4}x$

This will involve multiplying by $\frac{6}{4}$ and $\frac{5}{4}$, i.e. constant coefficients greater than 1; obviously this cannot be implemented by coefficient multipliers alone.
     We have so far considered only summers and integrators with INPUT GAINS of 1; in practice input gains of 1 and 10 are usually available. In addition, integrators may sometimes have an extra gain factor of 10; to show whether this is present or not the integrator symbol has a 1 or 10 inserted in its nose as shown in Figure 12(b) or (c). From its position, this factor is referred to as the NOSE-GAIN of the integrator. Summers almost always have nose-gains of 1; for some special purposes they may, on occasion, be required to have a nose-gain of 1/10.

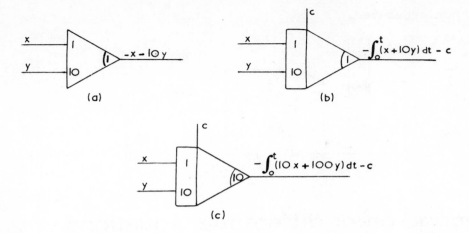

(a) (b)

(c)

Figure 12

To multiply by a constant $1 \leqslant a \leqslant 10$ a coefficient multiplier set to $\frac{a}{10}$ is followed by a gain of 10:

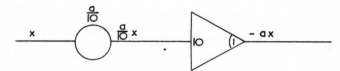

Figure 13

So to solve $\dot{x} = \frac{6}{4} - \frac{5}{4}x$

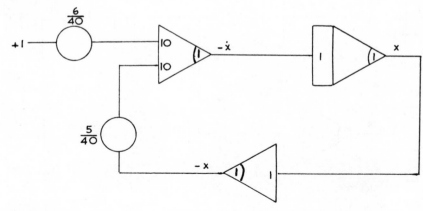

Figure 14

or if $\dot{x}$ is not generated,

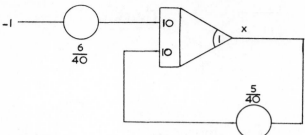

Figure 15

2.2 Second order differential equations

The procedure for second order differential equations (or, in fact, for equations of any order greater than one) is the same as for first order, i.e. the equation is first rearranged to make the highest derivative the subject.

Example 4

$$2\ddot{x} + 3\dot{x} + 4x = 1 \quad \text{given } x = 1, \ \dot{x} = 0 \text{ at } t = 0$$

Rearrange: $\quad \ddot{x} = \dfrac{1}{2} - \dfrac{3}{2}\dot{x} - 2x$

If $\ddot{x}$ is generated:

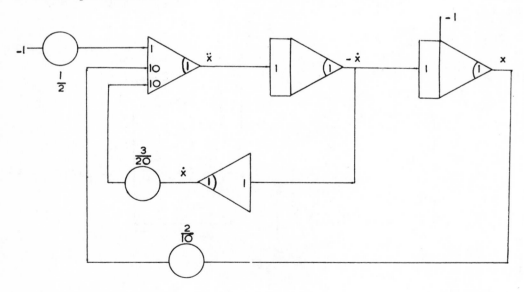

Figure 16

8

If $\ddot{x}$ is not generated:

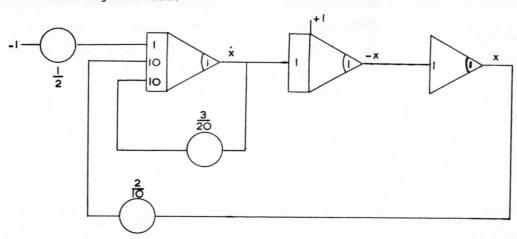

Figure 17

Exercise 3

Draw the closed loop diagram for the following equations:

(1) $4\ddot{x} + 3\dot{x} + 5x = 2$ given $\dot{x} = \frac{1}{3}$, $x = 0$ at $t = 0$

(2) $2\ddot{x} + 6\dot{x} + x = 4$ given $\dot{x} = \frac{1}{4}$, $x = 1$ at $t = 0$
                                   $\ddot{x}$ is required

(3) $\ddot{x} + 6x = 5$ given $\dot{x} = -\frac{1}{2}$, $x = \frac{1}{4}$ at $t = 0$

(4) $\ddot{x} + 3x = 4 - 2\dot{x}$ given $\dot{x} = 0$, $x = -\frac{1}{3}$ at $t = 0$
                                   $\ddot{x}$ is required

(5) $3\ddot{x} + k\dot{x} + 2x = 4$ given $\dot{x} = x = 0$ at $t = 0$
                                   solve for $0 < k < 10$

(6) $2\ddot{x} + k\dot{x} + 4x = 2$ for $k = 6$, 3, 0 in turn, for the cases
          (i) given $\dot{x} = x = 0$ at $t = 0$
       (ii) given $\dot{x} = \frac{7}{8}$ and $x = -\frac{1}{2}$ at $t = 0$

(7) $5\ddot{x} + \lambda\dot{x} + 80x = 25$ for λ in the range $5 < \lambda < 50$ and
                                   computing $\ddot{x}$, $\dot{x}$ and x for the cases
          (i) given $\dot{x} = x = 0$ at $t = 0$
       (ii) given $\dot{x} = \frac{1}{4}$, $x = -\frac{1}{4}$ at $t = 0$

2.3 Simultaneous differential equations

These equations lead to two equation diagrams which are inter-connected.

Example 5

$$\ddot{x} + 4\dot{x} + 2x - 2y = 0 \brace 3x + \dot{y} + y = 0$$ given that $x = y = 0$, $\dot{x} = 1$ at $t = 0$

Rearrange:

$$\ddot{x} = 2y - 4\dot{x} - 2x$$
$$\dot{y} = -y - 3x$$

Consider first the open loop diagrams shown in Figure 18 opposite.
All the inputs on the left-hand side of the diagram appear as outputs on the right-hand side and can be cross-connected to produce the closed loop diagram shown in Figure 19.

Exercise 4

Draw closed loop diagrams for:

(1) $\ddot{x} + 3\dot{x} + 4y = 6 \brace \dot{y} + 2x = 1$ given $\dot{x} = 0$, $x = -\frac{1}{2}$, $y = +\frac{1}{3}$ at $t = 0$.

(2) $\ddot{x} + 4x + 3\dot{y} = 7 \brace \ddot{y} + 4y + x = 2$ given all I.C.s $= 0$; $\ddot{x}$ and $\ddot{y}$ required.

(3) $4\dot{x} + 3y = 0 \brace \ddot{y} + 3x + 4\dot{y} = 7$ given $\dot{y} = 0$, $x = \frac{1}{2}$, $y = 1$ at $t = 0$.

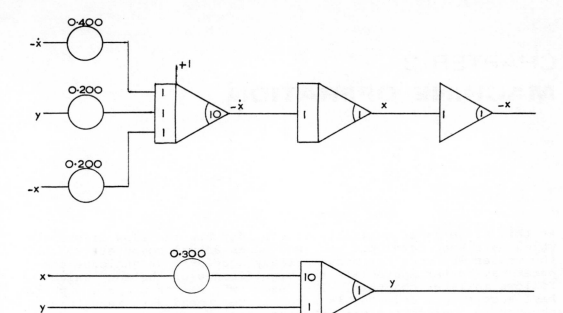

Figure 18

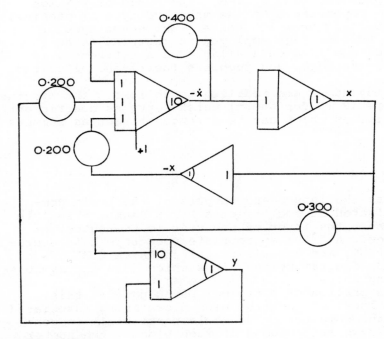

Figure 19

CHAPTER 3
MACHINE OPERATION

At this stage it is desirable to consider how the flow diagrams which have been developed are used on an actual computer, so that the reader who does not possess ready access to an analogue computer may better appreciate the significance of the work which follows in later chapters. The reader who is fortunate enough to have access to a computer is strongly recommended to read this chapter in conjunction with the computer manufacturer's instructions and to put some simple problems on the machine, even at this early stage.

Voltages within the analogue computer are used to represent the variables of the problem being solved. The range of voltage variation is limited; depending upon the make and type of machine, the limits may be ± 10, ± 50 or ± 100 volts. Whichever type of machine is used, the limit voltage employed is referred to as the MACHINE UNIT; this voltage is made available as a reference, in both positive and negative form, and supplies the +1 and -1 (first referred to on p.1).

The basic computing units are realized as follows: the machine contains potentiometers (POTS for short) which serve as coefficient multipliers, and amplifiers which can be arranged to act as summers or integrators.

3.1 Patching

In the actual computer, the inputs and outputs of the basic computing units are terminated at sockets on a PATCH PANEL. Flexible wires are used to connect the input of one unit to the output of another by being plugged into the appropriate sockets - this operation is known as PATCHING, and the wires, called PATCH CORDS, are represented on the flow diagram by the lines which join the symbols for the basic computing units.

Figure 20 shows a portion of a typical patch panel; this portion contains six blocks of sockets, each block being associated with an amplifier in the computer. The whole panel will, in general, possess several rows and columns of such blocks, the number depending upon the size of the machine concerned. The blocks are given a coordinate address, using letters and numbers.

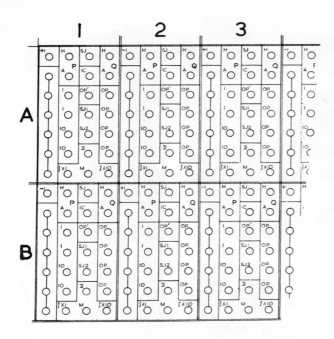

Figure 20

In the majority of cases, the blocks are colour-coded for rapid
identification, each section of sockets performing a certain function
having its own particular colour, i.e. all input sockets of one
colour, all output sockets another, and so on.

Each block shown in Figure 20 has 28 sockets, arranged in the
following colour-coded sections:

(*a*) Sections directly associated with the relevant amplifier (i.e.
with sockets having internal electrical connection to the
amplifier in some way):

4 inputs, two ×1 and two ×10.
4 "commoned" outputs, marked OP.
1 initial condition.
4 mode sockets: by coupling the one marked M to one of the
other three sockets in this section, the amplifier can be
arranged to sum, to integrate with a nose gain of 1, or to
integrate with a nose gain of 10. (On some computers, a
similar choice of amplifier operation is performed by using
switches on a control panel, and not by patching on the patch
panel.)
1 feedback socket, marked OP', and
3 summing-junction sockets, marked SJ, SJ$_1$ and SJ$_2$: the functions of these sockets may be ignored for the time being - for
most normal computing purposes OP' is patched to one of the OP
sockets and SJ$_1$ is patched to SJ$_2$; this applies to *all* blocks
on the patch panel whether or not all the amplifiers are being
used in a given problem.

13

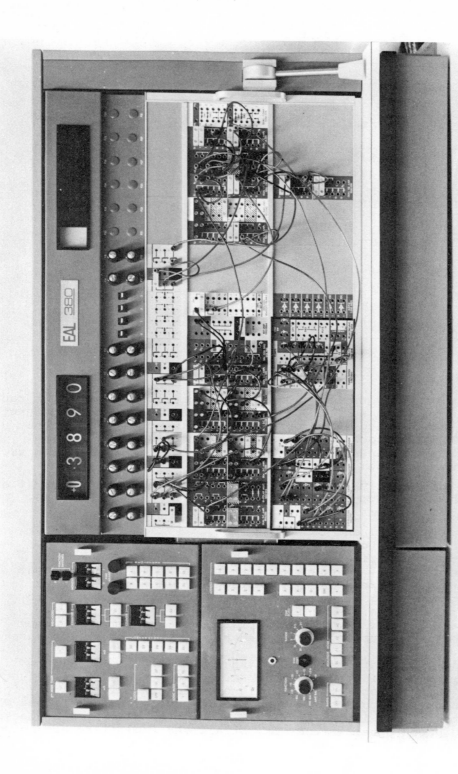

EAL 380 DESK TOP ANALOGUE COMPUTER

THE AUTHORS AT THE UNIVERSITY OF BATH RESEARCH HYBRID INSTALLATION (*b*) Sections not directly associated with the amplifier (i.e. with sockets which have no internal electrical connection to the amplifier):

1 reference, either positive (+1 MU) or negative (-1 MU).
6 sockets, internally connected to each other, to act as a commoning strip or bus-bar.
2 pairs of potentiometer sockets: each pair consists of an input (marked H, for high end) and an output (marked A, for arm). When giving the potentiometer an address, the left-hand pair is usually termed the P-pot, and the right-hand pair the Q-pot, of the block concerned.

ALLOCATION OF COMPUTING ELEMENTS

Before the computer is patched, the flow diagram already prepared must have the addresses of all computing elements to be used clearly marked in the appropriate element symbols. It is *essential* that the flow diagram be both neat and sufficiently large for everything shown on it to be easily read. Any untidiness in its presentation will almost inevitably lead to mistakes in the ensuing computation - it should always be remembered that the flow diagram acts as the Blueprint of the problem.

Taking care in the allocation of computing elements will result in a neatly patched panel; the 'flow' of patch cords across the panel should be kept as even as possible, for example:

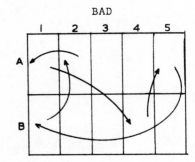
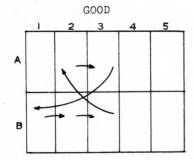

Figure 23

Consider the following example:

Example 6

Solve $\dot{x} + \frac{1}{2} + \frac{3}{2}x = 0$ given $x = \frac{1}{3}$ at $t = 0$, and computing $\dot{x}$.

Rearrange: $\dot{x} = -\frac{1}{2} - \frac{3}{2}x$

The machine flow diagram in which the pot settings are less than 1, showing amplifier gains and possible unit allocations, is:

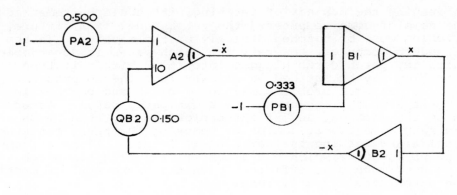

Figure 24

A pot list must next be made out:

Pot	Setting	Remarks
PA2	0·500	
QB2	0·150	
PB1	0·333	I.C./B1

Note that I.C. pots should always show the address of the relevant amplifier.

The problem may now be put on the computer by patching the flow diagram on the patch panel as shown in Figure 25:

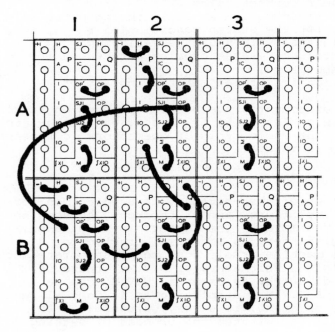

Figure 25

Before leaving the subject of patching, it should be remarked that, in the case of some computers, the patch panel is a fixture, i.e. each problem must be patched directly on the machine. In the majority of modern computers however, the patch panel is detachable (together with any patch cords plugged into it); with this type of panel, the problem may be patched on it away from the computer itself. In fact, several problems may be prepared and patched in advance of their computation, each on its own patch panel. After computation on the machine, any of these problems may then be stored for possible future re-investigation by removing the panel concerned from the machine and leaving the patch on it intact. It is evident that the type of computer which has a number of detachable patch panels can be used much more efficiently than can the type of machine in which the patch panel is a fixture.

3.2 Controls

Computer controls vary in detail from one make and model of machine to another, but are usually grouped together on a single CONTROL PANEL. A typical control panel comprises the following:

MODE SWITCH

This controls internal relays which set the computer into one of the following states: Pot Set, Problem Check, Compute, Hold and, possibly Repetitive Operation (Rep-Op).

In POT SET, the computer is in the correct state for setting the coefficient pots to their correct value.

In PROBLEM CHECK (sometimes called Re-Set), the computer solves the problem patched on it, for the static condition of $t = 0$, i.e. gives as outputs all the initial values of the variables.

In COMPUTE, the computer solves the problem patched on it against continuously variable time.

In HOLD, the computation is "frozen" at the instant of switching.

In REP-OP, the computer computes the problem patched on it for some pre-determined time (e.g. for 1, 5, or 10 sec, etc.), re-sets to $t = 0$ and re-computes; the whole cycle of operations is repeated as long as the Rep-Op mode is in use.

OUTPUT SELECTION

A selector switch, or a group of push-buttons, is used to monitor the outputs of any of the amplifiers, and of the pots, by showing the output concerned on a voltmeter. The latter, in many cases, displays the output in digital form as a decimal fraction of a Machine Unit; even if the machine itself does not incorporate such an instrument (called a Digital Voltmeter, or D.V.M.) there is usually a facility provided whereby an external D.V.M. can be connected to the machine. A D.V.M., displaying as it does all mon- itored values as fractions of an MU, is a very valuable aid to computation and also greatly facilitates the process of setting pots to their correct values.

OVERLOAD INDICATION

An indicator, one for each computer amplifier, will light up if the output of its associated amplifier should appreciably exceed 1 MU. Sometimes, in conjunction with the overload indicators, there is a switch; with this switch in its Hold position, the computer will automatically go into the Hold mode should any amplifier overload, so that the amplifier overload indicators may be inspected to discover which is the offending unit. If the computer does not have this facility, and an overload light shows during a computation, the computation should be repeated and the overload indicators carefully watched so that the amplifier(s) which is (are) overloading may be ascertained. With this information, the flow diagram, pot settings and patching of the problem, should be re-examined for possible mistakes.

3.3 Setting pots

Every potentiometer on the machine will have its own individual setting knob. The setting knobs are usually grouped together, on a pot panel or pot shelf.

Coefficient pots are set as soon as the complete patching has been put on the computer; the selector switch (or appropriate push-button) is used to monitor the pot to be set, with the mode switch in the Pot Set position. (On some computers, each pot setting knob may have its own individual button or key switch to be operated.) The appropriate pot setting knob is then adjusted until the D.V.M. shows the required setting as shown in the pot list.

INITIAL CONDITION SETTING

The I.C.s are set via pots, but on some machines they are not set in the same way as are the coefficient pots, and careful attention should be paid to the manufacturer's instructions regarding this point. In all cases, the setting of an I.C. gives the *output of the integrator concerned* some initial value, and it follows that the computer should be in the Problem Check mode. The value at the output of the pot being used is not important; it is the output of the integrator which matters. The integrator output is therefore monitored (using the output selector) and the I.C. pot setting knob adjusted until this output is of the correct value.

Following the setting of all coefficient pots and I.C.s, the computation may be run by switching the mode switch to Compute (or to Rep-Op, if desired and if the facility is available).

3.4 Recording solutions

One convenient way of displaying a solution, particularly for preliminary investigation, is on a cathode ray oscilloscope (C.R.O., or 'scope, for short). This instrument has a glass screen on which a spot of light can be moved in both horizontal (X) and vertical (Y) directions by varying the voltages to the X and Y inputs to the instrument (Fig.26).

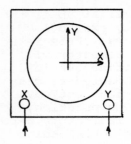

Figure 26

The 'scope controls may be adjusted so that

   (i) for $X = Y = 0$ the spot is in the centre of the screen,
 (ii) + 1 MU fed to X moves the spot to the extreme right of the
       screen,
(iii) + 1 MU fed to Y moves the spot to the top of the screen.

Thus:

Figure 27

In order to display a solution $f(t)$ against time t, the X deflection can represent t and the Y deflection can represent $f(t)$. The
X input must then be the ramp voltage shown in Figure 28:

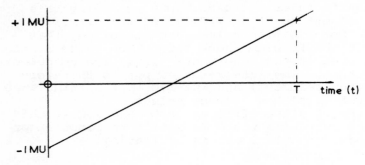

Figure 28

The equation of this function is $y = kt + c$, where $c = -1$ and
$k = 2/T$ (T being the required computing period). An easy way of
obtaining y is to write down the differential equation for which y
is the solution, and programme the computer to solve that equation:
evidently the equation required is:

20

$$\dot{y} = k \quad \text{given } y = c \text{ at } t = 0$$

$$\text{i.e.} \quad \dot{y} = \frac{2}{T} \quad \text{given } y = -1 \text{ at } t = 0$$

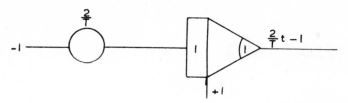

Figure 29

Thus, if computation is required for a 5 sec Rep-Op, the pot
allocated to the $2/T$ coefficient would be set to $2/5 = 0.400$; for
a 20 sec computing period the pot would be set to 0.100, and so on.
The 'scope is scaled for ± 1 MU along both axes by first
centring the spot with no inputs on X or Y, then plugging $+1$ MU
into X and Y and adjusting the relevant gain controls to give the
required amount of spot deflection in the two directions.
Another way of recording computer outputs is to use an $X-Y$
plotter. In this instrument, instead of a spot of light moving
across a screen, a pen is made to move across a sheet of graph
paper which has been inserted into the plotter. This produces a
permanent record of the computed solution, and one from which
measurements may be made. If desired, several solution curves may
be plotted on one piece of paper (using differently coloured inks
if need be), and a whole family of curves built up.
All $X-Y$ plotters have four basic controls:

Two SHIFT controls (sometimes marked Zero or Parallax): by using
these, one for X and one for Y, the pen may be moved to the
required position for zero inputs.
Two GAIN controls (sometimes marked Attenuator or Scale): by using
these, one for X and one for Y, the magnitude of pen deflection for
given inputs in the two directions may be varied.
Most $X-Y$ plotters also have a pen lift control, which enables the
pen to be lifted from the paper as and when required.

The same "drill" should be used for setting up both 'scopes
and plotters:

1. In the case of plotters ensure that the pen is lifted from the
    paper.
2. Set the spot, or pen, to the required zero position by using
    the shift controls with the input leads disconnected.
3. Apply $+1$ MU to both inputs, and adjust the gain controls to
    give the desired amount of deflection in the X and Y
    directions.
4. Remove the input leads and check that the spot, or pen,
    returns to the correct zero position. If necessary, steps 2
    and 3 are repeated.
Note. In the case of plotters, the final positions of the zero and
1 MU after steps 2 and 3 should be checked by dropping the pen on
to the graph paper, and lifting it again before each readjustment.

CHAPTER 4

AMPLITUDE SCALING

In Chapter 2 we discussed the preparation of simple flow diagrams
for first and second order linear differential equations and simultaneous differential equations. Before expanding this work further
to cover amplitude scaling and more complicated problems, it is
desirable to provide a set of individual machine equations each of
which will describe the function of a corresponding amplifier in the
flow diagram.

It will become apparent, as the work of this and later chapters
evolves, that there are two main reasons why this DECOMPOSITION process is of importance. First, it enables complicated problems to be
broken down into a group of simple first order differential equations
and simple algebraic (summation) equations. This in turn very greatly
simplifies the problem of fault-finding, and enables us to build up
a checking procedure which will isolate mistakes in programming which
otherwise might waste a considerable amount of commercially valuable
machine-time on the computer. Secondly (and to some extent related
to the reason first-mentioned) the decomposition process is of assistance in carrying out methodical AMPLITUDE SCALING of the problem,
as discussed later in this chapter. The word 'methodical' is used
advisedly - while it is true that many computer operators are able
to get by with a scaling "technique" largely composed of trial, error
and inspired guesswork, it is the authors' experience that such
'psychic' scaling is dangerously productive of mistakes, except in
the hands of thoroughly experienced programmers. Safety in scaling
demands a systematic approach, and the first step in this is the
reduction of the problem to a group of decomposed equations.

4.1 Decomposition

The flow diagram is prepared from the problem differential equation(s)
in the usual way, but does not show amplifier gains or pot settings;
we then write down separate equations, one for each amplifier with
the exception of inverters (whose equations are always trivial). In
writing the decomposed equations, we follow in this book the following conventions:

For INTEGRATORS

- $\frac{d}{dt}$ (Amplifier output) = Algebraic sum of amplifier inputs

For SUMMERS

- (Amplifier output) = Algebraic sum of amplifier inputs

EXAMPLE 7
Prepare flow diagram and decomposed equations for the simultaneous equations

$$2\ddot{x} + \dot{x} + 6x - 4y = 2$$
$$\ddot{y} + 4y - 4x = 0$$

given that all initial conditions are zero, and that $(x - y)$ is required as a solution.
Rewriting the problem equations:

$$\ddot{x} = -\frac{\dot{x}}{2} - x - 2(x - y) + 1$$

$$\ddot{y} = 4(x - y)$$

Flow diagram:

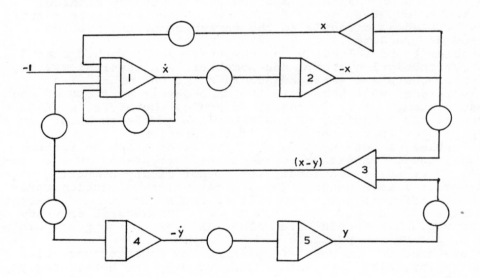

Figure 30

(Note that by arranging to compute $-x$ and $+y$ we have saved the use of two amplifiers.)

Numbering the amplifiers as shown (ignoring the inverter), we get the following

Decomposed problem equations:

Amplifier 1. $-\dfrac{d}{dt}(\dot{x}) = + x - 1 + 2(x - y) + \dfrac{\dot{x}}{2}$

Amplifier 2. $-\dfrac{d}{dt}(-x) = \dot{x}$

Amplifier 3. $-(x - y) = - x + y$

Amplifier 4. $-\dfrac{d}{dt}(-\dot{y}) = 4(x - y)$

Amplifier 5. $-\dfrac{d}{dt}(y) = - \dot{y}$

these should now be checked to see that they

(a) are consistent with the problem equations
(b) make mathematical "sense" within themselves.

In practice, these decomposed equations are processed further by being amplitude-scaled and then turned into MACHINE EQUATIONS; in their final form the machine equations will show the correct pot settings and amplifier gains to be used on the actual computer.
   Since the problem variables must be represented by machine variables in the computer, scale factors which are constants relating computer variables directly to the variables of the problem being studied are required.
   The problem to be solved on the computer can be regarded as a model of a mathematical system; the computer is a physical system, and if its components are arranged according to the model, its variables (voltages) will behave in the same manner as those of the mathematical system. It is necessary to scale, therefore, so that observations of the behaviour of the variables of the computer can be directly related to the variables of the problem.
   The variables of both systems may have limitations on their possible magnitudes. Magnitude scale factors are needed in the computer since, as we shall see later, the output of any computing unit must not exceed ± 1 machine unit (MU). The analogous problem variable will have different units and will be restricted to a different range i.e. -4 to +2 inches; or ± 100 ms^{-1}. For highest accuracy the computer variables should have values as near to the permissible maximum (i.e. ± 1 MU) as possible.
   There are a number of ways of relating the computer variables to the problem variables. We shall consider only one here, namely Machine Unit Scaling.

4.2 Normalized variables

We regard the outputs of the Computer Units as normalized or per unit quantities, the unit being 1 MU. If the output of a computing unit is θ (say) having a maximum value of θ_{max}, then the output is considered as a fraction of 1 MU, θ/θ_{max} (since by definition $\theta \leqslant \theta_{max}$, $|\theta/\theta_{max}|$ will always be $\leqslant 1$). Normalized variables may then be equated as follows:

e.g. for a problem variable x with a range of $\pm$ 10 metres,

$$\frac{x \text{ m}}{10 \text{ m}} = \left(\frac{\theta}{1}\right) \text{ MU}$$

The output of the computer unit in this case would be labelled $\left(\frac{x}{10}\right)$.
This means that if at some instant in time during a computation the
value of the computer variable $\left(\frac{x}{10}\right)$ is $0\cdot4$ MU the corresponding
value of x is given by

$$\frac{x}{10} = 0\cdot4 \qquad \text{i.e.} \quad x = 0\cdot4 \times 10 = 4 \text{ m}$$

The following examples will show the combined procedure of decomposition and the preparation of scaled machine equations.

EXAMPLE 8

$2\dot{x} + 14\cdot2x = 190$ given $x = 0$ at $t = 0$ and $\dot{x}$ is required

Suppose that $x_{max} = 20,$ $\dot{x}_{max} = 100$

Rearrange: $\dot{x} = -7\cdot1x + 95$

Unscaled flow diagram:

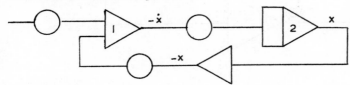

Figure 31

Decomposed equations:

Amplifier 1. $-(-\dot{x}) = -7\cdot1x + 95$

Amplifier 2. $-\frac{d}{dt}(x) = -\dot{x}$

Scaling: The machine variables will be $\left(\frac{x}{20}\right)$ and $\left(\frac{\dot{x}}{100}\right)$;   in terms
of these, the decomposed equations may be re-written as

Scaled equations:

1. $-\left(-\frac{\dot{x}}{100}\right) = \frac{7\cdot1}{100} \times 20\left(-\frac{x}{20}\right) + \frac{95}{100}$

2. $-\frac{d}{dt}\left(\frac{x}{20}\right) = \frac{100}{20}\left(-\frac{\dot{x}}{100}\right)$

The scaled equations may now be re-written in their final form,
separating pot settings from amplifier gains (we show the former in
square brackets) giving us the

Machine equations:

1. $\quad -\left(-\frac{\dot{x}}{100}\right) = [0\cdot142]10\left(-\frac{x}{20}\right) + [0\cdot95]1\,(1)$

2. $\quad -\frac{d}{dt}\left(\frac{x}{20}\right) = [0\cdot5]10\left(-\frac{\dot{x}}{100}\right)$

These are the actual equations that will be solved on the computer, the output of amplifier 1 (summer) being $\left(-\frac{\dot{x}}{100}\right)$ and that of amplifier 2 (integrator) being $\left(\frac{x}{20}\right)$. Inputs, with the necessary pot settings and input gains, are shown by the r.h.s. of the equations; we can now complete the full scaled flow diagram:

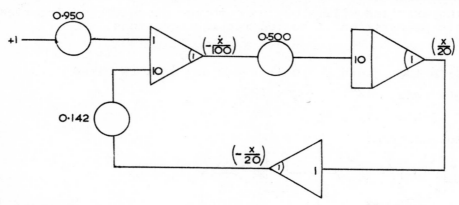

Figure 32

Note. The equation for amplifier 2 as written above suggests an input gain of 10, and implies therefore a nose-gain of 1. We can now add a further convention to our system of writing the machine equations, viz. that if an integrator having a nose-gain of 10 is required, the r.h.s. of its appropriate machine equation should be written with a nose-factor of 10. Thus machine equation 2 above could be re-written

$$-\frac{d}{dt}\left(\frac{x}{20}\right) = 10\left\{[0\cdot5]1\left(-\frac{\dot{x}}{100}\right)\right\}$$

which would imply the following slight change in the flow diagram:

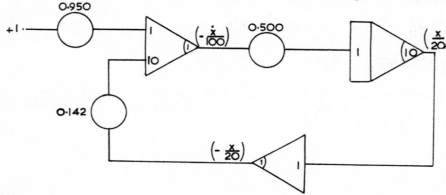

Figure 33

26

Example 9

$45\ddot{x} + 9\dot{x} + 900x = 400$ given $x = 0$, $\dot{x} = \frac{3}{4}$ at $t = 0$

Suppose that $\dot{x}_m = 2$, $x_m = 1$

Rearrange: $\ddot{x} = -\frac{1}{5}\dot{x} - 20x + \frac{80}{9}$

Unscaled flow diagram:

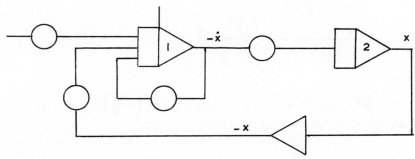

Figure 34

Decomposed equations:

Amplifier 1. $-\dfrac{d}{dt}(-\dot{x}) = -\dfrac{1}{5}\dot{x} - 20x + \dfrac{80}{9}$

Amplifier 2. $-\dfrac{d}{dt}(x) = -\dot{x}$

Machine variables will be $\left(\dfrac{\dot{x}}{2}\right)$ and $\left(\dfrac{x}{1}\right)$; hence we have the Scaled equations:

1. $-\dfrac{d}{dt}\left(-\dfrac{\dot{x}}{2}\right) = \dfrac{1}{5}\left(-\dfrac{\dot{x}}{2}\right) + \dfrac{20}{2}\left(-\dfrac{x}{1}\right) + \dfrac{40}{9}$

2. $-\dfrac{d}{dt}\left(\dfrac{x}{1}\right) = 2\left(-\dfrac{\dot{x}}{2}\right)$

From these we obtain the
Machine equations:

1. $-\dfrac{d}{dt}\left(-\dfrac{\dot{x}}{2}\right) = [0 \cdot 2]1\left(-\dfrac{\dot{x}}{2}\right) + 10\left(-\dfrac{x}{1}\right) + [0 \cdot 444]10(1)$

2. $-\dfrac{d}{dt}\left(\dfrac{x}{1}\right) = [0 \cdot 2]10\left(-\dfrac{\dot{x}}{2}\right)$

From which we get the completed scaled flow diagram:

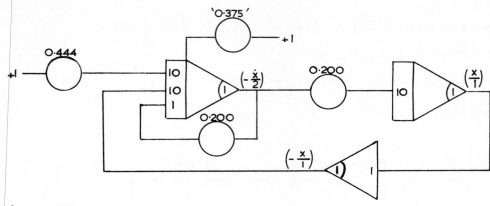

Figure 35

Note. Since the scaled output of amplifier 1 is $\left(-\frac{\dot{x}}{2}\right)$, and we are given that $\dot{x} = \frac{3}{4}$ at $t = 0$, we require that

$$\left(-\frac{\dot{x}}{2}\right) = -\frac{\frac{3}{4}}{2} = -\frac{3}{8} \text{ at } t = 0$$

Summarizing, the final machine equations for the problem will now show (by the conventions used) for every amplifier in the flow diagram other than inverters,

L.H.S. $\begin{cases} (a) & \text{whether the amplifier is a summer or an integrator} \\ (b) & \text{the magnitude and sign of the scaled output, in round} \\ & \text{brackets} \end{cases}$

R.H.S. $\begin{cases} (c) & \text{nose gain, in the case of integrators} \\ (d) & \text{pot settings, in square brackets} \\ (e) & \text{input gains, 1 or 10} \\ (f) & \text{number of inputs, their sign and their scaling, in} \\ & \text{round brackets.} \end{cases}$

When the solution is to be recorded on an *X-Y* plotter care should be taken to see that the scales of the graph axes are marked off in PROBLEM UNITS, *not* in Machine Units.

If a machine variable $\left(x/x_{max}\right)$ is to be plotted, it is advisable to choose units on the graph paper which fall easily and naturally into suitable decimal subdivisions. Since we almost always round off scaling factors to simple values such as $(1, 2$ or $5) \times 10^n$, this requirement can be met as follows:

Scaled variable	Graph paper divisions per MU
$\left(\dfrac{x}{1 \times 10^n}\right)$	1, 2, 5 or 10
$\left(\dfrac{x}{2 \times 10^n}\right)$	1, 2, 4 or 10
$\left(\dfrac{x}{5 \times 10^n}\right)$	1, 2½, 5 or 10

28

Exercise 5

Produce scaled flow diagrams for the following:

(1) $2\dot{x} + 3x = 4$ given $x = 0$ at $t = 0$.

    (Take $x_m = 2$)

(2) $\ddot{x} + 4\dot{x} + 10x = 20$ given $\dot{x} = x = 0$ at $t = 0$.

    (Take $\dot{x}_m = 10$, $x_m = 4$)

(3) $5\ddot{x} + 2\dot{x} + 25x = 60$ given $\dot{x} = 0$, $x = -1$ at $t = 0$.

    (Take $\dot{x}_m = 10$, $x_m = 5$)

(4) Question 3, but generating $\ddot{x}$.   (Take $\ddot{x}_m = 20$.)

4.3 Estimation of maximum values

One or more of the following sources of information should be used where possible.

  (i) Knowledge of the physical problem, where appropriate.
 (ii) Estimation based on a knowledge of the differential equations and their solutions.
(iii) Equal Coefficients Rule (see below).

If none of these can be applied, use Trial and Error. The machine will show up an error in scaling either by overloading (*under-estimate* of maxima) or by producing outputs $< \frac{1}{2}$ MU (*overestimate* of maxima). Remedy: *rescale the equations* in the light of this information, and try again.

    The following are helpful:

(a) $|x| \leqslant A$ if $x = Ae^{-kt}$ or $x = A\sin\omega t$ or $x = A\cos\omega t$

(b) $|\dot{x}| \leqslant kA$ if $x = Ae^{-kt}$

      $|\dot{x}| \leqslant \omega A$ if $x = A\sin\omega t$ or $A\cos\omega t$

(c) $|\ddot{x}| \leqslant k^2 A$ if $x = Ae^{-kt}$

      $|\ddot{x}| \leqslant \omega^2 A$ if $x = A\sin\omega t$ or $A\cos\omega t$.

Consider a second order differential equation with a constant driving function (step function) and zero initial conditions, e.g.

$$a\ddot{x} + b\dot{x} + cx = k \quad \text{given } x = \dot{x} = 0 \text{ at } t = 0$$

The equation can be rewritten

$$\ddot{x} + 2\zeta\omega_n\dot{x} + \omega_n^2 x = \frac{k}{a} \quad (\omega_n = \text{natural frequency})$$

where $\omega_n^2 = \frac{c}{a}$, $\zeta = \frac{b}{2\sqrt{(ac)}}$ (ζ = damping ratio)

If the solution of the differential equation is oscillatory, $b < 2\sqrt{(ac)}$ i.e. $\zeta < 1$; the system will oscillate with a frequency slightly smaller than the natural (undamped) frequency ω_n rad s^{-1} and with a damping time constant $= 1/\zeta\omega_n = 2a/b$ sec.

Then $x_{max} \leqslant 2 \times$ (Steady state value) $= \dfrac{2k}{c}$

(Note: 2 because of step - see Figure 36.)

Also $|\dot{x}| \leqslant \omega_n\left(\dfrac{k}{a\omega_n^2}\right) = \left(\dfrac{\omega_n k}{c}\right)$ not $\left(\dfrac{2\omega_n k}{c}\right)$

and $|\ddot{x}| \leqslant \omega_n^2\left(\dfrac{k}{a\omega_n^2}\right) = \omega_n^2\,\dfrac{k}{c}$

If solution of differential equation is overdamped $\left[b > 2\sqrt{(ac)}\right]$, the above maxima will be smaller but may still be used as first approximations for scaling purposes.

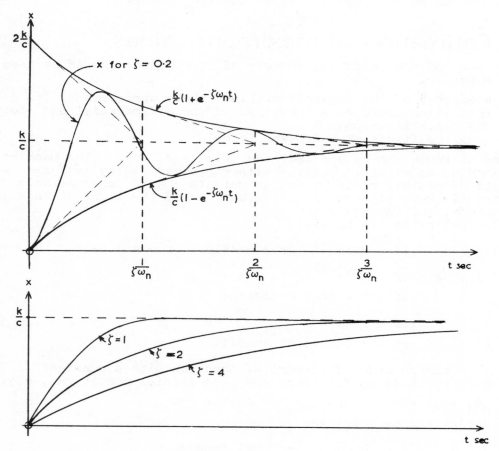

Figure 36

Important Note. Maxima estimated in these ways may result in numbers which are awkward to manipulate (e.g. $\dot{x}_{max} = 173$). It is therefore good practice to round up such maxima to a value which can be expressed as a power of 10×1, 2 or 5 (e.g. $x_{max} = 173 \simeq 200$).

30

It is, in general, bad practice to use maxima rounded up to values which contain factors such as 3, 7, 11, ... etc., since such factors lead to coefficients in the scaled equations which are of recurring decimal form, and these cannot accurately be set on potentiometers.

Let us now consider the general effect of introducing non-zero initial conditions in the case where $\zeta \ll 1$ (which will evidently produce the "worst" case as far as amplitudes are concerned).

For $\zeta = 0$, the analytic solution will be of the form

$$x = A\sin(\omega_n t + \phi) + \frac{k}{c} \tag{i}$$

$$\therefore \quad \dot{x} = \omega_n A\cos(\omega_n t + \phi) \tag{ii}$$

and $\quad \ddot{x} = -\omega_n^2 A\sin(\omega_n t + \phi) \tag{iii}$

When $t = 0$ these give

$$x_0 = A\sin\phi + \frac{k}{c} \tag{iv}$$

$$\dot{x}_0 = \omega_n A\cos\phi \tag{v}$$

$$\ddot{x}_0 = -\omega_n^2 A\sin\phi \tag{vi}$$

From (iv) $\quad \sin\phi = \frac{1}{A}\left(x_0 - \frac{k}{c}\right)$

From (v) $\quad \cos\phi = \dfrac{\dot{x}_0}{\omega_n A}$

Hence $\quad \left(x_0 - \frac{k}{c}\right)^2 + \left(\frac{\dot{x}_0}{\omega_n}\right)^2 = A^2$

i.e. $\quad A = \sqrt{\left[\left(x_0 - \frac{k}{c}\right)^2 + \left(\frac{\dot{x}_0}{\omega_n}\right)^2\right]} \tag{vii}$

We can now estimate the maxima of the variables, since into (i), (ii) and (iii) we can substitute from (vii) to find

$$x_{max} = A + \frac{k}{c}, \quad \dot{x}_{max} = \omega_n A \quad \text{and} \quad \ddot{x}_{max} = \omega_n^2 A$$

The value of A in (vii) has been derived for $\zeta = 0$; evidently when $0 < \zeta < 1$, the A obtained from (vii) will provide a safety margin when scaling. Note that ω_n is the *natural (undamped) frequency* of the system, and also that when $0 < \zeta < 1$, the k/c in the formula represents the *steady state value of x*.

EQUAL COEFFICIENTS RULE: (for use only in differential equations of order higher than two: Jackson in *Analog Computation* states that this rule is only an empirical generalization, but will serve the purpose in the case of most linear differential equations.)

Consider the equation

$$a_n \frac{d^n x}{dt^n} + a_{n-1} \frac{d^{n-1} x}{dt^{n-1}} + \ldots + a_1 \frac{dx}{dt} + a_0 x = K \cdot H(t)$$

The basis of the rule is to take $x_{max} \simeq \frac{2K}{a_0}$ (cf. second order equations), and for all the derivatives, to take $\left(\frac{d^m x}{dt^m}\right)_{max} \simeq \frac{K}{a_m}$ where $m = 1, 2, 3, \ldots n$.

The use of the rule is illustrated by Example 13, p.39.

Example 10

Solve $\quad 3\dot{y} + 4y = 6 \qquad$ given $y = -4$ at $t = 0$, and $\dot{y}$ is required.

$$\dot{y} = -\frac{4}{3} y + 2$$

Unscaled flow diagram:

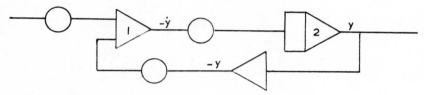

Figure 37

Decomposed equations:

Amplifier 1. $\quad -(-\dot{y}) = -\frac{4}{3} y + 2$

Amplifier 2. $\quad -\frac{d}{dt}(y) = -\dot{y}$

Scaling:

Now when $\dot{y} = 0$, $y = \frac{6}{4}$; but $y_0 = -4$. (See Figure 38.)

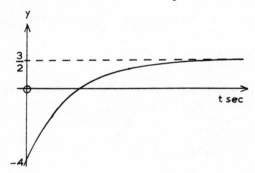

Figure 38

$\therefore y_m = 4$

Let us scale $\left(\frac{y}{5}\right)$

At $t = 0$, $\dot{y} = \frac{6 + 4 \times 4}{3}$

$\dot{y}_m = \frac{22}{3} \simeq 10$

Let us scale $\left(\frac{\dot{y}}{10}\right)$

32

Scaled equations:

1. $\quad -\left(-\dfrac{\dot{y}}{10}\right) = \dfrac{4 \times 5}{30}\left(-\dfrac{y}{5}\right) + \dfrac{2}{10}$

2. $\quad -\dfrac{d}{dt}\left(\dfrac{y}{5}\right) = \dfrac{10}{5}\left(-\dfrac{\dot{y}}{10}\right)$

which give

Machine equations:

1. $\quad -\left(-\dfrac{\dot{y}}{10}\right) = [0 \cdot 667]1\left(-\dfrac{y}{5}\right) + [0 \cdot 2]1(1)$

2. $\quad -\dfrac{d}{dt}\left(\dfrac{y}{5}\right) = [0 \cdot 2]10\left(-\dfrac{\dot{y}}{10}\right)$

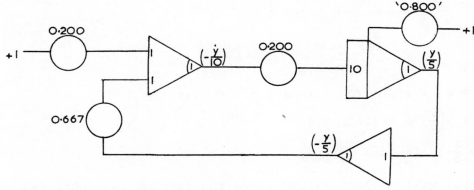

Figure 39

Note that the initial condition is $y_0 = -4$ $\therefore \left(\dfrac{y_0}{5}\right) = -\dfrac{4}{5}$

$\quad$ If $\dot{y}$ is not required:

Unscaled flow diagram:

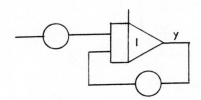

Figure 40

Decomposed equation:

Amplifier 1. $\quad -\dfrac{d}{dt}(y) = +\dfrac{4}{3}y - 2$

Scaled equation:

1. $\quad -\dfrac{d}{dt}\left(\dfrac{y}{5}\right) = \dfrac{4}{3}\left(\dfrac{y}{5}\right) - \dfrac{2}{5}$

Machine equation:

1. $-\frac{d}{dt}\left(\frac{y}{5}\right) = [0 \cdot 133]10\left(\frac{y}{5}\right) + [0 \cdot 4]1(-1)$

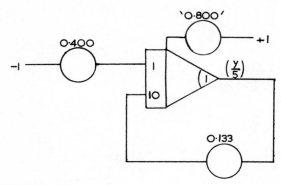

Figure 41

Example 11

Solve $\ddot{y} + 4\dot{y} + 25y = 40$ given $\dot{y} = y = 0$ at $t = 0$

i.e. $\ddot{y} + 2\left(\frac{2}{5}\right)5\dot{y} + (5)^2 y = 40$

where $\zeta = \frac{2}{5}$ (< 1) and $\omega_n = 5$.

The solution will be oscillatory since the damping is light, and the decay time constant $= 1/\zeta\omega_n = 1/2$ sec.

Unscaled flow diagram:

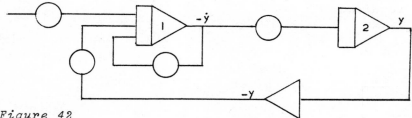

Figure 42

Decomposed equations:

Amplifier 1. $-\frac{d}{dt}(-\dot{y}) = -4\dot{y} - 25y + 40$

Amplifier 2. $-\frac{d}{dt}(y) = -\dot{y}$

Scaling: since y and $\dot{y}$ both have zero initial conditions

34

$$y_m \simeq \frac{2 \times 40}{25} \qquad \text{(i.e. twice steady state value)}$$

$$y_m \simeq \frac{16}{5} \qquad \text{Let us scale } \left(\tfrac{y}{5}\right)$$

$$\dot{y}_m \simeq \frac{40}{25} \times 5 \qquad \text{(i.e. } \omega_n \times y \text{ steady state)}$$

$$\dot{y}_m \simeq \frac{40}{5} = 8 \qquad \text{Let us scale } \left(\tfrac{\dot{y}}{10}\right)$$

Scaled equations:

1. $\quad -\dfrac{d}{dt}\left(-\dfrac{\dot{y}}{10}\right) = 4\left(-\dfrac{\dot{y}}{10}\right) + \dfrac{25 \times 5}{10}\left(-\dfrac{y}{5}\right) + \dfrac{40}{10}$

2. $\quad -\dfrac{d}{dt}\left(\dfrac{y}{5}\right) = \dfrac{10}{5}\left(-\dfrac{\dot{y}}{10}\right)$

Machine equations:

1. $\quad -\dfrac{d}{dt}\left(-\dfrac{\dot{y}}{10}\right) = 10\left\{[0\cdot4]1\left(-\dfrac{\dot{y}}{10}\right) + [0\cdot125]10\left(-\dfrac{y}{5}\right) + [0\cdot4]1(1)\right\}$

2. $\quad -\dfrac{d}{dt}\left(\dfrac{y}{5}\right) = [0\cdot2]10\left(-\dfrac{\dot{y}}{10}\right)$

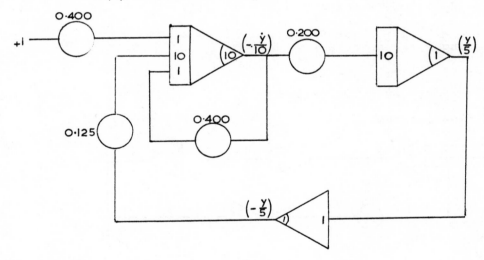

Figure 43

Suppose now that, in Example 11, the initial conditions are not as originally stated, but are (say), $y = -2$ and $\dot{y} = +2$ at $t = 0$. We have $\omega_n = 5$ and $\zeta = \frac{2}{5} < 1$.

As we saw on page 31, the amplitude of the solution when $\zeta \ll 1$ is given by

$$A = \sqrt{\left[\left(y_0 - \frac{k}{c}\right)^2 + \left(\frac{\dot{y}_0}{\omega_n}\right)^2\right]}$$

$$= \sqrt{\left[\left(-2 - \frac{40}{25}\right)^2 + \left(\frac{2}{5}\right)^2\right]}$$

$$= \sqrt{\left[\frac{8100}{625} + \frac{4}{25}\right]}$$

$$= \frac{\sqrt{8200}}{25} \simeq \frac{18}{5}$$

$$y_{max} \simeq \frac{18}{5} + \frac{40}{25} \simeq 5 \qquad\qquad \text{Let us scale } \left(\frac{y}{5}\right)$$

$$\dot{y}_{max} \simeq 5 \times \frac{18}{5} \qquad\qquad \text{Let us scale } \left(\frac{\dot{y}}{20}\right)$$

$\left[\text{Note that if } \ddot{y} \text{ were required, we should now scale } \left(\frac{\ddot{y}}{100}\right)\right].$

The decomposed problem equations may now be re-scaled in the light of these new scaling factors, and a new pair of machine equations obtained.

Example 12

Solve
$$\dot{x} + 3x + y = 10 \tag{i}$$
$$\ddot{y} + 2\dot{y} + 100y - 50x = 0 \tag{ii}$$

given $x = y = 0$, $\dot{y} = 10$ at $t = 0$
and computing $\dot{x}$, x, $\dot{y}$ and y.

Rearrange:
$$\dot{x} = -3x - y + 10$$
$$\ddot{y} = -2\dot{y} - 100y + 50x$$

Unscaled flow diagram:

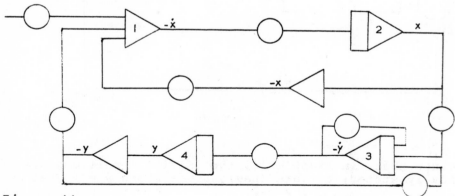

Figure 44

36

Decomposed equations:

Amplifier 1. $- (- \dot{x}) = - 3x - y + 10$

Amplifier 2. $- \dfrac{d}{dt}(x) = - \dot{x}$

Amplifier 3. $- \dfrac{d}{dt}(- \dot{y}) = - 2\dot{y} - 100y + 50x$

Amplifier 4. $- \dfrac{d}{dt}(y) = - \dot{y}$

Steady state solution may be found by solving the equations obtained by equating all the derivatives in the original equations to zero, assuming that the system is stable (this can be shown to be the case) and has step "driving" function:

$3x + y = 10$

$2y - x = 0$

Steady state $7x = 20$ $x = \dfrac{20}{7}$ Let us scale $\left(\dfrac{x}{5}\right)$

and $7y = 10$ $y = \dfrac{10}{7}$ Let us scale $\left(\dfrac{y}{2}\right)$

In estimating maxima, the two equations may be treated as separate entities - this procedure is, while evidently improper mathematically, a simple way of obtaining rough estimates for *scaling* purposes.

From equation (i) when $t = 0$

$\dot{x} = 10$ Let us scale $\left(\dfrac{\dot{x}}{10}\right)$

Equation (ii) can be written

$$\ddot{y} + 2\left(\dfrac{1}{10}\right)10\dot{y} + 10^2 y = 50x$$

hence $\omega_n \simeq 10$, $\zeta \simeq \dfrac{1}{10}$

$\dot{y}_m = 10 \times \dfrac{10}{7} \simeq 20$ Let us scale $\left(\dfrac{\dot{y}}{20}\right)$

(Note that the initial condition for $\dot{y}$ is "within" this scaling factor.)
The solution will also be lightly damped ($\zeta = 1/10$) and decay time-constant $= 1/\zeta\omega_n = 1$ sec.

Hence we have the
Scaled equations:

1. $\quad - \left(- \dfrac{\dot{x}}{10}\right) = \dfrac{3 \times 5}{10}\left(- \dfrac{x}{5}\right) + \dfrac{2}{10}\left(- \dfrac{y}{2}\right) + \dfrac{10}{10}$

2. $\quad - \dfrac{d}{dt}\left(\dfrac{x}{5}\right) = \dfrac{10}{5}\left(- \dfrac{\dot{x}}{10}\right)$

3. $\quad - \dfrac{d}{dt}\left(- \dfrac{\dot{y}}{20}\right) = 2\left(- \dfrac{\dot{y}}{20}\right) + \dfrac{100 \times 2}{20}\left(- \dfrac{y}{2}\right) + \dfrac{50 \times 5}{20}\left(\dfrac{x}{5}\right)$

4. $\quad - \dfrac{d}{dt}\left(\dfrac{y}{2}\right) = \dfrac{20}{2}\left(- \dfrac{\dot{y}}{20}\right)$

from which we get the
Machine equations:

1. $\quad - \left(- \dfrac{\dot{x}}{10}\right) = [0 \cdot 15]10\left(- \dfrac{x}{5}\right) + [0 \cdot 2]1\left(- \dfrac{y}{2}\right) + 1(1)$

2. $\quad - \dfrac{d}{dt}\left(\dfrac{x}{5}\right) = [0 \cdot 2]10\left(- \dfrac{\dot{x}}{10}\right)$

3. $\quad - \dfrac{d}{dt}\left(- \dfrac{\dot{y}}{20}\right) = 10\left\{[0 \cdot 2]1\left(- \dfrac{\dot{y}}{20}\right) + 1\left(- \dfrac{y}{2}\right) + [0 \cdot 125]10\left(\dfrac{x}{5}\right)\right\}$

4. $\quad - \dfrac{d}{dt}\left(\dfrac{y}{2}\right) = 10\left(- \dfrac{\dot{y}}{20}\right)$

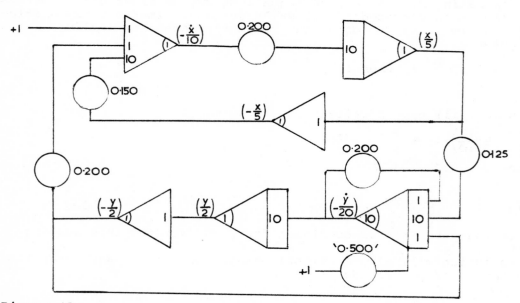

Figure 45

38

Example 13

Solve $\quad \dddot{x} + 4\ddot{x} + 30\dot{x} + 100x = 50 \quad$ given all I.C.s are zero

Rearrange: $\quad -\dddot{x} = +4\ddot{x} + 30\dot{x} + 100x - 50$

Unscaled flow diagram:

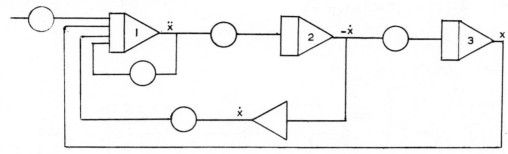

Figure 46

Decomposed equations:

Amplifier 1. $\quad -\dfrac{d}{dt}\dddot{x} = 4\ddot{x} + 30\dot{x} + 100x - 50$

Amplifier 2. $\quad -\dfrac{d}{dt}(-\ddot{x}) = +\ddot{x}$

Amplifier 3. $\quad -\dfrac{d}{dt}x = -\dot{x}$

By Equal Coefficients Rule

$x_m = \dfrac{2 \times 50}{100} = 1 \qquad\qquad$ Let us scale $\left(\dfrac{x}{1}\right)$

$\dddot{x}_m = \dfrac{50}{1} = 50 \qquad\qquad$ Let us scale $\left(\dfrac{\dddot{x}}{50}\right)$

Hence

$-\left(\dfrac{\dddot{x}}{50}\right) = +\dfrac{4\ddot{x}_m}{50}\left(\dfrac{\ddot{x}}{\ddot{x}_m}\right) + \dfrac{30\dot{x}_m}{50}\left(\dfrac{\dot{x}}{\dot{x}_m}\right) + \dfrac{100}{50}\left(\dfrac{x}{1}\right) - \dfrac{50}{50}$

For $\quad \dfrac{4\ddot{x}_m}{50} = 1 \quad \ddot{x}_m = \dfrac{50}{4} \qquad\qquad$ Let us scale $\left(\dfrac{\ddot{x}}{10}\right)$

For $\quad \dfrac{30\dot{x}_m}{50} = 1 \quad \dot{x}_m = \dfrac{50}{30} \simeq 2 \qquad\qquad$ Let us scale $\left(\dfrac{\dot{x}}{2}\right)$

Scaled equations:

1. $\quad -\dfrac{d}{dt}\left(\dfrac{\dddot{x}}{10}\right) = 4\left(\dfrac{\ddot{x}}{10}\right) + \dfrac{30 \times 2}{10}\left(\dfrac{\dot{x}}{2}\right) + \dfrac{100}{10}\left(\dfrac{x}{1}\right) - \dfrac{50}{10}$

2. $\quad -\dfrac{d}{dt}\left(-\dfrac{\dot{x}}{2}\right) = \dfrac{10}{2}\left(\dfrac{\ddot{x}}{10}\right)$

3. $\quad -\dfrac{d}{dt}\left(\dfrac{x}{1}\right) = \dfrac{2}{1}\left(-\dfrac{\dot{x}}{2}\right)$

Machine equations:

1. $-\dfrac{d}{dt}\left(\dfrac{\ddot{x}}{10}\right) = 10\left\{[0\cdot4]1\left(\dfrac{\ddot{x}}{10}\right) + [0\cdot6]1\left(\dfrac{\dot{x}}{2}\right) + 1\left(\dfrac{x}{1}\right) + [0\cdot5]1(-1)\right\}$

2. $-\dfrac{d}{dt}\left(-\dfrac{\dot{x}}{2}\right) = [0\cdot5]10\left(\dfrac{\ddot{x}}{10}\right)$

3. $-\dfrac{d}{dt}\left(\dfrac{x}{1}\right) = [0\cdot2]10\left(-\dfrac{\dot{x}}{2}\right)$

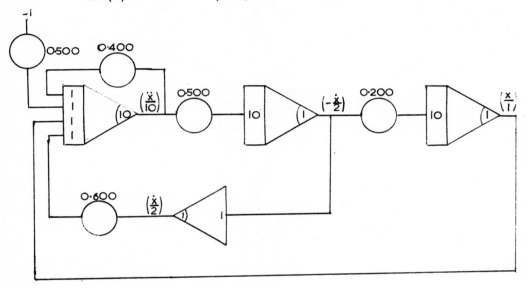

Figure 47

40

Exercise 6

(1) $4\ddot{y} + k\dot{y} + 37y = 99$ given $k = 4$ and $y = \dot{y} = 1$ at $t = 0$.

Examine for other values of k.

(2) $\left.\begin{array}{l} \dot{x} + 4x + 5y = 7 \\ \dot{y} + 4y - 5x = 8 \end{array}\right\}$ given $x = y = 0$ at $t = 0$.

(3) $\dddot{y} + 5\ddot{y} + 14\dot{y} + 10y = 20$ given all I.C.s zero.

(4) $\ddot{y} + 2\dot{y} + 49y = 120$ in the cases where
    (i) $y = \dot{y} = 0$ at $t = 0$
   (ii) $y = 2$, $\dot{y} = 0$ at $t = 0$
  (iii) $y = 0$, $\dot{y} = 20$ at $t = 0$.

(5) $\dddot{y} + 6\ddot{y} + 21\dot{y} + 26y = 50$ given $y = \ddot{y} = 0$, $\dot{y} = -2$ at $t = 0$.

(6) $\left.\begin{array}{l} \ddot{y} + \dot{y} + 16y + 6x = 50 \\ \dot{y} - 2\dot{x} + y - 2x = 0 \end{array}\right\}$ given $x = 5$, $y = 10$, $\dot{y} = -5$ at $t = 0$.

(7) $\left.\begin{array}{l} \ddot{x} + 15x + 3y + 30 = 0 \\ \ddot{y} + 2x + 10y + 4 = 0 \end{array}\right\}$ given $x = 5$, $\dot{x} = 0$, $y = 0$, $\dot{y} = 14$ at $t = 0$.

(8) $3\ddot{x} + f\dot{x} + 30x = 48$ for f in the range $6 \leqslant f \leqslant 18$ in the cases
    (i) $x = \dot{x} = 0$ at $t = 0$
   (ii) $x = 2$, $\dot{x} = -2$ at $t = 0$
  (iii) $x = -4$, $\dot{x} = 4$ at $t = 0$.

CHAPTER 5

ANALOGUE COMPUTING REPORTS

By this stage it is to be hoped that the reader has had some experience of solving simple differential equation problems on an actual analogue computer, preferably by patching up and running his own programme himself, rather than by merely watching a demonstration carried out by someone else. The authors believe - and practical experience confirms this - that analogue computing is best learned, and the learning more easily and thoroughly digested, when the student solves problems on an actual machine at a very early stage - the earlier the better.

Even if such early problems are of a simple character, a formal detailed report of the work carried out should be written; only in this way can good foundation habits be laid in terms of systematic working. Such a foundation will pay handsome dividends later when the problems (and their programming) become more difficult; and the acquisition of the ability to write problem reports in effective, unambiguous and concise terms is the surest way to turn the analogue computer from being merely an interesting toy into being an effective problem-solving tool.

In this chapter the authors present a specimen report on the analogue solution of a second order differential equation with a "step" forcing function. It is *not* suggested that this report is an ideal to be slavishly followed; but some of the principles which underlie its presentation are worthy of serious consideration, whatever format of report may be required by different operators in various circumstances.

What are these principles?

(*a*) PREPARATION
This should contain all details necessary for the ultimate solution of the problem, presented in such a way that another programmer could reproduce the problem at a later date, or indeed take over the problem from the original programmer at any stage, should that become necessary.

(*b*) RUNNING (or MACHINE) LOG
It is sometimes necessary to view in retrospect the work done on the machine, e.g. checking settings that have been used, checking alterations to the programme which may have been made during the running, and so on. It is not uncommon for such a retrospective

examination to take place perhaps days or even weeks after the original run; and this examination is only possible if detailed documentation has been carried out *at the time of the event*. Reliance on memory alone is futile.

(*c*) RESULTS
Sections (*a*) and (*b*) above are matters for the programmer, and are therefore machine-orientated. The graphs produced, and any results and conclusions deduced from them are matters for the consumption of the problem poser, and should therefore be completely *problem-orientated*; they should stand in their own right without need for reference to (*a*) or (*b*).

Let us examine the implementation of the above in some detail.

(*a*) BEFORE GOING TO THE COMPUTER
The following preparation work should have been done and already written up in the report:

(1) Unscaled flow diagram and decomposed equations.
(2) Estimation of maxima of *all* amplifier output signals.
(3) Scaled equations.
(4) Machine equations.
(5) Scaled machine flow diagram.
(6) Allocation of computer elements on (5), and a detailed Pot. List.
(7) A brief Procedure work-plan for tackling the problem on the machine, in order to save as much time as possible when on the machine itself; this plan should incorporate a list of all checks to be made on the machine, together with the expected numerical results of those checks.

(*b*) ON THE COMPUTER ITSELF
After patching the machine in accordance with (5) and (6) in (*a*) above, and after setting the pots from the previously prepared Pot. List, the Procedure plan of (7) above is carried out, keeping a meticulous Running Log as this is done. The Running (or Machine) Log should note results of all checks made - not by stating merely "so-and-so correct" or "such-and-such incorrect", but quoting *facts and figures* (e.g. as actual D.V.M. readings observed). Programming errors or machine faults discovered, and the means taken to rectify them, should be documented in detail. Any changes of scale factors which become necessary should be clearly stated, and the machine equations and scaled flow diagram brought up to date to suit. The Log should also refer to 'scope and plotter calibration, and in the latter case should state clearly the choice of graph scales to be used (see Chapter 4, p.28). Each variable as it is plotted should be logged, together with a note of which amplifier output is being used.

(*c*) AFTER LEAVING THE COMPUTER
Provided that the preparatory programming in (*a*) and the Running Log in (*b*) above have been neatly and carefully produced, there should be no need for them to be rewritten in "Fair Copy" form for the report; indeed, the authors regard such a practice as undesirable, since copying errors and omissions could occur. In other words, the report should virtually be complete by the time that the operator

leaves the machine. All that should remain to be done is the collating and editing of solution graphs from the X-Y plotter, together with a Results or Conclusions paragraph to interpret these graphs as concisely as possible.

In the example which follows, the Results paragraph is particularly brief owing to the simplicity of the problem concerned. Needless to say, a problem which is more complicated, or one which is a mathematical model of a physical system, may well require considerable expansion of this paragraph - the graphs for such a problem should not merely be dismissed with the comment "self-explanatory".

At the end of the specimen report which follows, an Appendix is provided to show the kinds of fault in graph production and editing which can - and occasionally do - occur, and which should be avoided by reasonable care and forethought.

Problem Specification :

To plot solutions of x and $\dot{x}$ against time, for the equation

$$\ddot{x} + \lambda\dot{x} + 13x = 26$$

for $\lambda = 0 ; 1 ; 10$, given that $x = \dot{x} = 0$ at $t = 0$

Unscaled flow diagram :

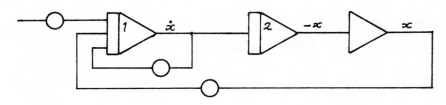

Decomposed equations :

1. $\quad -\dfrac{d}{dt}(\dot{x}) = -26 + \lambda\dot{x} + 13x$

2. $\quad -\dfrac{d}{dt}(-x) = \dot{x}$

Scaling :

natural (undamped) frequency $= \sqrt{13} \doteq 3.6$ rad s^{-1}

$\omega_n = 2\pi f$, $\therefore f = \dfrac{\omega_n}{2\pi} \doteq 0.57$ Hz

$\lambda = 2\zeta\omega_n$, $\therefore \zeta = \dfrac{\lambda}{2\omega_n}$

Now $0 \leqslant \lambda \leqslant 10$, hence $0 \leqslant \zeta \leqslant \dfrac{10}{7.2} \doteq 1.4$

and $x_{ss} = \dfrac{26}{13} = 2$

Sketch of expected solutions:

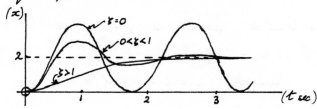

Scaling:

Maximum value of $x = 4$ when $\zeta = 0$

maximum value of $\dot{x} = 2\sqrt{13}$ when $\zeta = 0$

$\therefore$ scale $\left(\dfrac{x}{5}\right)$ and $\left(\dfrac{\dot{x}}{10}\right)$

Scaled equations:

1. $\quad -\dfrac{d}{dt}\left(\dfrac{\dot{x}}{10}\right) = -\dfrac{26}{10} + \lambda\left(\dfrac{\dot{x}}{10}\right) + \dfrac{13 \times 5}{10}\left(\dfrac{x}{5}\right)$

2. $\quad -\dfrac{d}{dt}\left(-\dfrac{x}{5}\right) = \dfrac{10}{5}\left(\dfrac{\dot{x}}{10}\right)$

Machine equations:

1. $\quad -\dfrac{d}{dt}\left(\dfrac{\dot{x}}{10}\right) = 10\left\{[0.260]\,1\,(-1) + \left[\dfrac{\lambda}{10}\right]\cdot\left(\dfrac{\dot{x}}{10}\right) + [0.650]\,1\left(\dfrac{x}{5}\right)\right\}$

2. $\quad -\dfrac{d}{dt}\left(-\dfrac{x}{5}\right) = 2\left(\dfrac{\dot{x}}{10}\right)$

<u>Scaled flow diagram :</u>   (allocations for EAL 380 machine)

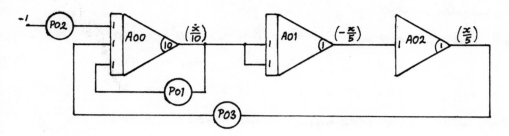

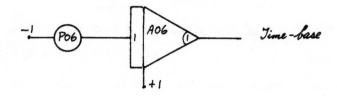

Time-base

<u>Pot. List</u> :

P06 :	$\frac{2}{T}$	(time-base)
P01 :	$\frac{\lambda}{10}$	
P02 :	0·260	
P03 :	0·650	

note : (see flow diagram and machine equation 2) : two ×1
inputs to A01 gives a gain of 1+1 = 2 , which is
more accurate than using [0·200]10

<u>Solution procedure</u> :

    Set $\lambda = 0$, check natural frequency $= \sqrt{13}$ rad s^{-1}

    Set $\lambda = 5$, check $x_{ss} = 2$, and time to reach
steady state (to within 1%) $\doteq 5 \times \frac{2}{5} = 2$ sec.

    Plot x for $\lambda = 0 ; 1 ; 10$ on same set of axes.

    Plot $\dot{x}$ for $\lambda = 0 ; 1 ; 10$ on same set of axes.

Machine Log :   Computer no 7 (EAL 380)

Problem patched . Pots. set from pot. list :

Compute time : $T = 5$ sec $\therefore \frac{2}{T} = 0.4$;   P06 = 0.400

$\lambda = 5$ $\therefore \frac{\lambda}{10} = 0.5$;   P01 = 0.500

DVM → A02 ;   CRO 'x' → A06, CRO 'y' → A02 .

At steady state DVM (A02 output) reads 0.401 m.v. $= \left(\frac{x}{5}\right)$

$\therefore x_{ss} = 2.005$ (checks).

Remove P01 → x1 of A00, putting $\lambda = 0$:

Compute time : $T = 10$ sec $\therefore \frac{2}{T} = 0.2$; P06 = 0.200

no of x cycles observed in 10 sec $\doteq 5\frac{3}{4}$ $\therefore f \doteq 0.575$ Hz

$\omega_n = 2\pi f = 2\pi \times 0.575 \doteq 3.6$ rad s^{-1} $\doteq \sqrt{13}$ (checks)

Replace P01 → x1 of A00, putting $\lambda = 5$:

Compute time : $T = 2$ sec . $\therefore \frac{2}{T} = 1$; P06 = 1.000

DVM (A02 output) reads 0.402 mv at end of compute time,

$\therefore x_{ss}$ reached (within 1%) at end of compute time (checks)

$\lambda = 10$ $\therefore \frac{\lambda}{10} = 1$;   P01 = 1.000

$T = 5$ $\therefore \frac{2}{T} = 0.4$; P06 = 0.400

Check solution on CRO : $T = 5$ reasonable for plotting .

Set X-Y plotter :   X: ±1 mv ≡ ± 5 (large) squares

$\therefore$ 1 square ≡ $\frac{1}{2}$ sec .

Y: +1 mv ≡ 10 (large) squares

$\therefore$ 1 square ≡ $\frac{1}{2}$ unit of x

Adjust Y-zero , to 1 sq. up from bottom of graph paper.

Plotter X → A06, y → A02 $(+\frac{x}{5})$

Plot Graph 1 :

λ	P01
0	0·000
1	0·100
2	0·200
3	0·300
4	0·400
5	0·500
6	0·600
7	0·700
8	0·800
9	0·900
10	1·000

Change plotter y-scale :   ±1 MU ≡ ±5 (large) squares,

y → A00 $(+\frac{\dot{x}}{10})$ ∴ 1 sq. ≡ 2 units of $\dot{x}$

Plot Graph 2 :

λ	P01
10	1·000
9	0·900
8	0·800
7	0·700
6	0·600
5	0·500
4	0·400
3	0·300
2	0·200
1	0·100
0	0·000

END OF LOG

Results :

The required plots of x and $\dot{x}$ against t are enclosed (Graphs 1 and 2), and are self-explanatory. The solutions shown verify those expected from theoretical considerations.

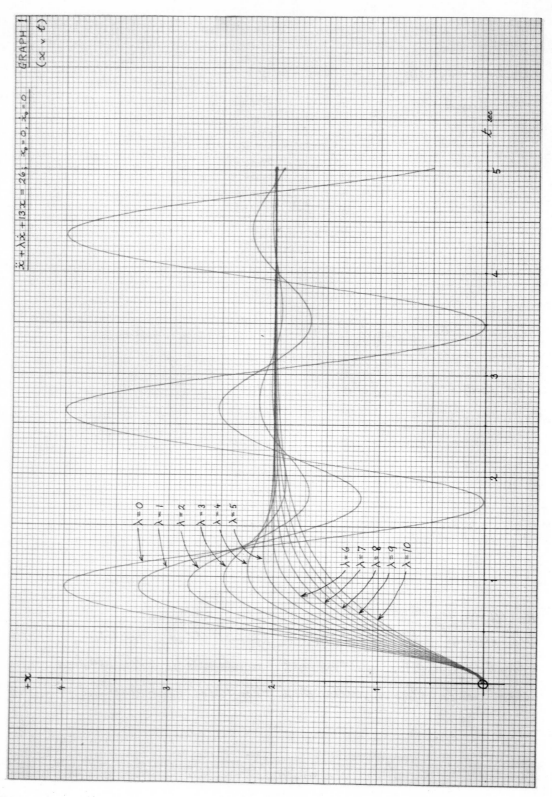

GRAPH I

$\ddot{x} + \lambda \dot{x} + 13x = 26, \quad x_0 = 0, \quad \dot{x}_0 = 0$

(x v t)

$\lambda = 0$
$\lambda = 1$
$\lambda = 2$
$\lambda = 3$
$\lambda = 4$
$\lambda = 5$

$\lambda = 6$
$\lambda = 7$
$\lambda = 8$
$\lambda = 9$
$\lambda = 10$

t sec

+x

4

3

2

1

50

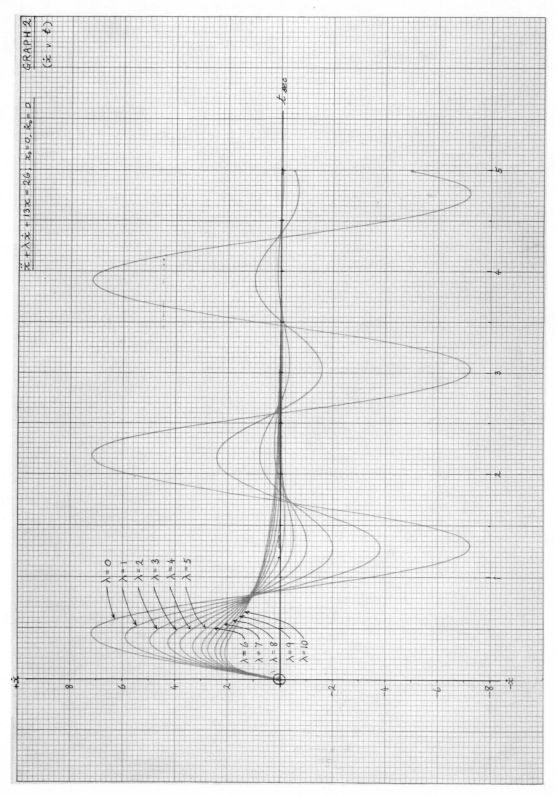

GRAPH 2

$\ddot{x} + \lambda \dot{x} + 13x = 26; \quad x_0 = 0, \dot{x}_0 = 0$

$(x \vee t)$

$\lambda = 0$
$\lambda = 1$
$\lambda = 2$
$\lambda = 3$
$\lambda = 4$
$\lambda = 5$

$\lambda = 6$
$\lambda = 7$
$\lambda = 8$
$\lambda = 9$
$\lambda = 10$

t sec

51

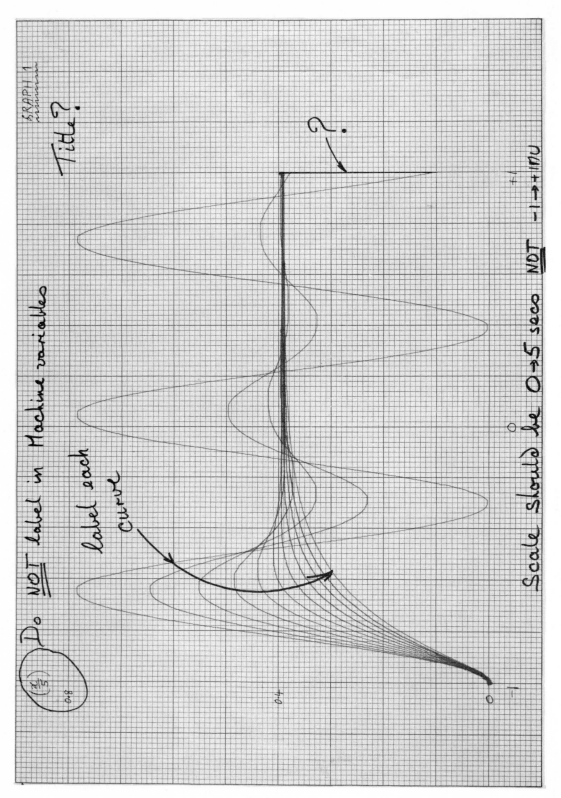

GRAPH 1

Title ?

Do NOT label in Machine variables

label each curve

$\left(\frac{x}{5}\right)$ 0·8

Scale should be 0→5 secs

NOT −1 → +1 in y

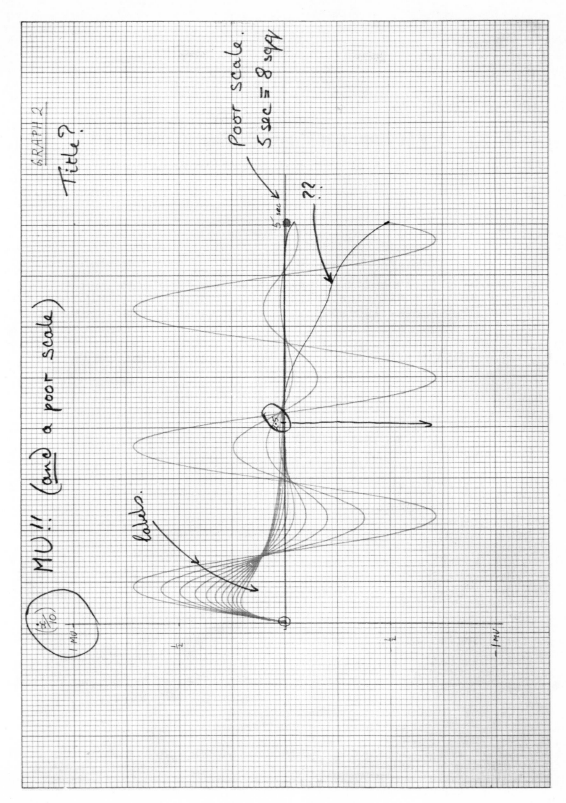

MU!! (and a poor scale)

GRAPH 2

Title?

Poor scale.
5 sec ≡ 8 sq/V

??

labels.

5 sec

$\frac{1}{2}$

$\frac{1}{4}$

1 mV

$\left(\frac{6}{10}\right)$

1 mV

CHAPTER 6
GENERATION OF FUNCTIONS (1)

The general procedure for generating simple functions of time is first to set up a differential equation for which the required function is the solution, and then solve the differential equation on the computer.

6.1 Ramp function (Used previously as a time base.)

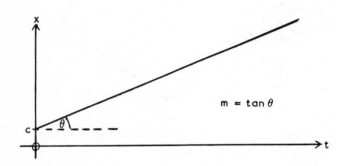

Figure 48

The equation of $f(t)$ is

$x = mt + c$

Differential equation: $\dot{x} = m$ with $x = c$ at $t = 0$

It follows that

$x_{max} = mT + c$ where T is the longest intended computing period.

or

$x_{max} = c$ whichever is the larger.

Decomposed equation: $-\dfrac{d}{dt}(x) = -m$

Machine equation: $-\dfrac{d}{dt}\left(\dfrac{x}{N}\right) = \left[\dfrac{m}{N}\right]1\,(-1)$

Hence the flow diagram required is

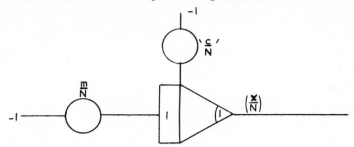

Figure 49

where N is the rounded up value of c or $mT + c$, whichever is the larger.

6.2 Exponential functions

EXPONENTIAL WITH NEGATIVE INDEX

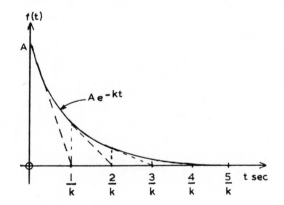

Figure 50

The equation of the function is

$f(t) = Ae^{-kt}$ where $k > 0$

Differential equation: $\dot{x} + kx = 0$ with $x = A$ at $t = 0$

For consider

$x = Ae^{-kt}$ $\dot{x} = -Ake^{-kt}$ $\therefore \dot{x} = -kx$

i.e. $-\dfrac{d}{dt}x = +kx$

Also at $t = 0$, $e^{-kt} = 1$, $\therefore x_0 = A$.

55

From Figure 50, $x_{max} = A$.

Machine equation is: $-\frac{d}{dt}\left(\frac{x}{A}\right) = [k]1\left(\frac{x}{A}\right)$

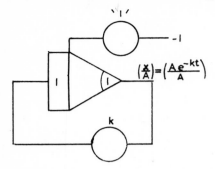

Figure 51

EXPONENTIAL WITH POSITIVE INDEX

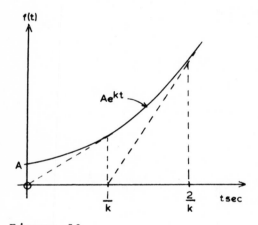

Figure 52

The equation of the function is

$$f(t) = Ae^{kt}$$

$$x = Ae^{kt}$$

$$\dot{x} = Ake^{kt} = kx$$

Hence the differential equation is

$$\dot{x} - kx = 0 \quad \text{with } x = A \text{ at } t = 0.$$

From Figure 52 it is evident that x_{max} will depend on t_{max}, the greatest duration of our computer time (T secs, say).   Then $x_{max} = Ae^{kT}$, which can be found from a set of exponential tables, and $\simeq N$, say.

56

Then
$$x_{max} < N$$

Machine equation is: $-\dfrac{d}{dt}\left(-\dfrac{x}{N}\right) = [k]1\left(\dfrac{x}{N}\right)$

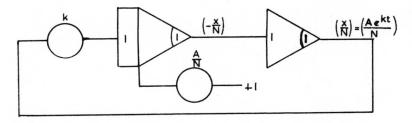

Figure 53

SATURATION EXPONENTIAL

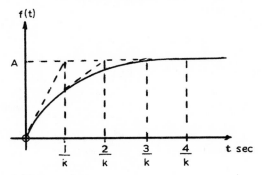

Figure 54

The equation of the function is

$$f(t) = A\left(1 - e^{-kt}\right) \quad \text{where } k > 0$$

Let $\quad x = A\left(1 - e^{-kt}\right)$

Therefore

$$\dot{x} = Ake^{-kt} = k(A - x)$$

Hence the differential equation is

$$\dot{x} + kx = kA \quad \text{with } x = 0 \text{ at } t = 0$$

i.e. $\quad -\dfrac{d}{dt}(x) = kx - kA$

From Figure 54 it is evident that x_{max} will not exceed A.
Therefore, Machine equation is

$$-\dfrac{d}{dt}\left(\dfrac{x}{A}\right) = [k]1\left(\dfrac{x}{A}\right) + [k]1(-1)$$

57

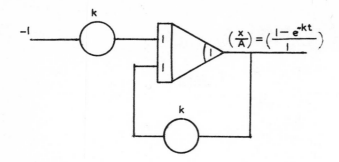

Figure 55

6.3 Sinusoids

$\cos\omega t$ and $\sin\omega t$

Now $\dfrac{d}{dt}(\sin\omega t) = \omega\cos\omega t$ (i)

$\dfrac{d^2}{dt^2}(\sin\omega t) = \dfrac{d}{dt}(\omega\cos\omega t) = -\omega^2(\sin\omega t)$ (ii)

The pair of equations (i) and (ii) can now be rewritten in the form

$-\dfrac{d}{dt}(-\sin\omega t) = \omega\cos\omega t$ (iii)

$-\dfrac{d}{dt}(\cos\omega t) = \omega\sin\omega t$ (iv)

It will be evident that equations (iii) and (iv) are decomposed equations for the flow diagram:

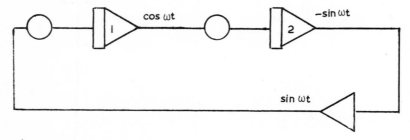

Figure 56

Since $-1 \leqslant \cos\omega t \leqslant 1$ and $-1 \leqslant \sin\omega t \leqslant 1$, the scaling now becomes simply $\left(\dfrac{\cos\omega t}{1}\right)$ and $\left(\dfrac{\sin\omega t}{1}\right)$ so that we have the

Machine equations:

(1) $-\frac{d}{dt}\left(\frac{\cos\omega t}{1}\right) = [\omega]1\left(\frac{\sin\omega t}{1}\right)$ where $\cos\omega t = 1$ at $t = 0$

(2) $-\frac{d}{dt}\left(\frac{-\sin\omega t}{1}\right) = [\omega]1\left(\frac{\cos\omega t}{1}\right)$ where $\sin\omega t = 0$ at $t = 0$

Scaled flow diagram:

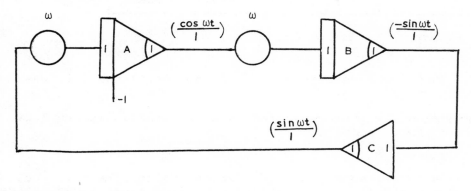

Figure 57

Note that for $1 \leqslant \omega \leqslant 10$ the machine equations can be written in the form:

(1) $-\frac{d}{dt}\left(\frac{\cos\omega t}{1}\right) = \left[\frac{\omega}{10}\right]10\left(\frac{\sin\omega t}{1}\right)$

(2) $-\frac{d}{dt}\left(\frac{-\sin\omega t}{1}\right) = \left[\frac{\omega}{10}\right]10\left(\frac{\cos\omega t}{1}\right)$

The flow diagram shows outputs of both $\sin\omega t$ and $\cos\omega t$; the frequency is set by two pots, one before each integrator (*not* one pot set to ω^2). Resetting the two ω pots changes the ω values (in rad s^{-1}), and retains the correct scaling $\left(\frac{\sin\omega t}{1}\right)$ and $\left(\frac{\cos\omega t}{1}\right)$ originally set by the I.C. on integrator A (Figure 57).

If the sign of the I.C. on integrator A is changed, the signs all the way round the loop are changed, so that outputs become:

A : $\left(-\frac{\cos\omega t}{1}\right)$

B : $\left(+\frac{\sin\omega t}{1}\right)$

C : $\left(-\frac{\sin\omega t}{1}\right)$

If the I.C. is now removed from A and put on B instead, the output functions change, and we get the following table:

59

I.C. (output)		Amplifier outputs		
Amplifier A	Amplifier B	A	B	C
+ 1	O	$\cos\omega t$	$-\sin\omega t$	$\sin\omega t$
− 1	O	$-\cos\omega t$	$\sin\omega t$	$-\sin\omega t$
O	+ 1	$\sin\omega t$	$\cos\omega t$	$-\cos\omega t$
O	− 1	$-\sin\omega t$	$-\cos\omega t$	$\cos\omega t$

$A\sin\omega t$ and $A\cos\omega t$

(i) for $\frac{1}{2} < A < 1$

In Figure 57 (for the generation of $\sin\omega t$ and $\cos\omega t$) the I.C. was always 1 since $\cos\omega t = 1$ at $t = 0$.
Now $A\cos\omega t = A$ at $t = 0$.
So $A\sin\omega t$ and $A\cos\omega t$ may be generated using Figure 57 with an I.C. of A, provided that $\frac{1}{2} < A < 1$.

(ii) for $A < \frac{1}{2}$

In theory the same method may be used for any value of $A < 1$; but for values of $A < \frac{1}{2}$ some loss of accuracy will be experienced, since the outputs of the amplifiers will always be less than $\frac{1}{2}$ MU. To eliminate this loss of accuracy we use the flow diagram of Figure 57 to generate $\sin\omega t$ and $\cos\omega t$ and then follow the required output with a pot set to A.

$a\sin\omega t + b\cos\omega t$

The flow diagram of Figure 57 may still be used; the outputs of integrator A $\left(\frac{\cos\omega t}{1}\right)$ and the inverter $\left(\frac{\sin\omega t}{1}\right)$ can be fed into a summer, via potentiometers set to a and b respectively, so that the summer output will be $- (a\sin\omega t + b\cos\omega t)$. Changing the sign of the I.C. on integrator A will convert this output to $+ (a\sin\omega t + b\cos\omega t)$ without the need for an additional inverter.

It is more elegant, and more economical in computer elements, to use a flow diagram similar to that of Figure 57 but with I.C.s on both integrators; now the function $a\cos\omega t + b\sin\omega t$ may be rewritten as

$R\sin(\omega t + \alpha)$ $\quad$ $\left[\text{or } R\cos(\omega t - \beta)\right]$

where $R = \sqrt{(a^2 + b^2)}$ $\quad$ $\alpha = \tan^{-1} b/a$ $\left[\text{and} \quad \beta = \tan^{-1} a/b\right]$

Initially ($t = 0$),

$\sin(\omega t + \alpha) = \sin\alpha$

$\cos(\omega t + \alpha) = \cos\alpha$

Hence the machine equations for Figure 57 become:

(1) $\quad -\dfrac{d}{dt}\left(\dfrac{\cos(\omega t + \alpha)}{1}\right) = [\omega]1\left(\dfrac{\sin(\omega t + \alpha)}{1}\right)$

(2) $\quad -\dfrac{d}{dt} -\left(\dfrac{\sin(\omega t + \alpha)}{1}\right) = [\omega]1\left(\dfrac{\cos(\omega t + \alpha)}{1}\right)$

60

and the flow diagram of Figure 57 becomes:

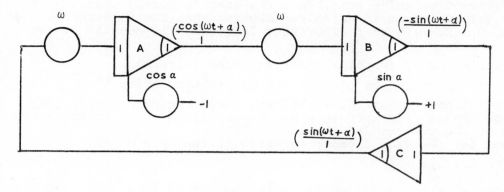

Figure 58

Similarly, to generate $\cos(\omega t - \beta)$ we should have the machine equations:

(1) $\quad -\dfrac{d}{dt}\left(\dfrac{\cos(\omega t - \beta)}{1}\right) = [\omega]\,1\left(\dfrac{\sin(\omega t - \beta)}{1}\right)$

(2) $\quad -\dfrac{d}{dt}\,-\left(\dfrac{\sin(\omega t - \beta)}{1}\right) = [\omega]\,1\left(\dfrac{\cos(\omega t - \beta)}{1}\right)$

which lead to the scaled flow diagram:

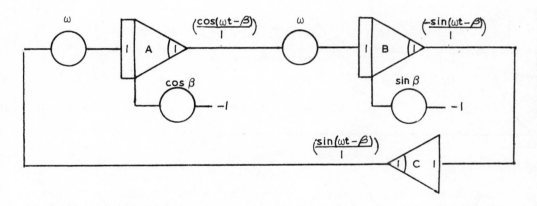

Figure 59

6.4 How driving functions
can affect scaling

We must now take a further look at the work on estimation of maxima covered in Chapter 4, in particular where second order differential equations are concerned. In Chapter 4 the examples discussed had "step" forcing functions; in practice we may meet problems in which the forcing functions are ramp, exponential, impulse or sinusoidal in character, and in such cases we may need to use scaling factors which differ from those suitable for a step function input.

At this point it is worth remembering that the solution to any stable L.O.D.E. with an $f(t)$ driving function will consist of two parts:

    Complementary function + Particular integral

i.e. Transient solution   + Steady state solution

When estimating maximum values the two components of the solution should be considered separately and the scaling factor taken as the maximum of the two results obtained.

Consider the second-order equation of the form

$$\ddot{x} + 2\zeta\omega_n\dot{x} + \omega_n^2 x = f(t)$$

As we have already seen, for the case where $f(t)$ is a step, say $C.H(t)$, we take

$$x_{max} \simeq 2\,\frac{C}{\omega_n^2} \qquad \dot{x}_{max} \simeq \frac{C}{\omega_n}$$

when $\zeta < 1$ and initial conditions are zero.

The following hints may be useful when $f(t)$ is not a step:

(a) f(t) A RAMP FUNCTION

If the ramp does not start at zero, i.e. $f(t) = At + B$, and has a relatively small slope, scaling may be estimated as for the step input case:

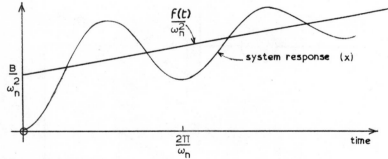

Figure 60

If the ramp does start at zero, one may be able to disregard the factor of 2 when scaling for x_{max}; but whether the ramp starts at zero or not, we must be careful to check its expected size at the end of the intended computing period - this value will assist us to estimate (roughly) the maximum value of x to which we should scale:

62

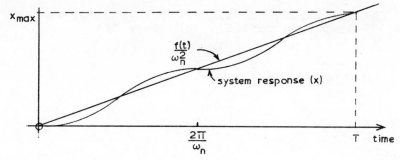

Figure 61

(Note also, that the steady state value of $\dot{x}$ is not zero, but will be proportional to the slope of the ramp input.)

(*b*) f(t) AN EXPONENTIAL FUNCTION

(i) $f(t) = Ae^{-kt}$ where $1/k$ is a relatively large time-constant compared to $2\pi/\omega_n$; scale x as for step input $A.H(t)$:

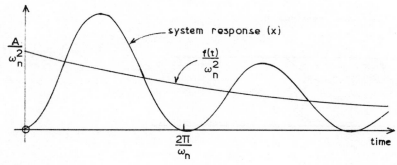

Figure 62

If $1/k$ is a relatively short time-constant compared to $2\pi/\omega_n$, the factor of 2 in scaling x_{max} may be disregarded:

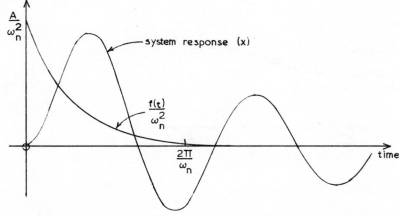

Figure 63

(ii) $f(t) = Ae^{+kt}$. The all-important value here is that of Ae^{kT} where T is the intended computing period: (cf. page 56)

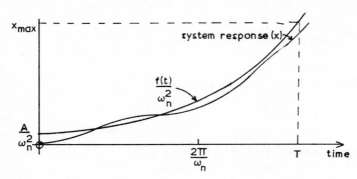

Figure 64

(iii) $f(t) = A\left(1 - e^{-kt}\right)$ where $1/k$ is a relatively short time-constant: Scale x as for step input $A.H(t)$:

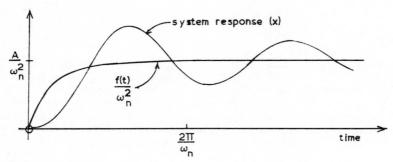

Figure 65

If $1/k$ is a relatively large time-constant, the factor of 2 in scaling for x_{max} may be disregarded:

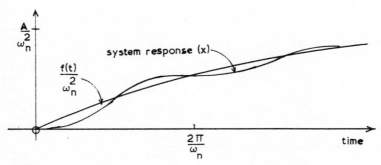

Figure 66

(c) f(t) AN IMPULSE

When $f(t) = A.\delta(t)$, for scaling purposes we can regard $f(t)$ as an exponential with an extremely small time constant:

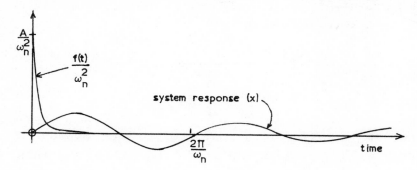

Figure 67

Note that when actually simulating the impulse response of any linear system of order n, such an exponential should not be used - instead, put the driving function equal to zero and the initial condition of the $(n-1)$th derivative equal to A. (The proof of this is easily established using Laplace Transforms.)

(d) f(t) A SINUSOID

With all the forcing functions considered so far the steady state value of x has been easy to estimate. This, however, is not the case with a sinusoidal driving function since the steady state amplitude varies dramatically with change of ω and ζ as reference to Figures 68 to 71 will show.

(i) $f(t) = A\cos\omega t$, ω small compared to ω_n; scale x as for step input $A.H(t)$:

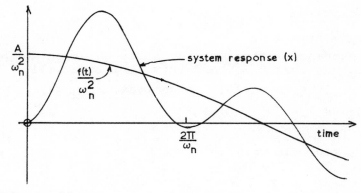

Figure 68

(ii) $f(t) = A\sin\omega t$, ω small compared to ω_n: the factor of 2 in scaling for x_{max} may be disregarded:

65

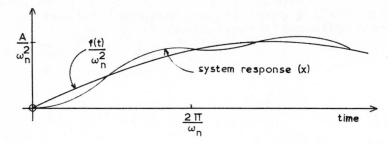

Figure 69

(iii) $f(t) = A\sin\omega t$ or $A\cos\omega t$, ω large compared to ω_n: Steady state solution for x will have less amplitude than A/ω_n^2, and this amplitude decreases as ω increases relative to ω_n; in general, x_{max} may be scaled for a value $< A/\omega_n^2$:

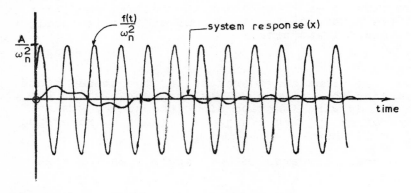

Figure 70

(iv) $f(t) = A\sin\omega t$ or $A\cos\omega t$, $\omega \simeq \omega_n$:

The resonance or near-resonance state: steady state solution for x may have a greater amplitude than A/ω_n^2, and this amplitude will increase to a large value if ζ is small: in general, x_{max} may require scaling for a value $\geqslant 2A/\omega_n^2$.

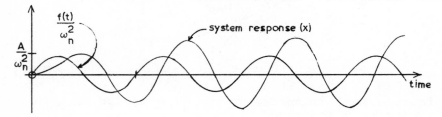

Figure 71

66

A very much better method of obtaining the steady state amplitude response of a second order system is to consult a normalized frequency response diagram such as that shown in Figure 72. For example, consider the case where we need to programme for the solution of

$$\ddot{x} + 4\dot{x} + 25x = 50\sin\omega t$$

given $\dot{x} = x = 0$ at $t = 0$, and $3 \leqslant \omega \leqslant 6$ rad s^{-1}.

Reducing the equation to standard form we have:

$$\ddot{x} + 2(2/5)(5)\dot{x} + (5)^2 x = 50\sin\omega t$$

If we now refer to the set of frequency response curves in Figure 72 we see that for $\zeta = 0.4$, the maximum gain (amplitude magnification ratio) will be 1.36 when $\omega/\omega_n = 0.85$, i.e. when $\omega = 4.25$ rad s^{-1} (and this latter value lies within the range of ω in the given problem).

Hence, for steady state, we can take:

$$x_{max} = \left(\frac{50}{25}\right)(1.36)$$

Let us scale $\left(\frac{x}{4}\right)$, or $\left(\frac{x}{5}\right)$

and $\left(\frac{\dot{x}}{16}\right)$, or $\left(\frac{\dot{x}}{20}\right)$

since $\dot{x}_{max} = (4.25)\left(\frac{50}{25}\right)(1.36)$

6.5 Initial rescaling

As has been said earlier, the first maximum value estimates may be found to be in error when eventually tried on the computer. The rescaling of *linear* problems is reasonably straightforward;

Consider the following example:

$$- \frac{d}{dt}\left(\frac{\dot{x}}{5}\right) = [0.5]10\left(\frac{\dot{x}}{5}\right) + [0.2]10\left(\frac{x}{1}\right) + [0.2]1\left(\frac{\sin\omega t}{1}\right)$$

Halving the driving function amplitude,

$$- \frac{1}{2}\frac{d}{dt}\left(\frac{\dot{x}}{5}\right) = \frac{1}{2}[0.5]10\left(\frac{\dot{x}}{5}\right) + \frac{1}{2}[0.2]10\left(\frac{x}{1}\right) + \frac{1}{2}[0.2]1\left(\frac{\sin\omega t}{1}\right)$$

$$- \frac{d}{dt}\left(\frac{\dot{x}}{10}\right) = [0.5]10\left(\frac{\dot{x}}{10}\right) + [0.2]10\left(\frac{x}{2}\right) + [0.1]1\left(\frac{\sin\omega t}{1}\right)$$

In general, increasing the input magnitudes (which implies those of the I.C.s as well as driving functions) by a factor n changes the scaling of every amplifier output within the system itself by a factor $1/n$.

This method is extremely useful when the values of maxima first chosen were underestimated, resulting in the overloading of one or more amplifiers. Reducing the magnitude of the driving function

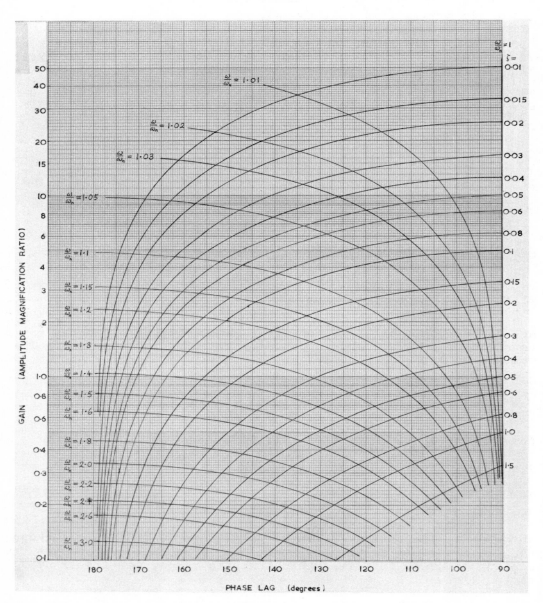

Figure 72

68

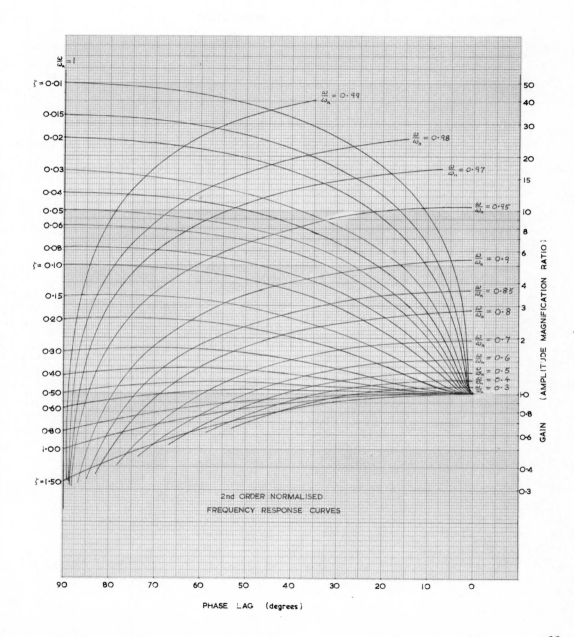

2nd ORDER NORMALISED
FREQUENCY RESPONSE CURVES

PHASE LAG   (degrees)

GAIN   (AMPLITUDE MAGNIFICATION RATIO)

$\frac{\omega}{\omega_n} = 0.99$

$\frac{\omega}{\omega_n} = 0.98$

$\frac{\omega}{\omega_n} = 0.97$

$\frac{\omega}{\omega_n} = 0.95$

$\frac{\omega}{\omega_n} = 0.9$

$\frac{\omega}{\omega_n} = 0.85$

$\frac{\omega}{\omega_n} = 0.8$

$\frac{\omega}{\omega_n} = 0.7$

$\frac{\omega}{\omega_n} = 0.6$

$\frac{\omega}{\omega_n} = 0.5$

$\frac{\omega}{\omega_n} = 0.4$

$\frac{\omega}{\omega_n} = 0.3$

$\frac{\omega}{\omega_n} = 1$

$\zeta = 0.01$

0.015

0.02

0.03

0.04

0.05

0.06

0.08

$\zeta = 0.10$

0.15

0.20

0.30

0.40

0.50

0.60

0.80

1.00

$\zeta = 1.50$

(and I.C.s) will provide a solution which is at least observable and from which the true maxima can be measured prior to a final rescale.

Exercise 7

1. Generate $0 \cdot 8e^{+kt}$ for 2 secs

   (i) for $k = \frac{1}{2}$
   (ii) for time-constant $\frac{1}{2}$ sec.

2. Generate $\sin \omega t$ and $\cos \omega t$ for 30 secs when

   (i) $\omega = \frac{1}{2}$ rad s^{-1}
   (ii) $\omega = 25$ rad s^{-1}

3. Generate $\sin(t + \phi)$ and $\cos(t + \phi)$ for 20 secs using *only three amplifiers* for the cases

   (i) $\phi = 30^{\circ}$
   (ii) $\phi = -\pi/4$

   Check in each case that both waveforms have the same amplitude.

4. Solve $\ddot{x} + \lambda \dot{x} + 25x = f(t)$, for $0 \leqslant \lambda \leqslant 10$, given that all I.C.s are zero, and taking

   (i) $f(t) = 10$
   (ii) $f(t) = 10e^{-0 \cdot 75t}$
   (iii) $f(t) = 10\sin t$
   (iv) $f(t) = 10t$
   (v) $f(t) = 10(1 - e^{-4t})$
   (vi) $f(t) = 10\cos 20t$
   (vii) $f(t) = 10\cos 4 \cdot 5t$.

5. Solve $\ddot{x} + 4\dot{x} + 36x = t^2 - 2t$, given $x = \dot{x} = 0$ at $t = 0$.

CHAPTER 7
MACHINE SOLUTION CHECKS

7.1 First order

Problem equation of the form $a\dot{x} \pm bx = f_1(t)$.

The analytic solution will be of the form

$x = Ae^{\mp kt} + f_2(t)$ where $k = b/a$

For equations arising from physical problems, the complementary function is usually of the form Ae^{-kt} (transient solution) and the particular integral $f_2(t)$ is the steady state solution.

The time constant of the transient will be $1/k$ sec.

When $t = \dfrac{1}{k}$ transient $= Ae^{-1} \simeq 0 \cdot 368A$

       $t = \dfrac{3}{k}$ transient $= Ae^{-3} \simeq 0 \cdot 050A$

       $t = \dfrac{5}{k}$ transient $= Ae^{-5} \simeq 0 \cdot 007A$

       $t = \dfrac{7}{k}$ transient $= Ae^{-7} \simeq 0 \cdot 001A$

It follows that after the elapse of 3 time constants the solution is within 5% of steady state,
after the elapse of 5 time constants the solution is within 1% of steady state,
after the elapse of 7 time constants the solution is within 0·1% of steady state.

If we now consider the case in which $f_1(t)$ is a *step function* input of the form $c.H(t)$ the steady state $f_2(t)$ will be constant and equal to c/b. This provides us with an opportunity for checking our work as follows.

Replace the original *amplitude-scaled version of* $f_1(t)$ by a step-function of 1 MU, compute this version of the problem, and from the C.R.O. trace estimate the time constant of the solution, and check that it is of the same order as $1/k$ from the analytic solution. Then with the D.V.M. read the value of the steady state and check that it is c/b.

Example 14

Solve $\quad 3\dot{x} + 7x = 5\cos 4t \qquad$ given $x = 0$ at $t = 0$

$$\dot{x} = \frac{5}{3}\cos 4t - \frac{7}{3}x$$

Unscaled flow diagram:

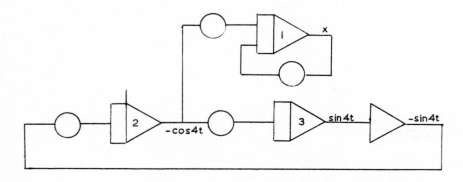

Figure 73

Decomposed equations:

Amplifier 1. $\quad -\dfrac{d}{dt}x = \dfrac{7}{3}x - \dfrac{5}{3}\cos 4t$

Amplifier 2. $\quad -\dfrac{d}{dt}(-\cos 4t) = -4\sin 4t$

Amplifier 3. $\quad -\dfrac{d}{dt}(\sin 4t) = -4\cos 4t$

Scaling:

$$x_{max} = \frac{5}{7} \simeq 1 \quad \text{hence we scale} \left(\frac{x}{1}\right)$$

and scale $\left(\dfrac{\sin 4t}{1}\right)$, $\left(\dfrac{\cos 4t}{1}\right)$

Scaled equations:

(1) $\quad -\dfrac{d}{dt}\left(\dfrac{x}{1}\right) = \dfrac{7}{3}\left(\dfrac{x}{1}\right) + \dfrac{5}{3}\left(-\dfrac{\cos 4t}{1}\right)$

(2) $\quad -\dfrac{d}{dt}\left(-\dfrac{\cos 4t}{1}\right) = 4\left(-\dfrac{\sin 4t}{1}\right)$

(3) $\quad -\dfrac{d}{dt}\left(\dfrac{\sin 4t}{1}\right) = 4\left(-\dfrac{\cos 4t}{1}\right)$

Machine equations:

(1) $\quad -\dfrac{d}{dt}\left(\dfrac{x}{1}\right) = [0\cdot233]\,10\left(\dfrac{x}{1}\right) + [0\cdot167]\,10\left(-\dfrac{\cos 4t}{1}\right)$

(2) $\quad -\dfrac{d}{dt}\left(-\dfrac{\cos 4t}{1}\right) = [0\cdot400]\,10\left(-\dfrac{\sin 4t}{1}\right)$

(3) $\quad -\dfrac{d}{dt}\left(\dfrac{\sin 4t}{1}\right) = [0\cdot400]\,10\left(-\dfrac{\cos 4t}{1}\right)$

Scaled flow diagram:

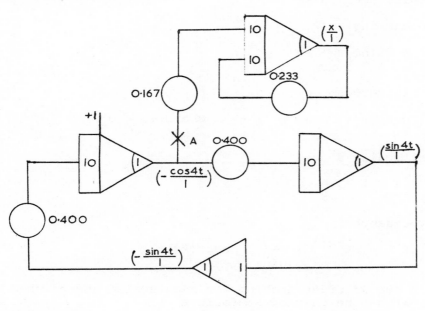

Figure 74

   To check on the machine: disconnect the $\left(-\dfrac{\cos 4t}{1}\right)$ input at the point on the patch panel which corresponds to point A on the flow diagram and run the problem with − 1 MU fed in its place: i.e. temporarily solve the differential equation

   $3\ddot{x} + 7x = 5.H(t)$

From this equation, the steady state solution should be $+\dfrac{5}{7}$ MU; the time-constant of the transient should be $\dfrac{3}{7}$ sec. (N.B. $k = \dfrac{7}{3}$)
Steady state should be approached, to within 5%, after $1\dfrac{2}{7}$ sec.
Check on the C.R.O. (and meter) that these results are obtained.

   The $\left(-\dfrac{\cos 4t}{1}\right)$ can now be checked for amplitude and period; if all is well, it is then reconnected at point A and the problem can be run.

7.2 Second order

Problem equation of the form $a\ddot{x} + b\dot{x} + cx = f(t)$.

For equations arising from physical problems, the terms on the l.h.s. are almost invariably positive, and as we have seen can be written in the form

$$\ddot{x} + 2\zeta\omega_n\dot{x} + \omega_n^2 x = \frac{1}{a}f(t)$$

If we replace $\frac{1}{a}f(t)$ by a suitably scaled step function $C.H(t)$, then depending on the values of the ζ the solution will fall into one of the following four categories:

(a) $\zeta = 0$ (no damping)

$$x = A\cos\omega_n t + B\sin\omega_n t + \frac{C}{\omega_n^2}$$

(b) $0 < \zeta < 1$ (under-damped)

$$x = e^{-\zeta\omega_n t}(A\cos\omega_1 t + B\cos\omega_1 t) + \frac{C}{\omega_n^2} \quad \text{where } \omega_1 < \omega_n$$

(c) $\zeta = 1$ (critically damped)

$$x = e^{-\zeta\omega_n t}(A + Bt) + \frac{C}{\omega_n^2}$$

(d) $\zeta > 1$ (over-damped)

$$x = e^{-\zeta\omega_n t}\left(Ae^{kt} + Be^{-kt}\right) + \frac{C}{\omega_n^2} \quad \text{where } |k| < \zeta\omega_n$$

When a given second order problem has been scaled and patched on the computer, it can be checked as follows:

(i) From the *problem* equation, the values of ω_n and ζ should be calculated.

(ii) On the computer, the driving function [scaled version of $f_1(t)$] is disconnected and replaced by a suitably scaled step function $C.H(t)$. Also the feedback loop of the first integrator (highest derivative of the second order equation) is temporarily removed, thus putting $\zeta = 0$. The computer is then put into compute, which enables the machine ω_n to be checked against the calculated value of ω_n.

(iii) The feedback loop is reconnected and the computer again put into compute. We can now check whether the transient output falls into either category (b) or (d) as predicted from the calculated value of ζ, and if under-damped some estimate of the damping time constant may be made and compared with $1/\zeta\omega_n$. Further, the steady state output can be measured against the calculated value of C/ω_n^2.

(iv) Provided that checks (ii) and (iii) show the expected behaviour, the step function can be disconnected, and the correctly scaled version of $f_1(t)$ reintroduced; the computer can then be run to solve the given problem.

Example 15

Solve $\quad 2\ddot{y} + \dot{y} + 18y = 5\cos t \quad$ given $y = 0$, $\dot{y} = \frac{1}{2}$ at $t = 0$.

From the equation, $\omega_n = 3$ and $\zeta = \frac{1}{12}$ (lightly damped)

Proceeding in the usual way, we can establish the machine equations:

(1) $\quad -\dfrac{d}{dt}\left(-\dfrac{\dot{y}}{1}\right) = [0\cdot5]1\left(-\dfrac{\dot{y}}{1}\right) + [0\cdot45]10\left(-\dfrac{y}{1/2}\right) + [0\cdot25]10\left(\dfrac{\cos t}{1}\right)$

(2) $\quad -\dfrac{d}{dt}\left(\dfrac{y}{1/2}\right) = [0\cdot2]10\left(-\dfrac{\dot{y}}{1}\right)$

(3) $\quad -\dfrac{d}{dt}\left(-\dfrac{\sin t}{1}\right) = 1\left(\dfrac{\cos t}{1}\right)$

(4) $\quad -\dfrac{d}{dt}\left(-\dfrac{\cos t}{1}\right) = 1\left(-\dfrac{\sin t}{1}\right)$

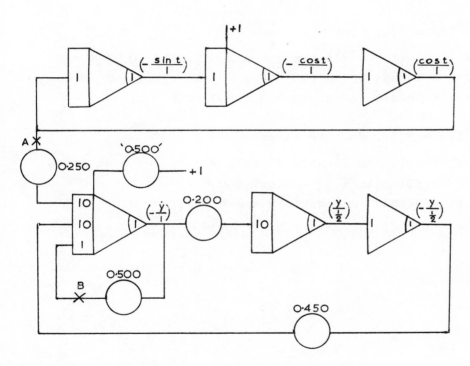

Figure 75

To check the machine: disconnect feedback loop at B and the $\cos t$ driving function at A and replace the latter by + 1 MU. Run the computer and check that $\left(\dfrac{y}{1/2}\right)$ output is a sinusoid with period $\dfrac{2\pi}{3} \simeq 2\cdot1$ sec. Reconnect feedback loop at B and rerun the computer. Solution shown should be a lightly damped sinusoid with a decay envelope of time constant $\dfrac{1}{\dfrac{1}{12} \times 3} = 4$ sec

This can be checked by observing the solution on the 'scope for 20 sec by which time the steady state value should be reached. The steady state value should be $y = \dfrac{5}{18}, \left[\left(\dfrac{y}{1/2}\right) = \dfrac{5}{9} \text{ MU}\right]$. If the check is satisfactory the step function can be removed, the cost driving function checked and then replaced, and the computer will then solve the given problem.

Exercise 8

Solve the following equations, giving a machine check in each case.

1. $\dot{x} + 2x = f(t)$, for the cases

    (i) $f(t) = -10$ and given $x = 8$ at $t = 0$

    (ii) $f(t) = \dfrac{1}{10} e^{2t}$ and given $x = -5$ at $t = 0$.

2. $\ddot{x} + 8\dot{x} + 16x = f(t)$, for the cases

    (i) $f(t) = 30\left(1 - e^{-\frac{1}{2}t}\right)$ and given $x = 0$, $\dot{x} = 10$ at $t = 0$

    (ii) $f(t) = 10\cos t$ and given $x = \dot{x} = 0$ at $t = 0$

    (iii) $f(t) = 5\cos 4t$ and given $x = \dot{x} = 0$ at $t = 0$.

3. $\ddot{x} + \dot{x} + 16x = f(t)$, for the cases

    (i) $f(t) = 10\left(1 - e^{-2t}\right)$ and given $x = -2$, $\dot{x} = 0$ at $t = 0$

    (ii) $f(t) = 10\sin\left(2t + \dfrac{\pi}{4}\right)$ and given $x = \dot{x} = 0$ at $t = 0$

    (iii) $f(t) = 5\sin 4t$ and given $x = \dot{x} = 0$ at $t = 0$.

CHAPTER 8
TIME-SCALING

8.1 Why we time-scale

The need for time-scaling may arise for one or both of the following reasons:

(*a*) The time occupied physically by the solution of the problem itself (problem time) and the time over which it is convenient to examine that solution on an analogue computer (computing time) may differ enormously. We may require to compute in less than a minute the solution of a problem which may take, physically, a few microseconds only (e.g. some electronic phenomena) or perhaps may take days or years (e.g. some biological or astronomical phenomena).

(*b*) The computing elements may subject their outputs to unacceptable errors if either

    too great a gain is employed, or
    they are used outside their "dynamic range".

Errors arising from either cause may be avoided, or at least mitigated, by time-scaling.

The use of time-scaling because of (*a*) above is self-evident; let us look at (*b*) in more detail.

Computing elements have physical limitations on the rate at which they can transfer information. For example, an X-Y pen recorder which has a maximum pen velocity of $0 \cdot 5 \text{ ms}^{-1}$ will not produce a reliable trace if we attempt to drive it at 1 ms^{-1}. Again, the response of an ideal inverter to a step function input would be a step function output; but, in practice, the actual inverter behaves much more like a first order lag, for example:

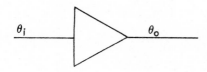

Figure 76

Ideally, $\theta_o = -\theta_i$. In practice it is more realistic to take
$$T\dot{\theta}_o + \theta_o = -\theta_i$$

Thus if $\theta_i = -H(t)$, then
$$\theta_o \simeq 1 - e^{-t/T}$$

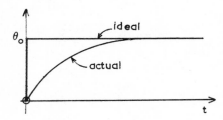

Figure 77

It follows that for $0 < t < \frac{1}{10}T$, resulting errors $\geqslant 90\%$

and for $t > 7T$, resulting errors $\leqslant 0 \cdot 1\%$

The value of the time-constant T depends on the type of computing element concerned; it may be as small as $0 \cdot 0001$ sec for an inverter but as large as $0 \cdot 1$ sec for a pen recorder; and high accuracy of solution during the interval $0 < t < 7T$ (where t is the computing time) cannot be obtained.

The approximation of computing elements to first order lags requires also that we consider their frequency response: for sinusoid inputs, as the frequency increases, the amplitude ratio (output/input) decreases and the phase change through the element increases. While it is difficult to quote hard-and-fast figures owing to the wide divergence in performance between different makes and types of equipment, the following table may be taken as a rough guide for the estimation of "safe" operating frequencies; if doubt exists in any case it is advisable to work the equipment *well below* the upper limits given.

High speed elements

Amplifiers (summers and integrators)	
Oscilloscopes	0 - 1 000 rad s^{-1}
Diodes and Diode Function Generators	
¼-Squares multipliers	

Medium speed elements

Strip recorders	
Relays	0 - 100 rad s^{-1}

Low speed elements

X-Y recorders	0 - 5 rad s^{-1}

To summarize: we must endeavour to see that

(i) total computing gains are not excessive;
(ii) computing frequencies are kept well within the frequency
     limitations of the *slowest* element in the group employed
     (not forgetting the type of recorder used).

8.2 How we time-scale

Let t = problem time, and let τ = machine time; to time-scale, let
$\tau = \beta t$ where β is the time-scaling factor.
 Then 1 problem second = β machine (computing) seconds.
 The expression "real time" should be avoided, otherwise
ambiguity may arise.
 Consider the typical integrator shown in Figure 78:

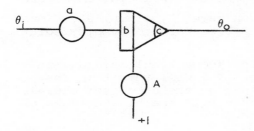

Figure 78

The Machine equation which relates to this will be

$$-\frac{d}{d\tau}(\theta_o) = c\left\{[a]b(\theta_i)\right\} \quad \text{with } \theta_o = -A \text{ at } \tau = 0$$

(Note that this equation is written in terms of τ; i.e. in machine
time, which is the time in which the integrator actually operates.)
 Integrating both sides of this equation with respect to τ and
incorporating the I.C., we get

$$\theta_o = -\left\{G\int_0^\tau \theta_i \; d\tau + A\right\} \qquad \text{(i)}$$

where $G = abc$, the Overall Gain of the integrator.
 We now relate machine time to problem time by putting $\tau = \beta t$,
so that equation (i) becomes

$$\theta_o = -\left\{G\int_0^{\beta\tau} \theta_i \; d(\beta t) + A\right\}$$

but $d(\beta t) = \beta dt$, so we have

$$\theta_o = -\left\{\beta G\int_0^{\beta\tau} \theta_i \; dt + A\right\} \qquad \text{(ii)}$$

 Equation (ii) is, of course, the same as equation (i), but is
written in terms of *problem* time (t), and the quantity βG can be
regarded as the Problem Gain of the integrator. When we prepare
the decomposed equations for a given problem, and amplitude-scale

them in the usual way, the resulting set of scaled equations will of course be in terms of problem time t and hence the coefficients of the terms on the right-hand side of the integrator equations will represent the problem gains of the integrators concerned, i.e. the βG value of equation (ii) above. It is evident that to time-scale by a factor of β we must revert to integrator equations of form (i) with overall machine gains G. Hence we *divide* all integrator problem gains by β to get the integrator machine gains.

There are several important points to note here:

(1) It will be seen from equations (i) and (ii) that the value of A is unaffected by time-scaling, i.e. initial conditions *remain unchanged* when the problem is time-scaled.

(2) Summers, and the equations relating to them, *remain unaffected* by time-scaling (since summers are not time-dependent elements).

(3) *All* integrators relating to the problem, including those concerned with driving functions such as e^{-kt}, $\sin\omega t$, etc., must be time-scaled; so must any time-base used to display solution read-out.

(4) Since 1 problem second = β machine (computing) seconds, it follows that choosing a value of $\beta < 1$ will result in the speeding-up of the problem when put on the computer, whereas choosing a value of $\beta > 1$ will result in the slowing-down of the problem when put on the computer.

The following example shows the conventions which should be followed when applying the above results in a practical case:

Example 16

Solve $\dfrac{d^2x}{dt^2} + 14\,\dfrac{dx}{dt} + 10\,000x = 50$ given $x = 0$ and $\dfrac{dx}{dt} = 1$ at $t = 0$

It follows that $\omega_n = 100$ rad s^{-1} and damping is light ($\zeta = 0\cdot07$) Proceeding in the usual way, we can establish the scaled equations:

(1) $-\dfrac{d}{dt}\left(-\dfrac{\dot{x}}{1}\right) = 14\left(-\dfrac{\dot{x}}{1}\right) + 100\left(-\dfrac{x}{0\cdot01}\right) + 50$

(2) $-\dfrac{d}{dt}\left(\dfrac{x}{0\cdot01}\right) = 100\left(-\dfrac{\dot{x}}{1}\right)$

From the scaled equations it is evident that we must time-scale, partly to reduce element gains from 100 and partly because $\omega \simeq 100$ rad s^{-1} is too high a frequency for satisfactory observation on a 'scope (and very much too high for an X-Y pen recorder).

Let $\tau = \beta t$

Time-scaled equations:

(1) $-\dfrac{1}{\beta}\dfrac{d}{dt}\left(-\dfrac{\dot{x}}{1}\right) = \dfrac{14}{\beta}\left(-\dfrac{\dot{x}}{1}\right) + \dfrac{100}{\beta}\left(-\dfrac{x}{0\cdot01}\right) + \dfrac{50}{\beta}$

(2) $-\dfrac{1}{\beta}\dfrac{d}{dt}\left(\dfrac{x}{0\cdot01}\right) = \dfrac{100}{\beta}\left(-\dfrac{\dot{x}}{1}\right)$

We now choose β so as to

    (*a*) reduce input gains to a reasonable level
and (*b*) suit the type of recording instrument we intend to use.

For (*a*) we should choose β = 10.
For (*b*) the use of a 'scope would be electronically satisfactory
        for β = 1, but only visually satisfactory for β > 5 (i.e.
        ω < 20 rad s⁻¹). For the use of an *X-Y* pen recorder, β > 20
        (i.e. ω < 5 rad s⁻¹).

Evidently a choice of β = 20 will meet all requirements. For
greater accuracy, or if a large-scale trace is required from a pen
recorder, β = 50 or 100 would be better.

Consider β = 50 (1 problem second = 50 computer seconds)

Machine equations:

(1) $- \dfrac{1}{50} \dfrac{d}{dt}\left(- \dfrac{\dot{x}}{1}\right) = [0 \cdot 280] 1\left(- \dfrac{\dot{x}}{1}\right) + [0 \cdot 200] 10\left(- \dfrac{x}{0 \cdot 01}\right) + 1(1)$

(2) $- \dfrac{1}{50} \dfrac{d}{dt}\left(\dfrac{x}{0 \cdot 01}\right) = [0 \cdot 200] 10\left(- \dfrac{\dot{x}}{1}\right)$

Flow diagram (for β = 50):

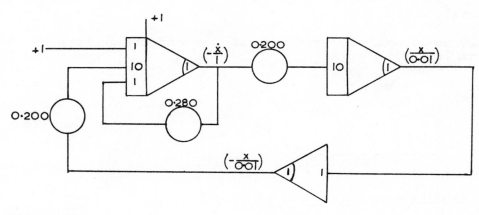

Figure 79

Note
  (i) Further change of time-scale can be done quite simply by
      altering all the integrator gains in unison.
      For example: if the two integrator elements in Figure 79 had
      nose gains of 10, the computer would run 10 times faster;
      i.e. β = 5.

 (ii) Inspection of the diagram shows that we are not only solving
      the given problem time-scaled by a factor of 50, but in effect
      we are solving many related problems. For example, we are
      solving at unity time-scale (β = 1) the problem

$$\left(\dfrac{\ddot{y}}{1}\right) = 0 \cdot 28\left(- \dfrac{\dot{y}}{1}\right) + 2\left(- \dfrac{y}{1/2}\right) + 1$$

    i.e. $\ddot{y} + 0 \cdot 28\dot{y} + 4y = 1$, with $y = 0$ and $\dot{y} = 1$ at $t = 0$.

Note that when a problem has been time-scaled, and its solution is drawn on an *X-Y* plotter, the time-axis on the graph paper *should be marked off in units of problem-time (t)*, and *not* of computer time (τ). A suitable scale should be chosen for the purpose (cf. table on page 28).

Exercise 9

1. Solve $\ddot{x} + 100\dot{x} + 10^4 x = 500\sin 50t$, given $x = \dot{x} = 0$ at $t = 0$ and computing $\ddot{x}$.

2. Solve $\ddot{x} + f\dot{x} + 150x = 6\cos\omega t$, given $x = \dot{x} = 0$ at $t = 0$, and where f can be varied over the range $4 \leqslant f \leqslant 8$, and ω can be varied over the range $9 \leqslant \omega \leqslant 15$.
   Use the computer to find which combination of f and ω, within the ranges quoted, will lead to maximum amplitude of steady-state x oscillations.

3. For the mass/spring/damper system shown, derive the equations of motion and show that they can be reduced to the form:
   $$\ddot{y} = -100(y - x) + 50\sin\omega t$$
   $$\dot{x} = 25(y - x) - 15x$$

   (It may be assumed that the mass of the connecting-bar is negligible.)

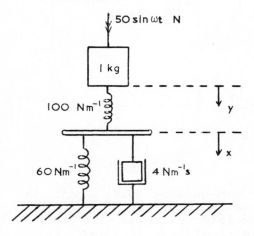

Investigate the motion of the system using an analogue computer, for values of ω in the range $5 \leqslant \omega \leqslant 10$ rad s^{-1}.

CHAPTER 9
TRANSFER FUNCTIONS

If the input θ_i and the output θ_o of a linear system are related by an equation of the form

$$\left(a_n D^n + a_{n-1} D^{(n-1)} + \ldots + a_1 D + a_0\right)\theta_o = \left(b_m D^m + \ldots + b_1 D + b_0\right)\theta_i$$

where $m \leqslant n$ and $D = d/dt$

then we may write this symbolically as

$$\theta_o = \frac{b_m D^m + \ldots + b_0}{a_n D^n + \ldots + a_0}\,\theta_i$$

Now if all the initial values which may be prescribed are zero, then the Laplace transforms of θ_i and θ_o are related by

$$\frac{\overline{\theta_o}(s)}{\overline{\theta_i}(s)} = \left(\frac{b_m s^m + \ldots + b_0}{a_n s^n + \ldots + a_0}\right)$$

where s is the Laplace parameter.

This ratio of the transform of the output to the transform of the input of an initially undisturbed system is defined as the transfer function of the system.

The system may now be represented in block diagram form by:

$$\overline{\theta_i} \longrightarrow \boxed{\dfrac{b_m s^m + \ldots + b_0}{a_n s^n + \ldots + a_0}} \longrightarrow \overline{\theta_o}$$

    The order of the transfer function is taken to be n (the degree of the denominator). In general, practical problems lead in the first instance to first and second order transfer functions or to cascaded combinations of them. The latter may (though seldom with profit for simulation purposes) be replaced by a single higher order transfer function.

Thus the system

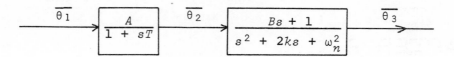

$$\theta_1 \rightarrow \boxed{\frac{A}{1 + sT}} \xrightarrow{\theta_2} \boxed{\frac{Bs + 1}{s^2 + 2ks + \omega_n^2}} \xrightarrow{\theta_3}$$

is equivalent to

$$\theta_1 \rightarrow \boxed{\frac{A(Bs + 1)}{(1 + sT)(s^2 + 2ks + \omega_n^2)}} \xrightarrow{\theta_3}$$

which in turn could be expressed as

$$\theta_1 \rightarrow \boxed{\frac{ABs + A}{Ts^3 + (2kT + 1)s^2 + (2k + \omega_n^2 T)s + \omega_n^2}} \xrightarrow{\theta_3}$$

9.1 First order transfer functions

(a) $\dfrac{\bar{x}}{\bar{y}} = \dfrac{A}{1 + sT}$ which is called a first order lag.

By taking the inverse Laplace transform we may obtain the first order differential equation

$$x + T\dot{x} = Ay$$

which may then be treated in the same way as any other first order differential equation

(b) $\dfrac{\bar{x}}{\bar{y}} = \dfrac{A + sB}{C + sD}$

This transfer function may be modified to give

$$\frac{\bar{x}}{\bar{y}} = \frac{A/C + sB/C}{1 + sD/C} = \frac{1}{1 + sD/C} \cdot (A/C + sB/C)$$

We now introduce a dummy variable z so that

$$\frac{\bar{x}}{\bar{y}} = \frac{\bar{z}}{\bar{y}} \cdot \frac{\bar{x}}{\bar{z}}$$

Then let $\dfrac{\bar{z}}{\bar{y}} = \dfrac{1}{1 + sD/C}$

so that $\dfrac{\bar{x}}{\bar{z}} = \dfrac{A}{C} + s\dfrac{B}{C}$

Taking the inverse transform for each equation gives the two equations

$$z + \frac{D}{C}\dot{z} = y \quad \text{and} \quad x = \frac{A}{C}z + \frac{B}{C}\dot{z}$$

which can be solved by normal methods.

84

Unscaled flow diagram

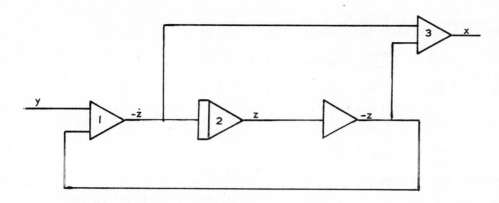

Figure 80

Decomposed equations

(1) $- (- \dot{z}) = \frac{C}{D} y - \frac{C}{D} z$

(2) $- \frac{d}{dt} (z) = - \dot{z}$

(3) $- (x) = - \frac{A}{C} z - \frac{B}{C} \dot{z}$

Scaling considerations will depend on the form of the input variable y.

For a step input

$$\dot{z}_{max} = \frac{C}{D} y \qquad z_{max} = y$$

and $|x_{max}| \leqslant |\frac{A}{C} z_{max}| + |\frac{B}{C} \dot{z}_{max}|$

But since it is unlikely that z and $\dot{z}$ will be a maximum at the same time, this maximum for x may well be an overestimate. As the following analysis will show a more realistic maximum would be either $(A/C) z_{max}$ or $(B/C) \dot{z}_{max}$ whichever is the greater.

By inspection it can be seen that:

when $\dot{z}$ is a maximum $(t = 0)$, $z = 0$ and

when z is a maximum (at z_{ss}), $\dot{z} = 0$

Now since z will have the form

$$z = z_{ss} \left(1 - e^{-kt} \right) \qquad \text{and} \qquad \dot{z} = \dot{z}_0 e^{-kt}$$

then $\quad x = \frac{A}{C} z_{ss}\left(1 - e^{-kt}\right) + \frac{B}{C} \dot{z}_0 e^{-kt}$

$$= \frac{A}{C} z_{ss} + e^{-kt}\left(\frac{B}{C} \dot{z}_0 - \frac{A}{C} z_{ss}\right)$$

Hence the solution will be exponential, with

$$x_0 = \frac{B}{C} \dot{z}_0 = \frac{B}{D} y \qquad \text{and} \qquad x_{ss} = \frac{A}{C} z_{ss} = \frac{A}{C} y$$

Therefore

$$x_{max} = \frac{B}{D} y \quad \text{or} \quad x_{max} = \frac{A}{C} y$$

whichever is the greater.

For y a sinusoidal input, frequency response considerations must be taken into account, and the reader is advised to consult the appropriate Bode plot or the first order normalized frequency response diagram shown in Figure 81.

9.2 Second order transfer functions

(a) $\quad \dfrac{\bar{x}}{\bar{y}} = \dfrac{A}{as^2 + bs + c}$

which is called a second order lag.

Taking the inverse transform gives the differential equation

$$a\ddot{x} + b\dot{x} + cx = Ay$$

It is more usual to consider second order transfer functions in the standard form

$$\frac{\bar{x}}{\bar{y}} = \frac{k\omega_n^2}{s^2 + 2\zeta\omega_n s + \omega_n^2}$$

which gives the differential equation

$$\ddot{x} + 2\zeta\omega_n\dot{x} + \omega_n^2 x = k\omega_n^2 y$$

where ζ is the damping ratio, ω_n is the natural frequency and k is usually referred to as the DC gain (gain at zero frequency).

(b) $\quad \dfrac{\bar{x}}{\bar{y}} = \dfrac{A + sB}{s^2 + 2\zeta\omega_n s + \omega_n^2}$

modifying the transfer function to extract a standard form second order lag gives

$$\frac{\bar{x}}{\bar{y}} = \frac{\omega_n^2}{s^2 + 2\zeta\omega_n s + \omega_n^2} \cdot \frac{A + sB}{\omega_n^2}$$

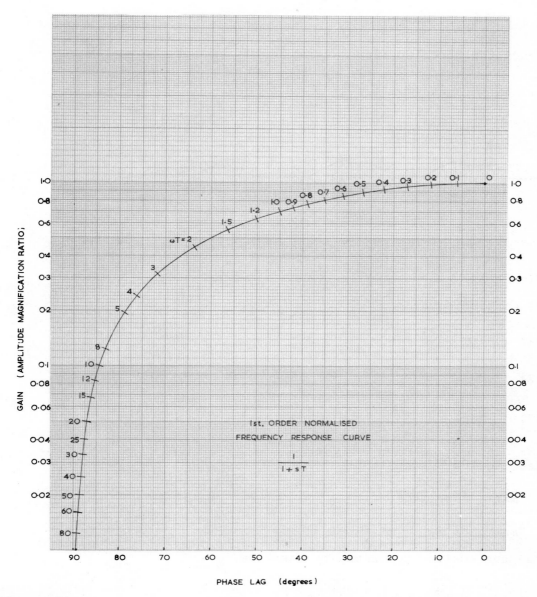

Figure 81

Introducing the dummy variable z, we have

$$\frac{\bar{z}}{\bar{y}} = \frac{\omega_n^2}{s^2 + 2\zeta\omega_n s + \omega_n^2}$$

and $\quad \dfrac{\bar{x}}{\bar{z}} = \dfrac{A + sB}{\omega_n^2}$

Taking inverse transforms

$$\ddot{z} + 2\zeta\omega_n\dot{z} + \omega_n^2 z = \omega_n^2 y$$

$$x = \frac{A}{\omega_n^2} z + \frac{B}{\omega_n^2} \dot{z}$$

Hence the unscaled flow diagram

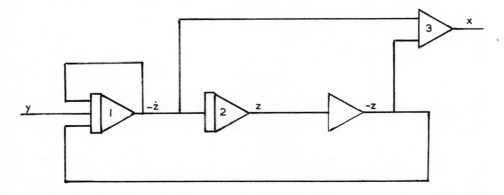

Figure 82

Decomposed equations

(1) $\quad -\dfrac{d}{dt}(-\dot{z}) = \omega_n^2 y - 2\zeta\omega_n\dot{z} - \omega_n^2 z$

(2) $\quad -\dfrac{d}{dt}(z) = -\dot{z}$

(3) $\quad -(x) = -\dfrac{A}{\omega_n^2} z - \dfrac{B}{\omega_n^2} \dot{z}$

Scaling for a step input

$$z_{max} = 2z_{ss} = 2y$$

$$\dot{z}_{max} = \omega_n z_{ss} = \omega_n y$$

and the scaling for x may be taken as

$$|x_{max}| \leqslant \left|\frac{A}{\omega_n^2} z_{max}\right| + \left|\frac{B}{\omega_n^2} \dot{z}_{max}\right|$$

88

If the numerator contains a term in s^2 then the second derivative of the dummy variable must be generated.

Example 17

Simulate $\dfrac{\bar{x}}{\bar{y}} = \dfrac{100(s^2 + 2s + 4)}{s^2 + 10s + 100}$

$\dfrac{\bar{x}}{\bar{y}} = \dfrac{100}{s^2 + 10s + 100} \cdot (s^2 + 2s + 4)$

Let $\dfrac{\bar{z}}{\bar{y}} = \dfrac{100}{s^2 + 10s + 100}$

$\dfrac{\bar{x}}{\bar{z}} = s^2 + 2s + 4$

Therefore $\ddot{z} + 10\dot{z} + 100z = 100y$

and $x = \ddot{z} + 2\dot{z} + 4z$

Unscaled flow diagram

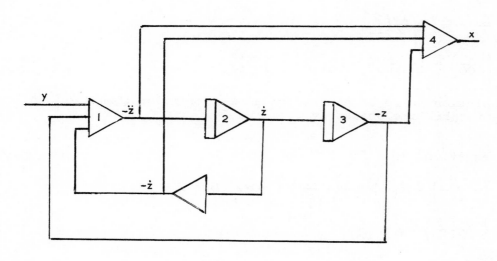

Figure 83

Decomposed equations

(1) $\quad - (- \ddot{z}) = 100y - 10\dot{z} - 100z$

(2) $\quad - \dfrac{d}{dt}(\dot{z}) = - \ddot{z}$

(3) $\quad - \dfrac{d}{dt}(- z) = \dot{z}$

(4) $\quad - (x) = - \ddot{z} - 2\dot{z} - 4z$

Scaling for step input $y = 1$

$$z_{max} < 2z_{ss} = 2y$$

$$\dot{z}_{max} < \omega_n z_{ss} = 10y$$

$$\ddot{z}_{max} < \omega_n^2 z_{ss} = 100y$$

$$x_{max} < \ddot{z}_{max} + 2\dot{z}_{max} + 4z_{max}$$
$$= 100y + 20y + 8y = 128y$$

Scale $\left(\dfrac{y}{1}\right), \left(\dfrac{z}{2}\right), \left(\dfrac{\dot{z}}{10}\right), \left(\dfrac{\ddot{z}}{100}\right), \left(\dfrac{x}{100}\right)$

Scaled equations

(1) $-\left(-\dfrac{\ddot{z}}{100}\right) = \dfrac{100}{100}\left(\dfrac{y}{1}\right) - \dfrac{100}{100}\left(\dfrac{\dot{z}}{10}\right) - \dfrac{100}{100}\cdot 2\left(\dfrac{z}{2}\right)$

(2) $-\dfrac{d}{dt}\left(\dfrac{\dot{z}}{10}\right) = 10\left(-\dfrac{\ddot{z}}{100}\right)$

(3) $-\dfrac{d}{dt}\left(-\dfrac{z}{2}\right) = \dfrac{10}{2}\left(\dfrac{\dot{z}}{10}\right)$

(4) $-\left(\dfrac{x}{100}\right) = \left(-\dfrac{\ddot{z}}{100}\right) - \dfrac{2}{10}\left(\dfrac{\dot{z}}{10}\right) - \dfrac{8}{100}\left(\dfrac{z}{2}\right)$

If the solution is to be plotted on an X-Y recorder then the problem must be time scaled by $\beta = 2$ or 5.

Let $\beta = 5$.

Machine equations ($\beta = 5$)

(1) $-\left(-\dfrac{\ddot{z}}{100}\right) = 1\left(\dfrac{y}{1}\right) + 1\left(-\dfrac{\dot{z}}{10}\right) + [0 \cdot 2]10\left(-\dfrac{z}{2}\right)$

(2) $-\dfrac{1}{\beta}\dfrac{d}{dt}\left(\dfrac{\dot{z}}{10}\right) = 2\left(-\dfrac{\ddot{z}}{100}\right)$

(3) $-\dfrac{1}{\beta}\dfrac{d}{dt}\left(-\dfrac{z}{2}\right) = 1\left(\dfrac{\dot{z}}{10}\right)$

(4) $-\left(\dfrac{x}{100}\right) = \dfrac{1}{10}\left\{10\left(-\dfrac{\ddot{z}}{100}\right) + [0\cdot 2]10\left(-\dfrac{\dot{z}}{10}\right) + [0\cdot 8]1\left(-\dfrac{z}{2}\right)\right\}$

Scaled flow diagram

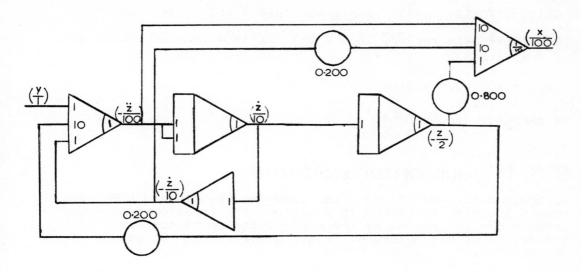

Figure 84

Let us now consider the scaling necessary if $y = \sin6t$. Consideration of Figure 72 shows that at $\omega = 6$, i.e. $\omega/\omega_n = 0\cdot6$ and for $\zeta = 10/(2 \times 10) = 0\cdot5$ the gain (A.M.R.) is $1\cdot15$ and the phase lag is $42\cdot5^{O} = 0\cdot74$ rad.

$z_{ss} = 1\cdot15\sin(6t - 0\cdot74)$

$z_{max} = 1\cdot15 \simeq 2$

$\dot{z}_{max} = 6 \times 1\cdot15 = 6\cdot9 \simeq 10$

$\ddot{z}_{max} = 36 \times 1\cdot15 = 41\cdot5 \simeq 50$

Scale $\left(\dfrac{z}{2}\right)$, $\left(\dfrac{\dot{z}}{10}\right)$, $\left(\dfrac{\ddot{z}}{50}\right)$

We can now use Figure 72 to give the gain of the second order lead

In standard form we have:

$\dfrac{\overline{x}}{\overline{z}} = 4 \cdot \dfrac{s^2 + 2s + 4}{4}$

i.e. $\omega_n = 2$, $\zeta = 2/(2 \times 2) = 0\cdot5$, $k = 4$

but since Figure 72 is drawn for a second order *lag* we must take the reciprocal of the gain and read the phase as a lead.

From the curves for $\omega/\omega_n = 6/2 = 3$ and $\zeta = 0.5$

Gain $= 1/0.115 = 8.7$ and phase lead $= 160^{\circ} = 2.8$ rad

The total gain for $\bar{x}/\bar{y}$ is $4 \times 8.7 \times 1.15 = 40$ and phase angle $= -0.74 + 2.8$

$$x_{ss} = 40\sin(6t + 2.06)$$

We therefore scale $\left(\dfrac{x}{50}\right)$.

9.3 Higher order systems

Although first and second order lead/lag systems are the most common transfer functions in practice, any transfer function of order n may be treated by the dummy variable method provided that the degree of the numerator is not greater than the degree of the denominator.

Exercise 10

Simulate the following transfer functions:

(1) $\dfrac{\bar{x}}{\bar{y}} = \dfrac{5}{6 + 7s}$ where $y = 2$

(2) $\dfrac{\bar{x}}{\bar{y}} = \dfrac{5 + 7s}{2 + 4s}$ where $y = 3\sin0.6t$

(3) $\dfrac{\bar{x}}{\bar{y}} = \dfrac{4 + 3s}{s^2 + 3s + 7}$ where $y = 4\sin2t$

(4) $\dfrac{\bar{x}}{\bar{y}} = \dfrac{1}{4}\left\{\dfrac{s^2 + 20s + 400}{s^2 + 5s + 100}\right\}$ where $y = \sin\omega t$, for ω in the range $5 \leqslant \omega \leqslant 50$

(5) $\theta_i \rightarrow \boxed{\dfrac{50}{1 + 3s}} \rightarrow \boxed{\dfrac{3 + 5s}{s^2 + 10s + 106}} \rightarrow \theta_o$

where $\theta_i = \sin\omega t$, for ω in the range $0 \leqslant \omega \leqslant 20$.

CHAPTER 10
COMPUTING ELEMENT CIRCUITS

10.1 High gain amplifier

As has been previously stated, the summer and integrator elements
are based on amplifiers. Each amplifier is a High Gain D.C.
amplifier (H.G.A.):

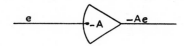

Figure 85

Ideally the H.G.A. would have an infinite D.C. gain A, but in
practice A is of the order 10^8 - 10^9 for D.C. inputs, and may fall
to as low as 4×10^4 for inputs of frequency 1 kHz.
   If e is the input to the H.G.A. and if A is *very large*, and if
the output $- Ae$ is held within the limits of $\pm$ 1 MU, it follows
that e will always be nearly zero, i.e. virtually at earth potential.
This type of amplifier is therefore often referred to as a "virtual
earth" amplifier.

10.2 Summer

Consider an H.G.A. with resistive inputs and feedback as shown in
Figure 86:

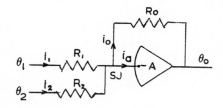

Figure 86

The H.G.A. input current i_a is in practice less than 5×10^{-11} amps; if therefore we assume the input to the H.G.A. to be at earth potential, and that the H.G.A. input current is zero, then from Kirchoff's law, the current at the junction of the input resistors (the summing junction SJ) is equal to the feedback current; i.e.

$$i_0 = i_1 + i_2$$

Then applying Ohm's law we have

$$-\frac{\theta_0}{R_0} = \frac{\theta_1}{R_1} + \frac{\theta_2}{R_2}$$

$$\theta_0 = -\left(\frac{R_0}{R_1}\theta_1 + \frac{R_0}{R_2}\theta_2\right)$$

where R_0/R_1 and R_0/R_2 are the input gains for the input variables θ_1 and θ_2.

10.3 Integrator

Consider the circuit of Figure 86 modified by the inclusion of an alternative capacitative feedback path as shown in Figure 87. When the capacitative path is selected:

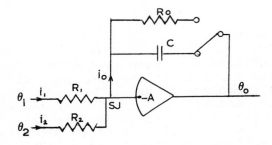

Figure 87

The voltage across the capacitor at any instant is $\frac{1}{C}\int i_0 d\tau$.

Assuming a virtual earth at the input to the H.G.A., and that the capacitor has no initial charge, then

$$\theta_0 = -\frac{1}{C}\int_O^\tau i_0 d\tau$$

but from Kirchoff's law

$$i_0 = i_1 + i_2 = \frac{\theta_1}{R_1} + \frac{\theta_2}{R_2}$$

Therefore

$$\theta_0 = -\frac{1}{C}\int_0^{\tau}\left(\frac{\theta_1}{R_1} + \frac{\theta_2}{R_2}\right) d\tau$$

We have already defined the values R_0/R_1 and R_0/R_2 as the input gains; we may therefore write

$$\theta_0 = -\frac{1}{R_0 C}\int_0^{\tau}\left(\frac{R_0}{R_1}\theta_1 + \frac{R_0}{R_2}\theta\right) d\tau$$

We now define $1/R_0 C$ as the INTEGRATOR NOSE GAIN. In some computers one of two capacitors can be selected, to give nose gains of 1 or 10.

10.4 Potentiometers

A coefficient multiplier is in fact an electrical potentiometer:

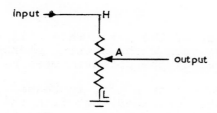

Figure 88

This may be considered to be two resistors with A at the junction:

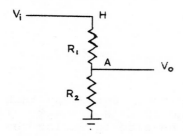

Figure 89

Movement of the pot knob in the clockwise direction has the effect of increasing the value of R_2 and decreasing R_1 and vice versa. Assuming that no current is taken from the output, then $i_1 = i_2$ where i_1 is the current in R_1 and i_2 is the current in R_2. Hence

$$\frac{V_i - V_o}{R_1} = i_1 = i_2 = \frac{V_o}{R_2}$$

$$\text{Output voltage } V_o = \frac{R_2}{R_1 + R_2} V_i$$

The pots are set up with 1 MU on the high end of the pot and monitoring the wiper voltage V_o (computer in Pot Set mode).

When the pot is used on the computer, the output will be connected to the input of an amplifier:

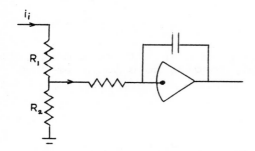

Figure 90

Some current will be drawn from the output of the pot. This will increase the current through R_1 and hence change the setting of the pot. It is essential then that the output of the potentiometer be patched, before the latter is set.

When small values are required to be set on a pot, increased accuracy may be obtained by using two pots (cascaded) but from the above it is obvious that care must be taken to avoid errors due to loading. When using cascaded pots to set 0·06 (say):

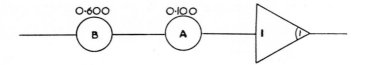

Figure 91

pot A may be set with its genuine amplifier load. Pot B may then be set in the knowledge that the correct load on B is present. If the pot setting combination is one that may be altered during the problem the variation should be made *on pot B*, leaving A unaltered.

On some computers, the cascading of pots is not possible, due to the way in which the + 1 MU is switched to the high end of the pot in the Pot Set mode. If all the pots on the computer have + 1 MU switched to their high ends when Pot Set is selected, then the second pot in a cascaded pair loses its genuine load, making it impossible to set that pot accurately. If, on the other hand, the + 1 MU is only switched to the high end of one particular pot when that pot is addressed, then provided that the correct order of setting is adhered to, all will be well when cascading. The pots of many computers are arranged in groups, and the high end of every pot in a particular group is switched to + 1 MU when any one pot in that group is addressed in the Pot Set mode; on such a machine, it follows that pots may be cascaded provided that they are chosen from separate groups. Should there be any doubt as to which of these Pot Set methods applies to the machine which the reader is likely to use, reference should be made to the relevant manual or to the manufacturer of the computer.

10.5 Controls

To use the circuits discussed above, the computer is put into one of the following modes:

Pot set:

(1) All input resistors have their amplifier ends disconnected from the amplifier and taken to genuine earth, thus presenting a true load to any preceding potentiometer, and avoiding overloads during the setting of the pot.

Problem check (on some computers, called I.C.):

(1) All summers are summing.
(2) All integrator outputs are fixed at their values for $t = 0$, and must not integrate their inputs.

Compute:

(1) All summers are summing.
(2) All integrators integrate the sums of their inputs.

Hold:

(1) All summers are summing.
(2) All integrator outputs are held static.

These four modes may be achieved by means of a set of relays as shown in Figure 92. The normally closed contact of each contact pair is shown shaded. The table shows which relays change over in which states, e.g. in Pot Set for a summer the wiper of contacts 3 changes from the shaded contact to the white one.

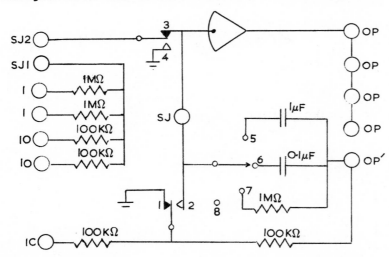

Figure 92

	SUMMER			INTEGRATOR × 1			INTEGRATOR × 10		
POT SET	1	4	7	2	4	5	2	4	6
PC (I.C.)	1	3	7	2	4	5	2	4	6
C	1	3	7	1	3	5	1	3	6
HOLD	1	3	7	1	4	5	1	4	6

The resistor values shown are typical for a 100 V machine. On a
10 V machine the resistor values are normally 100 kΩ and 10 kΩ
while the capacitors are 10 µF and 1 µF.

Figure 93 shows the equivalent circuits for eight of the
twelve states.

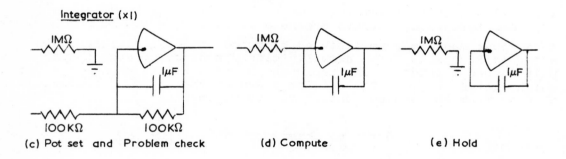

Figure 93

Let us look further at Figure 93(c):

Consider

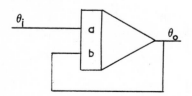

Figure 94

From Figure 94 we have

$$- \frac{d\theta_o}{dt} = b\theta_o + a\theta_i$$

i.e. $(D + b) \theta_o = - a\theta_i$

This first order differential equation has steady state solution
$\theta_o = - \frac{a}{b} \theta_i$ and the transient time-constant is $1/b$ sec.
Thus when $a = b = \dfrac{1}{0 \cdot 1 \times 1} = 10$ from Figure 93(c),

steady state $\theta_o = - \theta_i$

and time-constant is $0 \cdot 1$ sec.

Hence after, say, $0 \cdot 5$ secs (5 time-constants) $\theta_o \simeq - \theta_i$ where θ_i is the voltage at the I.C. socket.

Reference to Figure 92 will show that the scope of the amplifier can be greatly extended by using external components. For example

(a) Extra inputs may be obtained by plugging appropriate resistors into SJ_1 as shown (note:- SJ_1 and SJ_2 will thus still be linked).

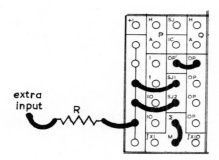

Figure 95

(b) The overall gain of a summer may be changed by using a different feedback resistor e.g. for a summer with a nose gain of 1/10 remove M and OP-OP' links, thus removing the feedback components, and insert 100 kΩ resistor between OP and SJ; then the summer becomes

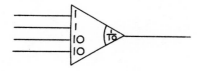

Figure 96

(c) If one amplifier is not required in a problem its input resistors may be "borrowed" by another amplifier to give 4 inputs of $\times$ 1 and 4 inputs of $\times$ 10. This may be done as shown in Figure 97.

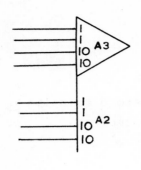

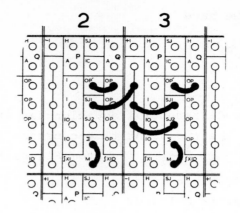

Figure 97

CHAPTER 11
STATIC CHECK PROCEDURE

It is good practice to have the scaled flow diagram fully prepared
before coming to the computer. In this way time spent at the computer is kept to a minimum - an important point in industry where
the cost of actual machine-time is high compared with the cost of
preparation work done in an office; the point has importance also
for students whose time in the computer laboratory is necessarily
limited.

Such practice demands that the paper-work should be correct,
and *known to be correct*, before any machine-time is used. It implies
further that once the problem has been set up on the machine it
should be possible (with reasonable ease and speed) to check that
the machine will correctly obey the equations of the problem.

Computer elements can give rise to errors due to malfunction,
e.g. defective resistors, burned-out pots, etc.; but the most
frequently occurring errors are those caused by the computer's human
elements - its operators and/or programmers. It is essential that
all such errors should be discovered before machine-time is wasted
in producing solutions to the wrong equations; checking procedures
which do this are carried out as a matter of routine by the majority
of experienced computer operators.

Earlier in this book (Chapter 7) a checking method for first
and second order equations was considered - a more general procedure
applicable to all orders or combinations of orders is clearly desirable. It is convenient to divide the checking process into two
parts:

(i) a check that the final flow diagram correctly represents the
     given equations

(ii) a check on the machine itself to see that it correctly obeys
     the given equations.

11.1 Paper check

By considering three examples we shall now develop a Static Check
procedure:

Example 18

$$\ddot{y} + 0\cdot8\dot{y} + 9y = 35 \quad \text{given } \dot{y} = +9, \ y = -2 \text{ at } t = 0$$

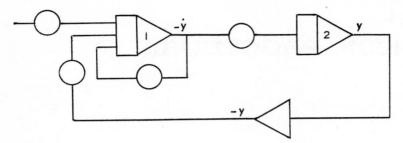

Figure 98

Decomposed equations:

Amplifier 1. $-\dfrac{d}{dt}(-\dot{y}) = 35 - 0\cdot8\dot{y} - 9y$

Amplifier 2. $-\dfrac{d}{dt}y = -\dot{y}$

Scaling:

Let us scale $\left(\dfrac{y}{10}\right)$, $\left(\dfrac{\dot{y}}{20}\right)$ (see page 31)

Scaled equations:

(1) $-\dfrac{d}{dt}\left(-\dfrac{\dot{y}}{20}\right) = \dfrac{35}{20} + 0\cdot8\left(-\dfrac{\dot{y}}{20}\right) + \dfrac{9\times10}{20}\left(-\dfrac{y}{10}\right)$

(2) $-\dfrac{d}{dt}\left(\dfrac{y}{10}\right) = \dfrac{20}{10}\left(-\dfrac{\dot{y}}{20}\right)$

Machine equations:

(1) $-\dfrac{d}{dt}\left(-\dfrac{\dot{y}}{20}\right) = [0\cdot175]10(1) + [0\cdot800]1\left(-\dfrac{\dot{y}}{20}\right) + [0\cdot450]10\left(-\dfrac{y}{10}\right)$

(2) $-\dfrac{d}{dt}\left(\dfrac{y}{10}\right) = [0\cdot200]10\left(-\dfrac{\dot{y}}{20}\right)$

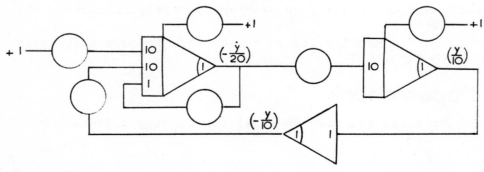

Figure 99

102

Note: at this stage pot settings should *not* appear on the flow diagram. This ensures that only the settings shown on the pot sheet are used in the static check; this is an important point since the computer pots are set from the pot sheet itself.

Computer elements are now allocated to suit the machine to be used, showing these allocations on both the flow diagram and the machine equations.

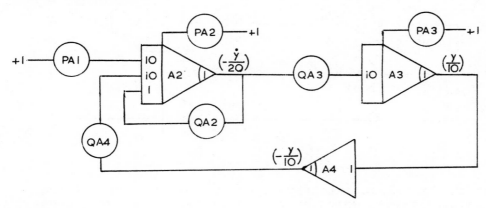

Figure 100

Machine equations:

A2 (1) $\quad -\dfrac{d}{dt}\left(-\dfrac{\dot{y}}{20}\right) = \underset{PA1}{[0.175]}10(1) + \underset{QA2}{[0.800]}1\left(-\dfrac{\dot{y}}{20}\right) + \underset{QA4}{[0.450]}10\left(-\dfrac{y}{10}\right)$

A3 (2) $\quad -\dfrac{d}{dt}\left(\dfrac{y}{10}\right) = \underset{QA3}{[0.200]}10\left(-\dfrac{\dot{y}}{20}\right)$

From the machine equations we produce the pot list:

Pot	Setting	Gain	Amplifier
PA1	0·175	10 × 1	
PA2	0·450	I.C.	A2
PA3	0·200	I.C.	A3
QA2	0·800	1 × 1	
QA3	0·200	10 × 1	
QA4	0·450	10 × 1	

The static check now begins with the substitution of the I.C.s into the decomposed problem equations and a calculation of the initial rates of change:

(1) $\quad -\dfrac{d}{dt}(-\dot{y}) = 35 - 0.8 \times 9 - 9 \times (-2)$

$\qquad\qquad = 35 - 7.2 + 18 = 45.8$

(2) $\quad -\dfrac{d}{dt}y = -9$

The outputs of integrators in the initial condition state are now inserted on the flow diagram (preferably using a distinctive colour; in this book italics are used):

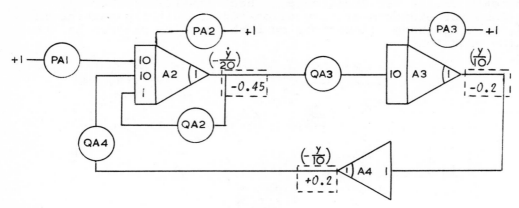

Figure 101

Note that the inputs to integrators are scaled versions of the problem initial rates, which have been calculated above; hence from the flow diagram and pot list we have:

$$- \frac{d}{dt} \text{(output)} = \sum \left\{ [\text{pot}] \times \text{gain} \times \text{(signal)} \right\}$$

Thus for A2:

$$- \frac{d}{dt} \left(- \frac{\dot{y}}{20} \right) = [\text{PA1}] \times 10 \times (1) + [\text{QA4}] \times 10 \times (+0 \cdot 2) + [\text{QA2}] \times 1 \times (-0 \cdot 45)$$

$$= 1 \cdot 75 + 0 \cdot 9 - 0 \cdot 36 = 2 \cdot 29 \text{ MU}$$

$$- \frac{d}{dt} (- \dot{y}) = 20 \times 2 \cdot 29 = 45 \cdot 8$$

This last figure agrees with the value calculated from the original decomposed equation 1 above, and gives us our first check.

Then for A3:

$$- \frac{d}{dt} \left(\frac{y}{10} \right) = [\text{QA3}] \times 10 \times (-0 \cdot 45)$$

$$= 0 \cdot 200 \times 10 \times (-0 \cdot 45) = - 0 \cdot 900 \text{ MU}$$

$$- \frac{d}{dt} y = 10 \times (-0 \cdot 9) = - 9 \quad \text{Checks with (2) above.}$$

With the possible exception that two, mutually cancelling, mistakes have been made in the above check, we can now be certain that the flow diagram is correct.

The integrator rates of change (2·29 and - 0·90 MU) just calculated, will be used later when checking that the computer is correctly set up for the problem.

In practice the successive modifications to the flow diagram as shown in Figures 100 and 101 would be incorporated on Figure 99; the three stages of modification have been shown separately in this

104

example in order better to illustrate the development. Similarly the machine equations need not be rewritten each time, but can be modified as they stand, as will be shown in the following two examples; in the first of these we show an extension of the above treatment to take account of problems in which the given initial conditions are zero.

Example 19

(See Example 13, page 39)

$$\dddot{x} + 4\ddot{x} + 30\dot{x} + 100x = 50 \quad \text{given } \ddot{x} = \dot{x} = x = 0 \text{ at } t = 0$$

Decomposed equations:

(1) $\quad -\dfrac{d}{dt}\ddot{x} = 4\ddot{x} + 30\dot{x} + 100x - 50$

(2) $\quad -\dfrac{d}{dt}(-\dot{x}) = +\ddot{x}$

(3) $\quad -\dfrac{d}{dt}x = -\dot{x}$

(For scaling, and machine equations, see pages 39 and 40)

Flow diagram:

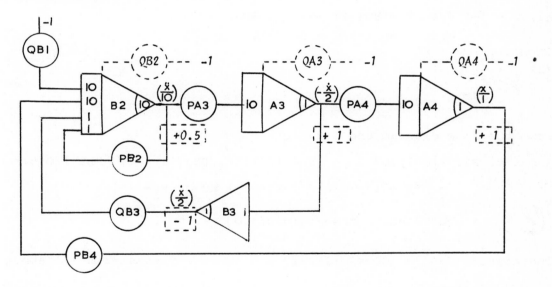

Figure 102

Pot list:

Pot	Setting	Gain	Amplifier
PA3	0·500	10 × 1	
PA4	0·200	10 × 1	
QA3		S.C.	A3
QA4		S.C.	A4
PB2	0·400	1 × 10	
PB4	0·100	10 × 10	
QB1	0·050	10 × 10	
QB2		S.C.	B2
QB3	0·600	1 × 10	

Since the integrators have zero I.C.s as given, we assume non-zero values for checking purposes, called 'static check initial conditions' (S.C.I.C.s). These non-zero assumed values must be less than the maxima for the variables concerned.

Let $\ddot{x} = + 5$, $\dot{x} = - 2$, $x = 1$, then

$$\left(\frac{\ddot{x}}{10}\right) = + 0\cdot5 \qquad \left(- \frac{\dot{x}}{2}\right) = + 1 \qquad \left(\frac{x}{1}\right) = + 1$$

Substitute these values into the decomposed equations:

(1) $\quad -\dfrac{d}{dt}\ddot{x} = 4 \times 5 + 30(-2) + 100 - 50$

$\qquad\qquad = 20 - 60 + 100 - 50 = 10$

(2) $\quad -\dfrac{d}{dt}(- \dot{x}) = + 5$

(3) $\quad -\dfrac{d}{dt}x = + 2$

From the flow diagram and pot list:

Input to B2: $[QB1]10(-1) + [PB4]10(1) + [QB3]1(-1) + [PB2]1(0\cdot5)$

$\qquad = - 0\cdot5 + 1 - 0\cdot6 + 0\cdot2 = 0\cdot1$ MU $= - \dfrac{1}{10}\dfrac{d}{dt}\left(\dfrac{\ddot{x}}{10}\right)$

$\left(\dfrac{1}{10}\dfrac{d}{dt}, \text{ since B2 has a nose gain of } 10\right)$

Therefore $- \dfrac{d}{dt}\ddot{x} = 100 \times 0\cdot1 = 10$ $\qquad$ Checks with (1) above

Input to A3: $[PA3]10(0\cdot5) = 2\cdot5$ MU $= - \dfrac{d}{dt}\left(- \dfrac{\dot{x}}{2}\right)$

Therefore $- \dfrac{d}{dt}(- \dot{x}) = 2 \times 2\cdot5 = 5$ $\qquad$ Checks with (2) above

Input to A4: $[PA4]10(1) = 2$ MU $= - \dfrac{d}{dt}\left(\dfrac{x}{1}\right)$

Therefore $- \dfrac{d}{dt}x = 2$ $\qquad$ Checks with (3) above

In the next example, we show how the presence of variable problem parameters, and the existence of time-scaling, may be incorporated within the static check procedure.

Example 20

Solve
$$\dot{x} + 60x + 20y = 200$$
$$\ddot{y} + K\dot{y} + 40\,000y = 20\,000x$$

given $x = y = 0$, $\dot{y} = 200$ at $t = 0$

Compute x, $\dot{x}$, y, $\dot{y}$, for $20 \leqslant K \leqslant 60$

Unscaled flow diagram

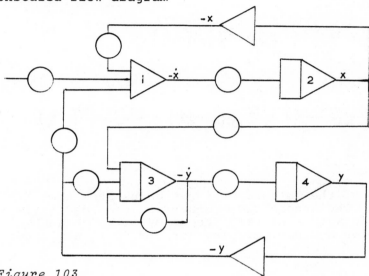

Figure 103

Decomposed equations:

(1) $\quad - (- \dot{x}) = 200 - 60x - 20y$

(2) $\quad - \dfrac{d}{dt}x = - \dot{x}$

(3) $\quad - \dfrac{d}{dt}(- \dot{y}) = 20\,000x - K\dot{y} - 40\,000y$

(4) $\quad - \dfrac{d}{dt}y = - \dot{y}$

Scaling:

At steady state (since the system is stable)
$$60x + 20y = 200$$
$$40\,000y - 20\,000x = 0$$

Therefore $\quad 2y = x$

Therefore $\quad x = \dfrac{20}{7} \quad$ and $\quad y = \dfrac{10}{7}$

107

Since, initially, x and y are zero: let us scale $\left(\dfrac{x}{5}\right)$, $\left(\dfrac{y}{5}\right)$.

As has been seen before, the equations may be treated in isolation for scaling purposes.

The first order equation has a decay time constant of 1/60 second. Therefore

$$\dot{x}_{max} \simeq 60 \times \frac{20}{7} \simeq 200 \qquad\qquad \text{Let us scale } \left(\frac{\dot{x}}{200}\right)$$

The second order equation has $\omega_n = 200$ and $\dfrac{1}{20} \leqslant \zeta \leqslant \dfrac{3}{20}$. Therefore

$$\dot{y}_{max} \simeq 200 \times \frac{10}{7} \simeq 300 \qquad\qquad \text{Let us scale } \left(\frac{\dot{y}}{500}\right)$$

Amplitude-scaled equations:

(1) $\qquad -\left(-\dfrac{\dot{x}}{200}\right) = \dfrac{200}{200} + \dfrac{60 \times 5}{200}\left(-\dfrac{x}{5}\right) + \dfrac{20 \times 5}{200}\left(-\dfrac{y}{5}\right)$

(2) $\qquad -\dfrac{d}{dt}\left(\dfrac{x}{5}\right) = \dfrac{200}{5}\left(-\dfrac{\dot{x}}{200}\right)$

(3) $\qquad -\dfrac{d}{dt}\left(-\dfrac{\dot{y}}{500}\right) = \dfrac{20\,000 \times 5}{500}\left(\dfrac{x}{5}\right) + \dfrac{500K}{500}\left(-\dfrac{\dot{y}}{500}\right) + \dfrac{40\,000 \times 5}{500}\left(-\dfrac{y}{5}\right)$

(4) $\qquad -\dfrac{d}{dt}\left(\dfrac{y}{5}\right) = \dfrac{500}{5}\left(-\dfrac{\dot{y}}{500}\right)$

The large values of the integrator input gains show that time-scaling is necessary. The second order equation, regarded in isolation, is lightly damped with a natural frequency of 200 rad s^{-1}, this suggests $\beta = 20$ for a C.R.O. display (or $\beta = 50$ if a plotter is to be used).

Consider the case $\beta = 20$:

Machine equations:

A4 (1) $\quad -\left(-\dfrac{\dot{x}}{200}\right) = 1\,(1) + \underset{QA3}{[0\cdot150]}10\left(-\dfrac{x}{5}\right) + \underset{PA4}{[0\cdot500]}1\left(-\dfrac{y}{5}\right)$

A2 (2) $\quad -\dfrac{1}{\beta}\dfrac{d}{dt}\left(\dfrac{x}{5}\right) = \underset{PA2}{[0\cdot200]}10\left(-\dfrac{\dot{x}}{200}\right)$

B2 (3) $\quad -\dfrac{1}{\beta}\dfrac{d}{dt}\left(-\dfrac{\dot{y}}{500}\right) = 10\left\{1\left(\dfrac{x}{5}\right) + \underset{PB2}{\left[\dfrac{K}{200}\right]}1\left(-\dfrac{\dot{y}}{500}\right) + \underset{QB4}{[0\cdot200]}10\left(-\dfrac{y}{5}\right)\right\}$

B3 (4) $\quad -\dfrac{1}{\beta}\dfrac{d}{dt}\left(\dfrac{y}{5}\right) = 10\left\{\underset{PB3}{[0\cdot500]}1\left(-\dfrac{\dot{y}}{500}\right)\right\}$

(Note: for pot list, see page 111.)

Flow diagram:

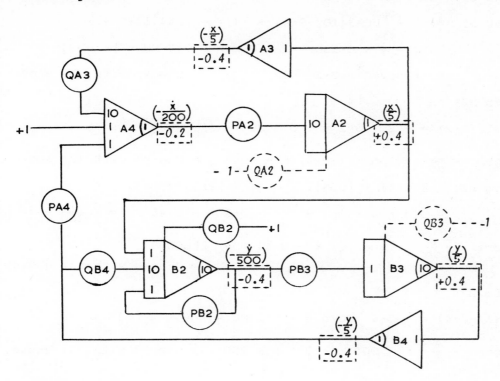

Figure 104

Static check:

Choose $K = 20$, $x = 2$, $y = 2$, $\dot{y} = 200$

Substituting these values into the decomposed equations:

(1) $\dot{x} = 200 - 120 - 40 = 40$

(2) $-\dfrac{d}{dt}x = -\dot{x} = -40$

(3) $-\dfrac{d}{dt}(-\dot{y}) = 20\,000 \times 2 - 20 \times 200 - 40\,000 \times 2$
$$= -4\,000 - 40\,000 = -44\,000$$

(4) $-\dfrac{d}{dt}y = -\dot{y} = -200$

S.C.I.C.s:

Let $x = 2$, $\left(\dfrac{x}{5}\right) = 0\cdot400$ Let $y = 2$, $\left(\dfrac{y}{5}\right) = 0\cdot400$

Let $\dot{y} = 200$, $\left(-\dfrac{\dot{y}}{500}\right) = -0\cdot400$ Let $K = 20$, $\left[\dfrac{K}{200}\right] = 0\cdot100$

Before calculating the inputs to integrators it is necessary to calculate the outputs of all the summers and insert the values on the flow diagram.

109

From the flow diagram and pot sheet

Output of A4: $- \left\{ [QA3]10(-0\cdot4) + 1(1) + [PA4]1(-0\cdot4) \right\}$

$$= 4 \times 0\cdot150 - 1 + 0\cdot2 = -0\cdot2 \text{ MU} = \left(-\frac{\dot{x}}{200} \right)$$

Therefore $\dot{x} = 200 \times 0\cdot2 = 40$ Checks with (1) above.

Input to A2:

$$[PA2]10(0\cdot2) = -2 \times 0\cdot2 = -0\cdot4 \text{ MU} = -\frac{1}{20}\frac{d}{dt}\left(\frac{x}{5}\right)$$

Therefore $-\frac{d}{dt}x = 100 \times (-0\cdot4) = -40$ Checks with (2) above.

Input to B2: $1(0\cdot4) + [QB4]10(-0\cdot4) + [PB2]1(-0\cdot4)$

$$= 0\cdot4 - 4 \times 0\cdot2 - 0\cdot4 \times 0\cdot1 = -0\cdot44 \text{ MU} = -\frac{1}{200}\frac{d}{dt}\left(-\frac{\dot{y}}{500}\right)$$

Therefore $-\frac{d}{dt}(-\dot{y}) = 10^5 \times -0\cdot44 = -44\,000$

Checks with (3) above.

Input to B3:

$$[PB3]1(-0\cdot4) = -0\cdot4 \times 0\cdot5 = -0\cdot2 \text{ MU} = -\frac{1}{200}\frac{d}{dt}\left(\frac{y}{5}\right)$$

Therefore $-\frac{d}{dt}y = 1\,000 \times -0\cdot2 = -200$ Checks with (4) above.

It should be a routine procedure to enter the inputs to integrators
and outputs from summers (and inverters) as calculated during the
static check, on the pot and amplifier sheets. An example of this
is shown below.

Complete problem preparation incorporating the static check
procedure so far described, may be summarized as follows:

1. Prepare: Unscaled flow diagram
              Decomposed equations
              Amplitude scaling
              Scaled equations
              Time scaling
              Machine equations
              Scaled flow diagram
              Pot list.

2. Assign arbitrary values to variable parameters (magnitudes to
    be within the scaled range).

3. Assume arbitrary values for those variables which correspond to
    integrator outputs. (Keep within the scaled range; problem
    initial values can be used if not zero.)

4. Substitute in *decomposed equations* and so calculate values for
    the derivatives.

5. Scale the values from 2. and 3. above, and put them on the
    flow diagram.

AMPLIFIER SHEET

Name ASC
Problem Example 20
Computer No. 5
Time scale β = 20

	Function	O/P Variable	P.C.	STATIC CHECK Calculated O/P	Calculated $\frac{1}{10}\frac{d}{dt}$	Measured O/P	Measured $\frac{1}{10}\frac{d}{dt}$
A1							
A2	$\int \times 1$	$\left(\dfrac{x}{5}\right)$	0		$-0\cdot040$		
A3	$\Sigma \times 1$	$-\dfrac{x}{5}$	0	$-0\cdot400$			
A4	$\Sigma \times 1$	$\left(-\dfrac{\dot{x}}{200}\right)$	0	$-0\cdot200$			
A5							
A6							
B1							
B2	$\int \times 10$	$\left(-\dfrac{\dot{y}}{500}\right)$	$-0\cdot400$		$-0\cdot044$		
B3	$\int \times 10$	$\dfrac{\dot{y}}{5}$	0		$-0\cdot020$		
B4	$\Sigma \times 1$	$\left(-\dfrac{\dot{y}}{5}\right)$	0	$-0\cdot400$			
B5							
B6							
C1							
C2							
C3							
C4							
C5							
C6							
D1							
D2							
D3							
D4							
D5							
D6							

POTENTIOMETER SHEET

Name ASC
Problem Example 20
Computer No. 5
Time scale β = 20

POT.	Setting	Gain	S.C.	Amplifier	Remarks
PA1					
PA2	$0\cdot200$	10×1			
PA3		1×1			
PA4	$0\cdot500$	1×1			
PA5					
PA6					
QA1					
QA2	$0\cdot150$		$0\cdot400$	A 2	$(x = 2)$
QA3		10×1			
QA4			$\cdot$		
QA5					
QA6					
PB1					
PB2	$\dfrac{K}{200}$	1×10	$0\cdot100$		$(K = 20)$
PB3	$0\cdot500$	1×10			
PB4					
PB5					
PB6					
QB1					
QB2	$0\cdot400$	IC		B 2	
QB3			$0\cdot400$	B 3	$(y = 2)$
QB4	$0\cdot200$	10×10			
QB5					
QB6					

6. *Using the flow diagram and pot list*, calculate the outputs from summers, and then the initial values of integrator rates. From the latter calculate the derivatives of the unscaled variables and check with 4. above.

Note: If the results of 4., when scaled, exceed 1 MU for summers or 10 MU for integrators (the reason for the latter will become apparent from the next section), or are equal to zero for either, the values chosen in 3. must be modified and the calculations repeated.

11.2 Machine check

So far the checking procedure has shown that the machine flow diagram is (most probably) correct; in addition, the expected values of the sum-of-inputs to each integrator are known. The check on the computer itself consists of measuring the sum-of-inputs, and comparing them with the values already calculated. In this way, errors of the following kind will be eliminated (but note that, as in the paper static check, it is just conceivable that two mutually cancelling errors could occur and remain undetected):

1. Incorrect patching
2. Incorrect pot settings
3. Incorrect summer/integrator settings
4. Defective patch cords
5. Unserviceable units.

The way in which S.C.I.C.s are set on the computer varies from one make of computer to another. On some machines the S.C.I.C.s are patched and set up in the same way as are the normal non-zero problem I.C.s, using patch cords of a distinctive colour to facilitate easy location and removal after the checking procedure has been completed. On some computers the S.C.I.C. pots are fed from a special reference supply socket; on these machines the S.C.I.C.s become effective only when a Static Check button or switch is operated, and thus the S.C.I.C. patching may be left in place during the running of the problem. There are also other methods in use - the appropriate computer handbook should be consulted in all cases. We now require to measure the outputs of all summers, and the sum-of-inputs to all integrators (in the problem check mode), and ensure that these agree with the calculated values from the paper check. The outputs of summers are measured in the usual way; it might be thought that we could measure the sum-of-inputs to integrators by switching them to Sum and reading the outputs. If this were done, however, their I.C.s or S.C.I.C.s would be lost, thereby invalidating the check. The I.C.s and S.C.I.C.s can however be retained by disconnecting the junction of the summing resistors from the input of the integrating amplifier to be checked, and connecting it instead to the input of a Check Amplifier:

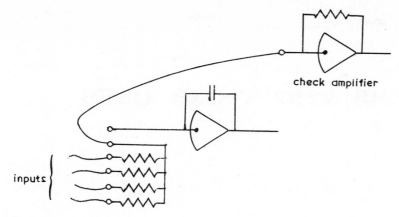

Figure 105

    In some computers a check amplifier is provided as a special unit in addition to the complement of normal computing amplifiers, and the connection of the check amplifier to the input resistors of the integrators is effected by a series of switches, one for each integrator. In computers without such provision, one of the normal computing amplifiers must be used as the check amplifier, and the necessary connection made with a patch cord. (This amplifier can conveniently be patched as the C.R.O. or Plotter time base if required, after the machine check has been completed.)

    It often happens that the sum of the inputs to an integrator exceeds 1 MU; although this may not cause an overload when running the problem, since the input to an integrator is only a rate, it would mean that the check amplifier would overload when checking. In computers incorporating a separate check amplifier this difficulty is obviated by arranging the check amplifier to have an alternative nose gain of 1/10. In computers where one of the normal computing amplifiers has to be used for checking purposes, the nose gain of 1/10 must be arranged by suitable patching (see page 99).

    As the outputs and inputs are measured they should be entered in the appropriate columns of the amplifier sheet.

    Having completed the Static Check it only remains for the S.C.I.C.s to be removed, and the outputs of all amplifiers checked with the P.C. column of the amplifier sheets, before the computation of the problem is commenced.

CHAPTER 12
MULTIPLIERS AND THEIR USES

12.1 Some problem non-linearities

Linear differential equations with constant coefficients may provide useful although often crude mathematical models of physical systems. Such an equation· describes the one-dimensional motion of a mass-spring system:

$$M\ddot{x} = - Kx + \text{(External force acting in } x \text{ direction)} \qquad \text{(i)}$$

(M = mass; K = stiffness = force per unit displacement).

Equation (i) implies that the spring is accurately linear in characteristic throughout the whole possible range of displacement x; it implies further that the whole system is operating in vacuo and that there is no friction acting anywhere in the system, not even internally within the material of the spring. It is evident from everyday experience that such a system does not exist in physical fact, although it can exist as a mental concept - in the same world as exist the weightless smooth pulley, the light inextensible string and the undeformable and perfectly elastic billiard ball.

Equation (i) can be made a somewhat less crude model of a physically viable mass-spring system if we include a velocity damping term:

$$M\ddot{x} = - f\dot{x} - Kx + \text{(External disturbing force)} \qquad \text{(ii)}$$

The additional force proportional to velocity (f a constant) which occurs in the equation enables us, by suitable choice of the parameter f, to introduce into the mathematical model a representation of the effect of air resistance, friction, and the deliberate inclusion of some physical damping device such as a piston moving in an oil-filled dashpot. Equation (ii) does in fact take us a significant step towards an authentic mathematical model of very many physical systems which occur in nature; of course, equation (ii) may be solved analytically, and as we have seen it presents few difficulties when solved on an analogue computer.

The trouble starts (from an analytic solution point of view) when we further improve equation (ii) in an attempt to make it a still closer representation of certain physical systems. Suppose, for example, that the shape, size and velocity of the mass concerned result in the damping due to air resistance becoming significantly large and better represented as proportional to (velocity)^2; the equation of motion becomes:

$$M\ddot{x} = - f\dot{x}|\dot{x}| - Kx + \text{(External disturbing force)} \qquad \text{(iii)}$$

(The reason for using $\dot{x}|\dot{x}|$ instead of $(\dot{x})^2$ is one to which the reader may usefully devote some thought.)

Suppose now that we include the effect of a double-acting damper as well, in which, while being linear in characteristic, the damping effect as the piston moves one way differs from that as it moves in the opposite direction. Equation (iii) may now be modified to read

$$M\ddot{x} = - f\dot{x}|\dot{x}| - f_1\dot{x} - Kx + \text{(External disturbing force)}$$
$$\text{for } \dot{x} < 0 \qquad \text{(iv)(a)}$$
$$M\ddot{x} = - f\dot{x}|\dot{x}| - f_2\dot{x} - Kx + \text{(External disturbing force)}$$
$$\text{for } \dot{x} > 0 \qquad \text{(iv)(b)}$$

Suppose further that the spring in the system is a compound spring, so designed that upon compression the stiffness increases as the cube of the displacement, whereas in extension the stiffness increases as the square of the displacement; our system will now require four equations to represent it:

$$M\ddot{x} = - f\dot{x}|\dot{x}| - f_1\dot{x} - K_1x|x| + \text{(External disturbing force)}$$
$$\text{for } \dot{x} < 0, \ x < 0 \qquad \text{(v)(a)}$$
$$M\ddot{x} = - f\dot{x}|\dot{x}| - f_1\dot{x} - K_2x^3 + \text{(External disturbing force)}$$
$$\text{for } \dot{x} < 0, \ x > 0 \qquad \text{(v)(b)}$$
$$M\ddot{x} = - f\dot{x}|\dot{x}| - f_2\dot{x} - K_1x|x| + \text{(External disturbing force)}$$
$$\text{for } \dot{x} > 0, \ x < 0 \qquad \text{(v)(c)}$$
$$M\ddot{x} = - f\dot{x}|\dot{x}| - f_2\dot{x} - K_2x^3 + \text{(External disturbing force)}$$
$$\text{for } \dot{x} > 0, \ x > 0 \qquad \text{(v)(d)}$$

This process of elaboration may evidently be taken further still - for example, the mass may be constrained to move between end-stops; the latter may be elastic or virtually inelastic, and if elastic they may themselves have non-linear characteristics.

The more elaborate models represented by equations (iii), (iv) and (v) are difficult to solve analytically; however, their solution by analogue computer is little, if any, more difficult than in the case of equation (ii). It is true that one or more further items of "hardware" will be required - e.g. multipliers, diodes, function generators - but the principles of problem layout and development of the final machine equations, scaled flow diagram and pot and amplifier lists are exactly as described in earlier chapters. If difficulties do arise they are usually concerned with scaling, because maxima are often more difficult to assess when non-linearities are present.

It is for solving problems in which non-linear aspects occur that the analogue computer really "comes into its own"; analogue methods are often the most elegant and powerful available for their solution.

Differential equations arising from physical problems can be classified as follows:

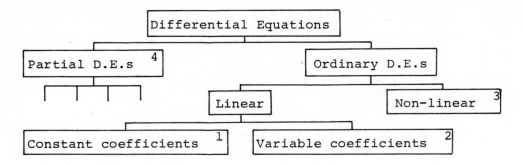

Figure 106

The analogue computer programming of the equations of block 1 has already been discussed in some detail; in this chapter we shall consider how the computer may be used to investigate the solution of the kind of equations referred to in blocks 2 and 3.

The equations in block 4 can themselves be subdivided into several groups, but the treatment of these equations falls outside the scope of this book. The reader who wishes to pursue further the study of analogue computer solution of partial differential equations should consult one or more of the more advanced textbooks which deal with the topic.

A few examples of the type of equation in blocks 2 and 3 are quoted below:

Linear with variable coefficients

(i) $\ddot{y} + (a - 2\theta\cos\omega t)y = 0$ where a, θ and ω are constants

(Mathieu's equation; can describe an oscillator circuit in which capacitance or inductance are time-variant; occurs in some frequency modulation problems)

(ii) $(1 - t^2)\ddot{y} - 2t\dot{y} + n(n + 1)y = 0$ where n is a positive constant (usually an integer)

(Legendre's equation: occurs in boundary value problems in spherical coordinates, in potential and radiation theory)

Non-linear

(i) $mr\ddot{\theta} + mg\sin\theta = 0$

(Simple pendulum, not confined to small angles of oscillation)

(ii) $m\ddot{x} + f\dot{x} + (Ax + Bx^3) = F\cos\omega t$

(Duffing's equation; mass/spring/damper system with a particular non-linear spring characteristic)

(iii) $\ddot{x} - \varepsilon(1 - x^2)\dot{x} + x = 0$

      (Van der Pol's equation; one of several equations which describe various electronic self-exciting oscillators).

As a brief study of the above examples will show, the computer must produce the product of two quantities which are simultaneously varying. So far in this book, only multiplication by a constant has been considered i.e. by setting, before computation has commenced, a potentiometer to the required (constant) coefficient value. If the constant coefficient is to be replaced by a variable coefficient, we can arrange for the pot setting to be automatically and continuously adjusted during the computation; such an adjustment takes place in the Servo multiplier.

12.2 Servo multiplier

The servo multiplier (now largely obsolescent) consists basically of a potentiometer, the spindle of which is driven by a small electric motor:

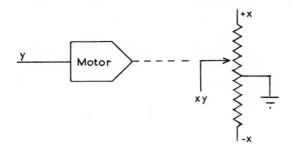

Figure 107

The potentiometer winding is usually earthed at its centre; $+ x$ is applied to one end and $- x$ to the other. The motor is then arranged so that when the motor input variable y is zero, the shaft drives the wiper to the centre; when y is positive, the wiper moves towards the $+ x$ end of the pot and when y is negative the wiper moves towards the $- x$ end; the amount of this movement is proportional to the magnitude of the y input. The voltage at the wiper is consequently proportional to xy. It will be remembered that great care must be taken when using pots to avoid loading errors (see page 96); the manufacturers of servo multipliers consequently arrange that the wiper voltage will always be a true xy provided that the wiper is taken only to a × 1 input of an amplifier.

    In practice the motor usually drives several pots on a common spindle (four is the number most often encountered). American books on analogue computing frequently refer to the pots of a servo multiplier as "cups".

On the flow diagram these are shown thus:

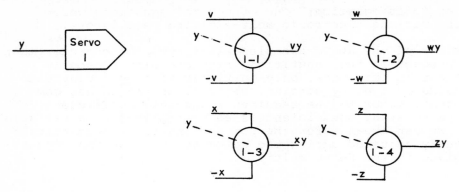

Figure 108

This means that up to four computer variables can be multiplied by
a single computer variable.

It will be seen from the unscaled flow diagram, Figure 109,
that the production of powers of a variable is very easy using a
servo multiplier:

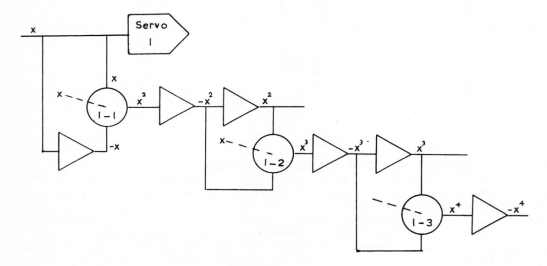

Figure 109

SERVO RESOLVER

This (now obsolescent) is a variation on the servo multiplier.
Servo resolvers are servo multipliers with the linear pots replaced
by specially wound sine/cosine pots, with two wipers:

118

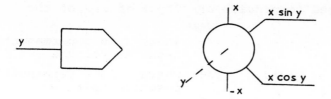

Figure 110

These have the same loading restrictions as the servo multiplier.

12.3   Mark-space multiplier

From the operator's point of view, a mark-space multiplier (now largely obsolescent) may be considered as a more versatile electronic version of the servo multiplier. Physically it consists of two types of unit, a master and a slave. The master replaces the servo motor and the slaves the potentiometers; both units require only a single input and have (unlike the servo multiplier) no loading limitations.

Mark-space multipliers are often housed in a six unit rack and the master and slave units may be placed in any of the six positions, except that only a master can hold the first position and only a slave the last. Each is driven by the first master to its left; hence a rack may be arranged as shown:

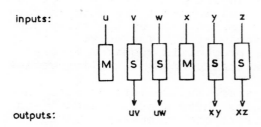

Figure 111

Only the slaves have outputs; the product of the slave's input and its master's input. The other possible master/slave combinations are:

```
M  S  M  S  M  S
M  S  S  S  S  S
M  S  S  S  M  S
M  S  M  S  S  S
```

12.4 Quarter squares multiplier

The quarter squares multiplier is also an all-electronic unit; it makes use of the identity

$$\frac{1}{4}\left\{(A + B)^2 - (A - B)^2\right\} = AB$$

119

The unit may be arranged to provide an output in one of the
following forms:

$+ AB$, $- AB$, $- A^2 + B^2$, $A^2 + B^2$, $\pm \sqrt{A}-$ where A is a permanently
                                                negative voltage

and $\pm \sqrt{A}+$ where A is a permanently
                                                positive voltage

The flow diagram symbol is:

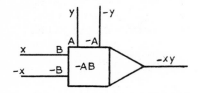

Figure 112

On some computers the $- A$ input is not required.

12.5 Accuracy

(1) Dynamic errors

Since the servo multiplier is essentially a mechanical device, its
performance is limited by maximum spindle acceleration and velocity.
Hence large errors will result if the servo motor input has a large
amplitude at a frequency above about 10 rad s^{-1}. On the other hand
the frequency response of the electrical input of the pots is very
high (i.e. up to about 10^4 rad s^{-1}), limited only by the stray capacity of the pots and their associated wiring. The servo is a
useful multiplier when more than one product is required from a
single multiplying factor, and where that common multiplier varies
only at low speed.
    The frequency response of mark-space multipliers is such that
they should not be used for frequencies above about 35 rad s^{-1} on
either master or slave inputs, if errors are to be kept within
$\pm$ 0·01 MU in the product.
    The quarter squares multiplier has a much higher maximum
operating frequency, of 10^3 rad s^{-1} or better, on both inputs.

(2) Static and zero errors

Static errors of the servo multiplier are primarily determined by
the mechanical registration of the pots on their common spindle,
which is set by the manufacturer. Errors of $\pm$ 0·005 MU are usually
quoted.
    Zero error of the servo multiplier can occur when the input to
the motor is zero, but not when the inputs to the pots are zero.
    On the slaves of mark-space multipliers there are usually a
number of adjustment controls, which are interdependent. Using
these with patience and care the zero error can be virtually eliminated; static errors may be reduced to about $\pm$ 0·001 MU.
    Quarter squares multipliers have a maximum static error of
about $\pm$ 0·0025 MU in the product, for all inputs (including zero).

Since a static error (in any multiplier) will produce a larger percentage error on small outputs than on large outputs, it follows that it is desirable to keep outputs as large as possible, if necessary by running the problem in two stages with a scale change in between.

12.6 Scaling

When a product is required in a problem the variables to be multiplied and the possibility of time-scaling must first be studied, so as to decide which type of multiplier should be used. Into this consideration must come the availability of units on the computer in question.

Amplitude scaling is elementary when using machine unit scaling, thus for a multiplier giving - AB output form,

- Output = Product of inputs

which gives rise to four possible decomposed equations:

$$-\left(\frac{xy}{50}\right) = \left(-\frac{x}{10}\right)\left(\frac{y}{5}\right)$$

$$-\left(\frac{xy}{50}\right) = \left(\frac{x}{10}\right)\left(-\frac{y}{5}\right)$$

$$-\left(-\frac{xy}{50}\right) = \left(\frac{x}{10}\right)\left(\frac{y}{5}\right)$$

$$-\left(-\frac{xy}{50}\right) = \left(-\frac{x}{10}\right)\left(-\frac{y}{5}\right)$$

where the terms on the right-hand side are the positive inputs to the multiplier.
Hence, if the inputs are correctly scaled the output will be scaled automatically; in spite of this it is necessary to write decomposed equations for multipliers, for static check purposes.

Example 21

Consider Mathieu's equation:

$$\ddot{y} + (a - 2\theta\cos\omega t)y = 0$$

where $a = 6 \cdot 25$, $\theta = 1 \cdot 5$, $\omega = 2$
and given $\dot{y} = 0$ and $y = 6$ at $t = 0$

Choice of multiplier:

Since only one multiplication is required the servo or mark-space multiplier has no advantage over the quarter squares multiplier.

The equation can be written as:

$$\ddot{y} + (6 \cdot 25 - 3\cos 2t)y = 0$$

Comparing this with the s.h.m. equation

$$\ddot{y} + \omega_n^2 y = 0$$

we have, as a rough approximation,

$\omega_n$max $\simeq \sqrt{9 \cdot 25} \simeq 3$ rad s^{-1}

The frequency of the two inputs to the multiplier are

3 rad s^{-1} for y and 2 rad s^{-1} for $(6 \cdot 25 - 3\cos2t)$

These are both within the capabilities of the servo multiplier, using unity time-scaling (β = 1); within the capabilities of a mark-space multiplier with a time scale of up to about β = 1/20; and within the capabilities of a quarter squares multiplier with a time scale of up to β = 1/1 000 (other factors permitting).

We shall assume that the solution is intended for oscilloscope display, and produce a suitable flow diagram.

Unscaled flow diagram (using a general symbol for the multiplier):

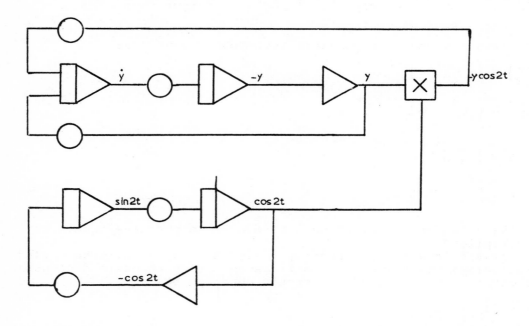

Figure 113

Decomposed equations:

Amplifier 1. $- \dfrac{d}{dt}\dot{y} = 6 \cdot 25y - 3y\cos2t$

Amplifier 2. $- \dfrac{d}{dt}(- y) = \dot{y}$

Amplifier 3. $- \dfrac{d}{dt}(\sin2t) = - 2\cos2t$

Amplifier 4. $- \dfrac{d}{dt}(\cos2t) = 2\sin2t$

Multiplier 5. $- y\cos2t = - y(\cos2t)$

122

Scaling:

Since the equation has no damping and ω_n is less than 3 rad s^{-1} it may be assumed that y_{max}, when excited by a frequency of 2 rad s^{-1}, may be slightly larger than the initial value of y:

Take $y_{max} = 10$ and scale $\left(\frac{y}{10}\right)$

Then $\dot{y}_{max} \simeq 10 \times 3 = 30$ Let us scale $\left(\frac{\dot{y}}{50}\right)$

and scale $\left(\frac{\cos 2t}{1}\right)$, $\left(\frac{\sin 2t}{1}\right)$

and scale $\left(\frac{y\cos 2t}{10}\right)$

Scaled equations:

(1) $\quad -\frac{d}{dt}\left(\frac{\dot{y}}{50}\right) = \frac{10 \times 6 \cdot 25}{50}\left(\frac{y}{10}\right) + \frac{30}{50}\left(-\frac{y\cos 2t}{10}\right)$

(2) $\quad -\frac{d}{dt}\left(-\frac{y}{10}\right) = \frac{50}{10}\left(\frac{\dot{y}}{50}\right)$

(3) $\quad -\frac{d}{dt}\left(\frac{\sin 2t}{1}\right) = 2\left(-\frac{\cos 2t}{1}\right)$

(4) $\quad -\frac{d}{dt}\left(\frac{\cos 2t}{1}\right) = 2\left(\frac{\sin 2t}{1}\right)$

(5) $\quad -\left(-\frac{y\cos 2t}{10}\right) = \left(\frac{y}{10}\right)\left(\frac{\cos 2t}{1}\right)$

Machine equations: (unity time scaling)

(1) $\quad -\frac{d}{dt}\left(\frac{\dot{y}}{50}\right) = [0 \cdot 125]10\left(\frac{y}{10}\right) + [0 \cdot 600]1\left(-\frac{y\cos 2t}{10}\right)$

(2) $\quad -\frac{d}{dt}\left(-\frac{y}{10}\right) = [0 \cdot 500]10\left(\frac{\dot{y}}{50}\right)$

(3) $\quad -\frac{d}{dt}\left(\frac{\sin 2t}{1}\right) = [0 \cdot 200]10\left(-\frac{\cos 2t}{1}\right)$

(4) $\quad -\frac{d}{dt}\left(\frac{\cos 2t}{1}\right) = [0 \cdot 200]10\left(\frac{\sin 2t}{1}\right)$

(5) $\quad -\left(-\frac{y\cos 2t}{10}\right) = \left(\frac{y}{10}\right)\left(\frac{\cos 2t}{1}\right)$

Flow diagram for the quarter squares multiplier case:

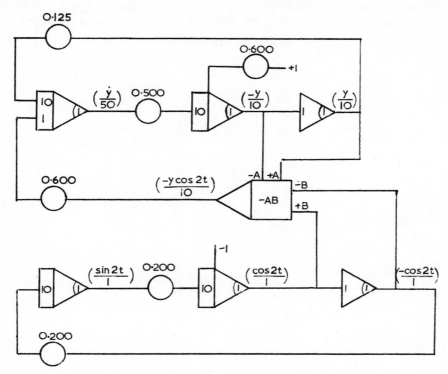

Figure 114

CHAPTER 13
GENERATION OF FUNCTIONS (2)

13.1 Generalized integration

When solving a differential equation such as

$$\frac{d^2y}{dx^2} + Ax\frac{dy}{dx} + By = f(x)$$

in which x is the independent variable, on an analogue computer, the substitution usually made is $x = t$, giving

$$\ddot{y} + At\dot{y} + By = f(t)$$

and the solution can be obtained by methods described in the earlier chapters.

If, however, it is required to solve equations such as

$$\frac{dy}{dx} = f(x) \qquad \frac{dy}{dx} = g(y) \qquad \text{or even } \frac{dy}{dx} = g(x,y)$$

as part of some larger problem in which both x and y are varying with time, the above procedure is inapplicable. Provided that $\dot{x}$ is available from the computer, integration with respect to x can be achieved as follows:

Consider $\quad \dfrac{dy}{dx} = f(x)$

then $\qquad \dfrac{dy}{dt} = f(x)\dfrac{dx}{dt} \quad$ with both y and x specified at $t = 0$

and hence $\quad -\dfrac{dy}{dt} = -f(x)\dot{x}$

This last equation is obeyed by the unscaled flow diagram:

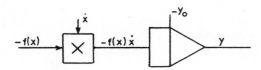

Figure 115

125

The system integrates $f(x)$ with respect to x, and is called *generalized integration* as it is more general than integration with respect to time.

Consider now two important applications of this principle:

(a) GENERATION OF e^{-ax}

Let $y = e^{-ax}$

Differentiating with respect to time, we have

$$\frac{dy}{dt} = -a(e^{-ax})\left(\frac{dx}{dt}\right) \quad \text{where } y = +e^{-ax_0} \text{ at } t = 0$$

i.e. $\quad -\frac{dy}{dt} = a(y\dot{x})$

which gives the unscaled flow diagram (Fig.116)

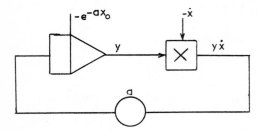

Figure 116

Evidently the technique can be modified quite simply to produce the function e^{+ax}.

(b) GENERATION OF $\sin nx$ AND $\cos nx$

Now $\quad \frac{d}{dt}(\cos nx) = -n\sin nx \frac{dx}{dt}$

and $\quad \frac{d}{dt}(\sin nx) = n\cos nx \frac{dx}{dt}$

This pair of equations can be rewritten in the form of decomposed equations:

(1) $\quad -\frac{d}{dt}(\cos nx) = n\dot{x}\sin nx$

(2) $\quad -\frac{d}{dt}(-\sin nx) = n\dot{x}\cos nx$

Evidently the terms on the r.h.s. of these equations may be computed using multipliers, provided that the variable $\dot{x}$ is available; we then have the unscaled flow diagram (Fig.117)

126

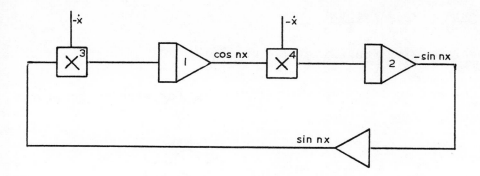

Figure 117

For the multipliers we must add the decomposed equations

(3) $-(\dot{x}\sin nx) = (-\dot{x})(\sin nx)$

(4) $-(\dot{x}\cos nx) = (-\dot{x})(\cos nx)$

Scaling: since $-1 \leqslant \sin nx \leqslant +1$ and $-1 \leqslant \cos nx \leqslant +1$,
we scale $\left(\dfrac{\sin nx}{1}\right)$, $\left(\dfrac{\cos nx}{1}\right)$

If the scaling of $\dot{x}$ is $\left(\dfrac{\dot{x}}{N}\right)$, where $N \geqslant \dot{x}_{max}$, then the multiplier

outputs will be scaled $\left(\dfrac{\dot{x}\sin nx}{N}\right)$ and $\left(\dfrac{\dot{x}\cos nx}{N}\right)$

Scaled equations:

(1) $-\dfrac{d}{dt}\left(\dfrac{\cos nx}{1}\right) = nN\left(\dfrac{\dot{x}\sin nx}{N}\right)$

(2) $-\dfrac{d}{dt}\left(-\dfrac{\sin nx}{1}\right) = nN\left(\dfrac{\dot{x}\cos nx}{N}\right)$

(3) $-\left(\dfrac{\dot{x}\sin nx}{N}\right) = \left(-\dfrac{\dot{x}}{N}\right)\left(\dfrac{\sin nx}{1}\right)$

(4) $-\left(\dfrac{\dot{x}\cos nx}{N}\right) = \left(-\dfrac{\dot{x}}{N}\right)\left(\dfrac{\cos nx}{1}\right)$

It may now be necessary to time-scale, the choice of β being
dependent on the value of the problem gains (nN) and, of course, on
criteria such as plotter speed limitations. Any larger problem
within which the $\sin nx$ and $\cos nx$ generation occurs may also require
to be time-scaled, and the final choice of β must be one which is
suitable for the problem *as a whole*.

"Generalized" machine equations:

(1) $-\dfrac{1}{\beta}\dfrac{d}{dt}\left(\dfrac{\cos nx}{1}\right) = \left[\dfrac{nN}{\beta M}\right]_M\left(\dfrac{\dot{x}\sin nx}{N}\right)$

(2) $-\dfrac{1}{\beta}\dfrac{d}{dt}\left(-\dfrac{\sin nx}{1}\right) = \left[\dfrac{nN}{\beta M}\right]_M\left(\dfrac{\dot{x}\cos nx}{N}\right)$

127

(3) $-\left(\dfrac{\dot{x}\sin nx}{N}\right) = \left(-\dfrac{\dot{x}}{N}\right)\left(\dfrac{\sin nx}{1}\right)$

(4) $-\left(\dfrac{\dot{x}\cos nx}{N}\right) = \left(-\dfrac{\dot{x}}{N}\right)\left(\dfrac{\cos nx}{1}\right)$

where M is the appropriate overall gain factor for each integrator.

"Generalized" scaled flow diagram:

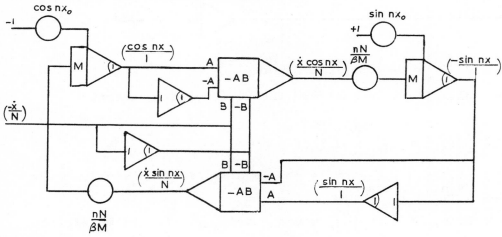

Figure 118

Notes

   (i)   The initial conditions for the two integrators are *not
          necessarily* 1 and 0;   they are in fact the values of $\cos nx$
          and $\sin nx$ at $t = 0$.   If, at $t = 0$, $x = x_0$, then $\cos nx_0$ and
          $\sin nx_0$ must be calculated (e.g. from tables) for the settings
          of the I.C. pots.

   (ii)   By suitable programming of the multiplier input/output signs,
          it is usually possible to dispense with the inverter shown in
          Figure 118.

  (iii)   A technique similar to this may be used to generate $\sinh nx$
          and $\cosh nx$.

   (iv)   It is important to use multipliers with *negligible zero
          errors*.   For example, if $\dot{x}$ has zero value at some stage of
          the computation, and one of the multipliers has a zero error
          of 0.001 MU, the latter will be steadily integrated with
          respect to time by the integrators of the system (see p.120).

13.2 Square root and division

Consider in principle the following circuits.

(a) SQUARE-ROOT:

Flow diagram:

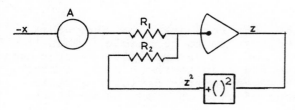

Figure 119

Note. Most multipliers have standard arrangements for producing either + ( )^2 or − ( )^2.

Applying Kirchhoff's law at the S.J.

$$- \frac{Ax}{R_1} + \frac{z^2}{R_2} = 0, \quad z^2 = \frac{R_2 Ax}{R_1}, \quad z \propto \sqrt{x}$$

(b) DIVISION:

Flow diagram:

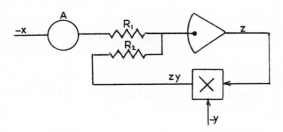

Figure 120

Summing the currents arriving at the S.J.

$$- \frac{Ax}{R_1} + \frac{yz}{R_2} = 0, \quad yz = \frac{R_2 Ax}{R_1}, \quad z \propto \frac{x}{y}$$

13.3 Practical difficulties with square root and division

(*a*) Evidently an amplifier cannot be expected to produce a signal involving $\sqrt{-1}$ at its output; it follows that in the case of the square-root circuit, the input $-x$ must remain a negative voltage throughout the computation.

(*b*) In both the circuits concerned, the feedback loop round the H.G.A. must remain negative for the system to be stable. Thus the z^2 multiplier output in Figure 119 and the yz multiplier output in Figure 120 must remain of the opposite sign to the $-x$ input signal *throughout the computation*. In the case of the division circuit this implies further that no change of sign of y may be permitted during the computation.

It may sometimes be necessary to have a division circuit which can handle possible changes in sign of *both* input variables; such a circuit is called a "four-quadrant" division circuit:

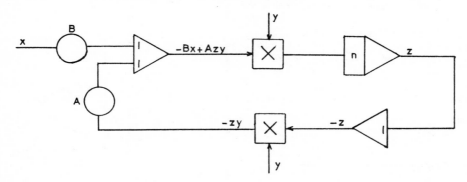

Figure 121

For a steady state value of z, the input to the integrator will be zero. In this state, the output of the summer is

$$- Bx + Azy = 0$$

$$z = \frac{B}{A}\frac{x}{y}$$

Negative feedback conditions are maintained at all times since when y is negative there are three sign reversals (three amplifiers) and when y is positive there are five sign reversals (three amplifiers plus two negative multiplications).

Inspection of Figure 121 shows that we are, in effect, solving the equation

$$\dot{z} + nAy^2z = nBxy$$

i.e.

$$\dot{z} + \lambda z = nBxy \qquad \text{where } \lambda > 0$$

Evidently the larger that λ can be made, the sooner will the steady state

$z = Bx/Ay$

be reached.   This suggests that a large value of n should be chosen; however any large decrease in the value of the feedback capacitor of the integrator will increase the drift of the steady state solution, thus the value of n will have to be chosen as a compromise. The multiplier before the integrator should be chosen for its ability to give a good zero when the output of the summer is zero.

(c) Both the circuits concerned may exhibit a tendency towards instability in practice;   if so it will be found necessary to inhibit that tendency by introducing a small feedback capacitor (e.g. 300pF) across the H.G.A.   Such an addition modifies the high-frequency response of the amplifier but no practical disadvantage arises in its use, except in very high speed computation.

(d) The division circuit (Figure 120) in particular, poses scaling problems.   Evidently the scaling factor chosen for the amplifier output z must be related to numerator maximum and *denominator minimum*;   thus, for example, to compute

$z = \dfrac{x}{y}$ where (say) $x_{max} \leqslant 10$ and $y_{max} \leqslant 5$

z itself cannot properly be scaled without having an estimated value of y_{min}.   Suppose that $y_{min} \geqslant 2$;   then $z_{max} \leqslant x_{max}/y_{min} \simeq 10/2$ and we scale $\left(\dfrac{y}{5}\right)$

Thus the decomposed equation

$- z = \dfrac{- x}{y}$

becomes the scaled equation

$-\left(\dfrac{z}{5}\right) = \dfrac{1}{5} \times \dfrac{10}{5} \times \dfrac{\left(-\dfrac{x}{10}\right)}{\left(\dfrac{y}{5}\right)}$

which gives the machine equation

$-\left(\dfrac{z}{5}\right) = \dfrac{[0.4]1\left(\dfrac{-x}{10}\right)}{1\left(\dfrac{y}{5}\right)}$

and the flow diagram:

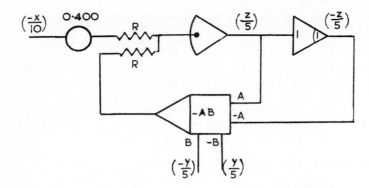

Figure 122

It is usual not to draw in the resistors but to show them as normal input gains (see Figure 123). The curved back to the amplifier implies no internal feedback.

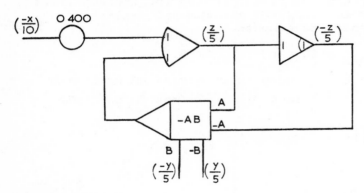

Figure 123

In the example just discussed we assumed $y_{min} \geqslant 2$; evidently if y_{min} is appreciably smaller than this, z may tend towards very large values. It will then be necessary to put an output limiter across the amplifier (see Section 14.1). The division circuit will then not provide a correct simulation while the limiter is in operation, but amplifier overload will be prevented.

It is important to examine the effects of errors due to the multiplier in a division circuit.
Consider:

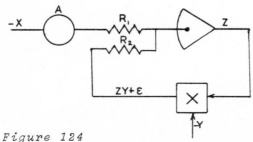

Figure 124

132

Let X, Y, and Z be machine variables: i.e. $X = \left(\dfrac{x}{x_{max}}\right)$, $Y = \left(\dfrac{y}{y_{max}}\right)$, $Z = \left(\dfrac{z}{z_{max}}\right)$. Let the output of the multiplier in Figure 124 be $ZY + \varepsilon$, where ε is an error introduced by the multiplier.

Then from Kirchhoff's law at the S.J.,

$$- \frac{AX}{R_1} + \frac{ZY + \varepsilon}{R_2} = 0$$

$$ZY + \varepsilon = \frac{R_2 AX}{R_1} = GX$$

where G is the overall X-input gain

$$Z = \frac{GX - \varepsilon}{Y}$$

Now the theoretical value of Z is GX/Y; hence the absolute error in Z will be

$$E = \varepsilon/Y$$

and the percentage error in Z will be

$$\frac{E \times 100}{\text{true } Z} = \frac{\varepsilon/Y}{GX/Y} \times 100 = \frac{100\varepsilon}{GX} \text{ \%}$$

Let us suppose that, for a given multiplier, there is an error of $\frac{1}{4}$% of 1 MU, i.e. $= 0.0025$ MU; then the percentage error in Z will be

$$\frac{100 \times 0.0025}{GX} = \frac{1}{4GX} \text{ \%}$$

Thus if $G = 1$, for less than 1% error in Z it follows that X must exceed 0.25 MU; hence Y also must exceed 0.25 MU (otherwise the amplifier would overload). An improvement may (apparently) be made by increasing G to nG ($n > 1$), by changing the A pot setting to nA (Figure 124). If this were done, one of three possible scaling changes would be implied, namely

$$\left(\frac{x}{nx_{max}}\right) \quad \text{or} \quad \left(\frac{y}{\dfrac{y_{max}}{n}}\right) \quad \text{or} \quad \left(\frac{z}{\dfrac{z_{max}}{n}}\right)$$

Since $n > 1$, y_{max} and z_{max} may not be decreased without overload ensuing; it follows that the scaling must be changed to $\left(\dfrac{x}{nx_{max}}\right)$.

Thus the input is no longer X but X/n; therefore the output of the pot is $\left[nA\right]\left(\dfrac{X}{n}\right) = AX$ as before, and no advantage at all has been gained.

Enough has been said to show that division circuits are troublesome in practice, and are best avoided if at all possible. There *may* be cases in which it is necessary to retain such a circuit - sometimes it is possible to mitigate the worst effects by a "trick" technique such as that shown in the following example:

Example 22

Bessel's equation of zero order:

$$t^2\ddot{y} + t\dot{y} + t^2 y = 0 \quad \text{given } y = 1, \ \dot{y} = 0 \text{ at } t = 0$$

Hence

$$\ddot{y} = -\frac{\dot{y}}{t} - y$$

Now at $t = 0$, both $\dot{y}$ and t are zero, thus causing difficulties in a division circuit.

Using L'Hôpital's rule

$$\lim_{t \to 0} \frac{\dot{y}}{t} = \lim_{t \to 0} \frac{\ddot{y}}{1}$$

$$= \lim_{t \to 0} \left(- \frac{\dot{y}}{t} - y\right)$$

$$= -\lim_{t \to 0} \frac{\dot{y}}{t} - 1$$

Therefore

$$2\lim_{t \to 0} \frac{\dot{y}}{t} = -1 \quad \text{i.e.} \quad \lim_{t \to 0} \frac{\dot{y}}{t} = -\frac{1}{2}$$

Using this result, the computer set-up can be modified by arranging for it to divide, not $\dot{y}$ by t, but $\dot{y} - \frac{1}{2} e^{-t/T}$ by $t + e^{-t/T}$ (where T is a small time-constant). Evidently, at $t = 0$, the quotient will be $-\frac{1}{2}$; and after a period of approx. $7T$, the quotient tends towards $\dot{y}/t$; for $0 < t < 7T$, the accuracy of the simulation is obviously affected adversely by the presence of the exponential terms.

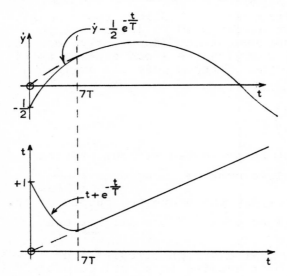

Figure 125

134

Whilst the technique described above overcomes the difficulty of starting the division at $t = 0$, inspection of the original equation suggests that the solution will be oscillatory (confirmation of this can be supplied by a knowledge of the behaviour of Bessel functions), thus $\dot{y}$ will periodically pass through zero; as we have seen (page 120) whenever $\dot{y}$ is small, the accuracy of the division circuit may be seriously affected.

There is an elegant technique which offers a powerful and effective alternative to the use of division circuits, and is applicable to many problems:

13.4 Variable time scaling

Consider in principle the generalized simultaneous equations

$$\left.\begin{array}{l} \dot{x} + f(x,y) = 0 \\ \dot{y} + g(x,y) = 0 \end{array}\right\}$$

where $f(x,y)$, $g(x,y)$ are functions which can be produced by analogue computing techniques; the unscaled flow diagram is

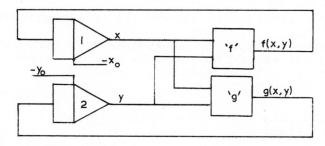

Figure 126

Decomposed equations:

(1) $\quad - \dfrac{d}{dt}(x) = f(x,y)$

(2) $\quad - \dfrac{d}{dt}(y) = g(x,y)$

Let us time-scale ($\tau = \beta t$); then the time-scaled equations (written in the usual form) are:

(1) $\quad - \dfrac{1}{\beta}\dfrac{d}{dt}(x) = \dfrac{1}{\beta} f(x,y)$

(2) $\quad - \dfrac{1}{\beta}\dfrac{d}{dt}(y) = \dfrac{1}{\beta} g(x,y)$

If, instead of $1/\beta$, both sides were multiplied by $dt/d\tau$, the equations would appear in the form:

(1) $\quad - \dfrac{d}{d\tau}(x) = \dfrac{dt}{d\tau} f(x,y)$

(2) $\quad - \dfrac{d}{d\tau}(y) = \dfrac{dt}{d\tau} g(x,y)$

So far, an arbitrary positive constant value for the time-scaling factor $dt/d\tau$ has always been chosen, the choice being determined by factors such as over-large integrator gains and the low frequency response of some of the computing elements (e.g. X/Y pen-recorders). However, there is no necessity for $dt/d\tau$ to be constant; if an awkward quotient of variables should occur in the generation of either $f(x,y)$ or $g(x,y)$ the divisor may be removed by choosing a suitable *variable* value for $dt/d\tau$. In general, this value would be the L.C.M. of the divisors occurring in the decomposed equations; let this L.C.M. be a variable z; there are then *three* equations describing the system:

(1) $- \dfrac{d}{d\tau}(x) = z.f(x,y)$

(2) $- \dfrac{d}{d\tau}(y) = z.g(x,y)$

(3) $- \dfrac{d}{d\tau}(t) = -z$

It follows at once that the right-hand sides of these equations contain no variable divisors. Thus all the disadvantages associated with the use of division circuits will be avoided.

N.B. (i) It is essential to operate in this way on *all* the integrator equations for the problem

(ii) t can no longer be produced via the usual time-base circuit, and must be obtained for recording purposes as the output of the integrator referred to by equation (3) above.

Example 23

The following (simplified) equations refer to vertical rocket flight, while fuel remains unburned:

$$\ddot{h} = \frac{CB}{M + m} - g$$

$$\dot{m} = - B$$

where h is height above launching pad,
   M is mass of rocket without fuel (constant),
   m is mass of unburned fuel,
   C is exhaust gas velocity relative to rocket (taken as constant),
   B is a given constant,
   g is gravitational acceleration (assumed to be constant for the purposes of this problem).

Initial conditions:
   $h = \dot{h} = 0$ and $m = m_0$ at $t = 0$

From practical considerations we may take h, $\dot{h}$ and m as being $\geqslant 0$; writing decomposed equations for these variables,

(1) $- \dfrac{d}{dt}(- \dot{h}) = \dfrac{CB}{M + m} - g$

136

(2) $- \dfrac{d}{dt}(h) = - \dot{h}$

(3) $- \dfrac{d}{dt}(m) = B$

Time-scaled equations:

(1) $- \dfrac{d}{d\tau}(- \dot{h}) = \dfrac{dt}{d\tau}\left(\dfrac{CB}{M + m} - g \right)$

(2) $- \dfrac{d}{d\tau}(h) = - \dfrac{dt}{d\tau} \dot{h}$

(3) $- \dfrac{d}{d\tau}(m) = \dfrac{dt}{d\tau} B$

If we now choose $\dfrac{dt}{d\tau} = M + m$, the division implicit in equation (1) is avoided, and there are then five equations:

(1) $- \dfrac{d}{d\tau}(- \dot{h}) = CB - (M + m)g$

(2) $- \dfrac{d}{d\tau}(h) = - (M + m)\dot{h}$

(3) $- \dfrac{d}{d\tau}(m) = (M + m)B$

(4) $- \dfrac{d}{d\tau}(t) = - (M + m)$

(5) $- \left(- (M + m)\dot{h} \right) = (- \dot{h})\left(- (M + m) \right)$

Unscaled flow diagram:

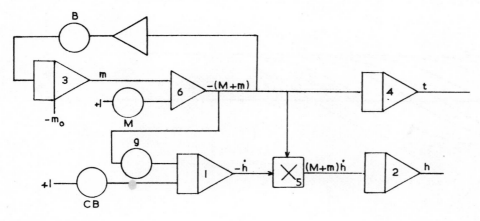

Figure 127

Amplitude scaling may now be carried out (using estimates based on given values of C, B, g and m_0), and six machine equations can be derived.

Note that (*a*) the machine equations may be further time-scaled (by any suitable constant factor β) should it be found desirable to do so, and

(b) when recording solutions for h, $\dot{h}$ and m against t, the X-input to the pen recorder (or 'scope) will be taken from the output of integrator 4. and *not* from the usual separate time-base circuit. Since t does not vary linearly with respect to τ (see equation (4) above) the pen will no longer move linearly in the X-direction with respect to *computer* time.

The next example (although easily solved by analytical techniques) is of interest as showing a special case of time-scaling in which $dt/d\tau = -1$ (i.e. "reverse-time" scaling).

Example 24

Solve the equation $\dot{y} + y^2 = 1$

given $y = C$ and $\dot{y} = 0$ at $t = 0$

where C is a parameter and solution is required for $0 < t < T$.

Solving this equation analytically (by separation of variables) there are two possible sets of solutions:

(i) $y = \tanh(t + k_1)$ where $\tanh k_1 = C$

This is valid for $|y| < 1$ and hence applies only when $|C| < 1$.

(ii) $y = \coth(t + k_2)$ where $\coth k_2 = C$

This is valid for $|y| > 1$ and hence applies only when $|C| > 1$.

This suggests that when plotting solutions from an analogue computer for the given problem, two sets of curves should (in general) be obtained:

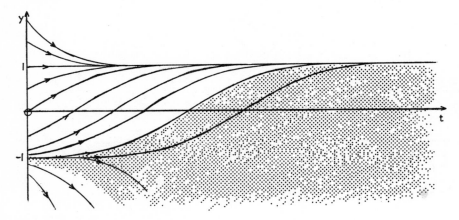

Figure 128

The particular regions of interest are likely to be those in the neighbourhood of $C = 1$ and $C = -1$. In practice no difficulty is found in the neighbourhood of $C = 1$, but as $C \to -1$ (from above or below) it will be found that the computer set-up becomes abnormally sensitive and the solution curves break away at random into one or other type of solution, making it virtually impossible to plot the curves in the region shown shaded in Figure 128.

138

This difficulty may be overcome by reversing the direction of computation, as follows:

Decomposed equation:

$$- \frac{d}{dt} y = y^2 - 1$$

Time-scaling:

$$- \frac{d}{d\tau} y = \frac{dt}{d\tau} (y^2 - 1)$$

Let us choose $dt/d\tau = -1$, so that

(1) $\quad - \frac{d}{d\tau} y = - y^2 + 1$

(2) $\quad - \frac{d}{d\tau} t = 1$

Unscaled flow diagram:

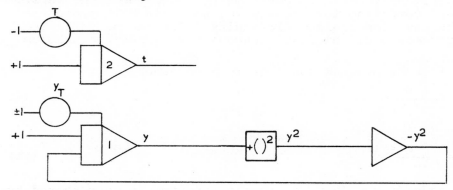

Figure 129

Since problem time t is thus reversed in direction relative to computer time τ, it follows that integrator 2 must have as its initial condition $t = T$ when $\tau = 0$. For the same reason, the initial condition on integrator 1 is not C, but the value of y when $t = T$; for each computer run, a value of this initial condition can be chosen by taking an arbitrary value on the ordinate $t = T$:

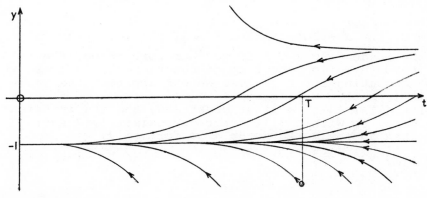

Figure 130

139

Note that the pen of an X/Y pen-recorder with X-input taken from the output of integrator 2 will start to move from right to left at the end of problem time, and will finish on the extreme left at the beginning of problem time.

Example 25

Solve the equation $(10 - w)\frac{dy}{dw} + y = 5w$, for $-10 \leqslant w < 10$,

given that $y = 0$ at $w = -10$.

Rewriting the equation we have

$$\frac{dy}{dw} = \frac{5w - y}{10 - w} \tag{i}$$

This equation could be programmed using a division circuit, but in this particular case such a circuit would present scaling difficulties since the divisor $\to 0$ as $w \to 10$. Furthermore, the conventional simulation $t = w$ is impossible for negative values of w. The latter difficulty could be overcome by using the time-transform $\tau = w + 10$ and computing for $0 \leqslant \tau < 20$, but this method does not help with the division scaling difficulty. The use of variable time-scaling removes all difficulties and simplifies the problem enormously:

Rewriting (i) in decomposed equation form we have

$$-\frac{d}{dw}(y) = \frac{y - 5w}{10 - w} \tag{ii}$$

Time-scaling (ii) we get

$$-\frac{d}{d\tau}(y) = \left(\frac{y - 5w}{10 - w}\right)\left(\frac{dw}{d\tau}\right) \tag{iii}$$

We now *choose* $dw/d\tau = 10 - w$, so that the system is represented by two decomposed equations, viz.:

(1) $-\frac{d}{d\tau}(y) = y - 5w$

(2) $-\frac{d}{d\tau}(w) = w - 10$

Scaling: equation (2) will have an analytic solution of the form

$$w = Ae^{-\tau} + 10$$

Hence, when $\tau = 0$, $w = A + 10$; and as $\tau \to \infty$, $w \to 10$.

To cover the range $-10 \leqslant w < 10$ we therefore choose $A = -20$, and since the (computer) time constant of equation (2) is 1 sec it follows that by computing for $\tau \geqslant 7$ sec we can approach the value $w = 10$ to within less than 0.1% error.

Now equation (1) is also a first order lag, and its transient will similarly decay to within 0.1% after approximately 7 sec; steady state y then approximates to $5w = 50$ for $\tau > 7$.

Hence we scale $\left(\frac{w}{10}\right)$ and $\left(\frac{y}{50}\right)$.

Scaled equations:

(1) $\quad - \dfrac{d}{d\tau}\left(\dfrac{y}{50}\right) = \left(\dfrac{y}{50}\right) - \dfrac{5 \times 10}{50}\left(\dfrac{w}{10}\right)$

(2) $\quad - \dfrac{d}{d\tau}\left(\dfrac{w}{10}\right) = \left(\dfrac{w}{10}\right) - 1$

which lead at once to the
Machine equations:

(1) $\quad - \dfrac{d}{d\tau}\left(\dfrac{y}{50}\right) = 1\left(\dfrac{y}{50}\right) + 1\left(- \dfrac{w}{10}\right)$

(2) $\quad - \dfrac{d}{d\tau}\left(\dfrac{w}{10}\right) = 1\left(\dfrac{w}{10}\right) + 1(- 1)$

Final scaled flow diagram:

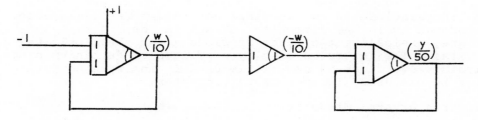

Figure 131

Note: For plotting y against w, a conventional time-base must *not*
be used.   The X-input to the 'scope or X/Y plotter must be driven
from the output of the first integrator $\left(\dfrac{w}{10}\right)$ of the flow diagram;
although the pen will not move linearly over the paper from left to
right, the resulting graph must have its horizontal axis *marked off
linearly* in terms of w, from -10 to $+10$.

CHAPTER 14

DIODE CIRCUITS

A diode is, in principle, a two-terminal non-return device; current
will pass through it in one direction but not in the other.
     There are, basically, two types of diode - the thermionic valve
and the crystal. The latter is usually a silicon or germanium diode;
the thermionic valve diode is now little used in analogue computing
and will not be discussed further in this chapter.

The symbol for a crystal diode is:

(the black arrowhead indicates the direction of permitted current
flow).
     In practice, diodes do not exhibit the perfect short- and open-
circuit characteristics referred to above; in fact, for silicon
diodes, the forward resistance is not zero, but varies (a little)
with the current and is of the order of 10 to 50 Ω, and the backward
resistance is not infinite, but is of the order of 50 to 200 MΩ.
If current through the diode is plotted against voltage across it,
the resulting curve is of the form:

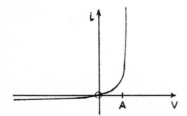

Figure 132

As can be seen from this curve, a small current (of the order of
0.1 to 1 μA) will flow for negative values of V, and the diode will
only conduct significantly when V exceeds the value at A (approximately + 0.5 volt). The effect of these imperfections will be
examined in more detail in the discussion of the individual circuits
which follows. In this discussion we shall use the convention that
upper case R denotes a resistor in the range 100 kΩ - 1 MΩ, whereas
lower case r denotes a resistor of much smaller value.

14.1 Limiters and comparators

These are of two types - *input* and *feedback*. Input limiters limit the input to an amplifier, whereas the feedback type limits the output of the amplifier with which it is associated. Each of the types can be developed into circuits which give either precision ("hard") limits or non-precision ("soft") limits.

1. INPUT LIMITER (SOFT)

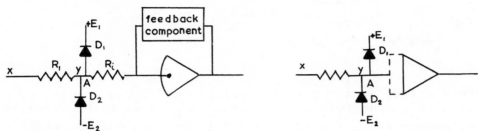

Figure 133

Note: Figure 133 shows both the circuit diagram and the corresponding patching diagram. This practice will be followed in the rest of this chapter, where appropriate. The reader is reminded that an amplifier symbol with a curved input end denotes a high gain amplifier with no implied feedback component; and that a dotted input inside the symbol denotes a connection to the summing junction.

If the input signal x is such that the voltage at A (i.e. y) lies in the range $- E_2 < y < + E_1$, both diodes will be in the non-conducting state ("off"). Then

$$y = \frac{R_i}{R_1 + R_i}\, x$$

Now suppose that x changes so that y tends to become greater than $+ E_1$; then D_1 will conduct (i.e. be "on") while D_2 remains off, and due to the low forward resistance of D_1,

$$y \simeq + E_1$$

Similarly, if x changes so that y tends to become less than $- E_2$, D_1 will be off and D_2 will conduct, so that

$$y \simeq - E_2$$

Sketching the graph of y against x for the circuit:

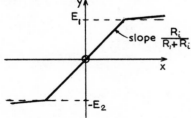

Figure 134

Note that the limits achieved have non-zero slopes, due to the non-ideal diode resistances.

2. INPUT LIMITER (HARD)

This circuit introduces the diode bridge circuit, which has several other important applications.

Consider first the *half-bridge* input limiter:

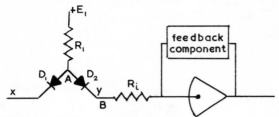

Figure 135

If the input signal x is a positive voltage and large enough, D_1 will be held off; the voltage at point A (V_A) will be positive, and since B is connected to the SJ (via R_i) it follows that D_2 will conduct. Then

$$y = V_A - \frac{1}{2} = \frac{R_i}{R_1 + R_i + r_F} E_1 \qquad \text{(i)}$$

(where r_F is the forward resistance of the diode).

Now suppose that x decreases so that $0 < x \leqslant V_A - \frac{1}{2}$; then D_1 will conduct and $V_A = x + \frac{1}{2}$; but we already have $y = V_A - \frac{1}{2}$, hence

$$y = x \qquad \text{(ii)}$$

If the two diodes are well matched, i.e. if both require exactly the same voltage to make them conduct (see A on Figure 132), then result (ii) is independent of this particular diode imperfection.

Now suppose that x decreases further so that $x \leqslant 0$: D_1 will remain on, but since V_A will then be $\leqslant \frac{1}{2}$ volt, D_2 will go off and therefore

$$y = 0 \qquad \text{(iii)}$$

Plotting y against x we have:

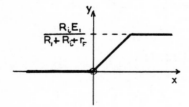

Figure 136

144

It follows that a similar argument, applied to the circuit shown in Figure 137 will lead to the y/x plot of Figure 138:

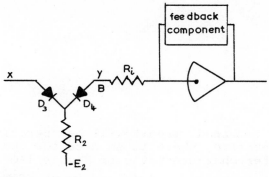

Figure 137

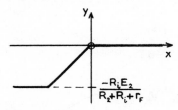

Figure 138

Adding together the circuits of Figures 135 and 137 we obtain:

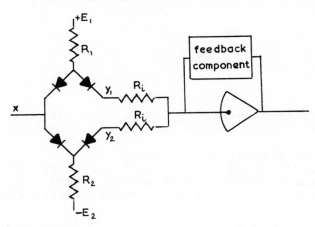

Figure 139

which will provide the y/x plot (or *Transfer Characteristic*):

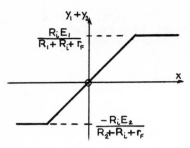

Figure 140

Effectively, only one half of the combined circuit will be operative
at any one time; in practice, therefore, there is no need for two
input resistors R_i, and the transfer characteristic of Figure 140 is

obtained from the circuit (the one actually used in practice) of
Figure 141:

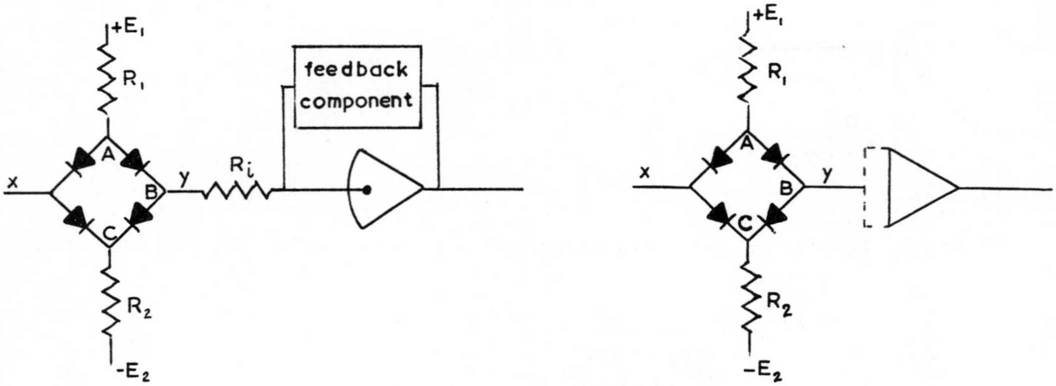

Figure 141

Note that in the transfer characteristics of Figures 136, 138
and 140 the limits achieved have (virtually) zero slopes, provided
that the diodes are well matched.

The behaviour of the final circuit of Figure 141 may be
summarized by considering the following four circuits, each one of
which corresponds to one of the possible states of the actual
circuit employed (in these "equivalent" circuits, diode imperfections
are ignored):

(i) $x > \dfrac{R_i E_1}{R_1 + R_i}$: bridge "open", or "in limit"

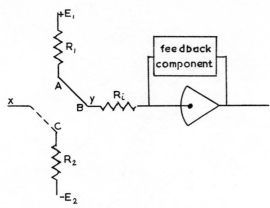

Figure 142(a)

y is held at the value $+ \dfrac{R_i}{R_1 + R_i} E_1$

N.B. the bridge may be considered as limiting the *current* to
$\dfrac{E_1}{R_1 + R_i}$ amps.

(ii) $0 < x < \dfrac{R_i E_1}{R_1 + R_i}$: bridge "closed", or "not in limit":

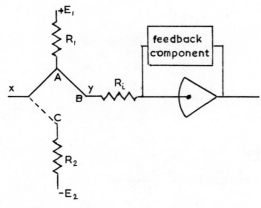

Figure 142(b)

$y = x$

(iii) $\quad -\dfrac{R_i E_2}{R_2 + R_i} < x < 0$: bridge "closed", or "not in limit":

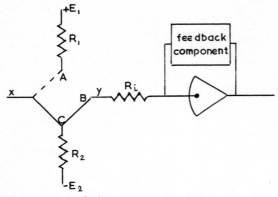

Figure 142(c)

$y = x$

(iv) $\quad x < -\dfrac{R_i E_2}{R_2 + R_i}$: bridge "open", or "in limit":

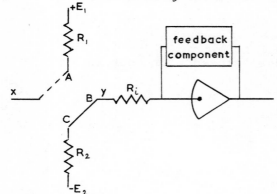

Figure 142(d)

y is held at the value $-\dfrac{R_i}{R_2 + R_i} E_2$

N.B. the bridge again limits the current, to $-\dfrac{E_2}{R_2 + R_i}$ amps.

3. FEEDBACK LIMITER (SOFT)

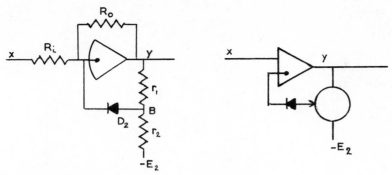

Figure 143

If the input signal x is such that y is zero, then the voltage at B (V_B) will be negative and D_2 will be off. The circuit then acts as a summer, and (while D_2 remains off) we have

$$y = -\frac{R_0}{R_i} x \qquad\qquad\qquad\qquad\qquad\qquad\qquad\qquad\text{(i)}$$

Since D_2 is connected between point B and the SJ, it will conduct if V_B becomes positive, and this will occur when

$$y > \frac{r_1}{r_2} E_2$$

(From (i) above this will happen when $x < -\dfrac{r_1}{r_2}\dfrac{R_i}{R_0} E_2$)

When D_2 does so conduct, the amplifier feedback consists of R_0 and r_1 in parallel (ignoring the diode resistance) and B becomes another summing junction, i.e. the equivalent circuit is:

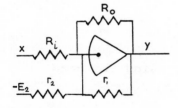

Figure 144

The equivalent feedback resistance is now $\dfrac{R_0 r_1}{R_0 + r_1}$, so

$$y = -\left(\frac{R_0 r_1 /(R_0 + r_1)}{R_i}\right) x + \left(\frac{R_0 r_1 /(R_0 + r_1)}{r_2}\right) E_2 \qquad\qquad\text{(ii)}$$

149

From (i) and (ii) the transfer characteristic will be:

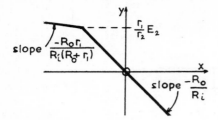

Figure 145

Consider the circuit:

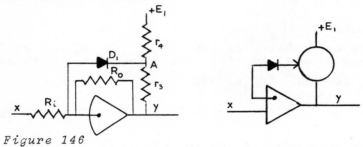

Figure 146

then a similar argument will show that the transfer characteristic is:

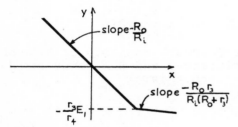

Figure 147

Combining the circuits of Figures 143 and 146, using the same amplifier, we have the circuit:

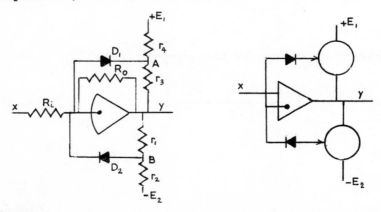

Figure 148

This will give a transfer characteristic which shows limiting of output for both signs:

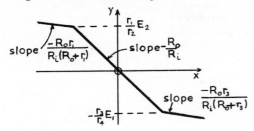

Figure 149

Evidently the "softness" of the limits can be minimized by making r_1 and r_3 small; it is therefore convenient to use "free pots" for $r_1 + r_2$ and $r_3 + r_4$, where A and B in Figure 148 are then the pot wipers.

Note that if either limit is required to be at zero, then r_1 (or r_3, as appropriate) = 0 and hence the pot concerned may be omitted and its diode connected directly to the amplifier output.

4. FEEDBACK LIMITER (HARD)

Consider first the circuit shown in Figure 150, in which a diode bridge has been placed in series with the feedback resistor:

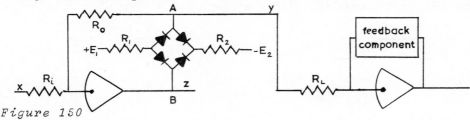

Figure 150

If the input x is such that the amplifier output z (at B) is within the limits to which the bridge has been set, the bridge will be closed, i.e. will be in either state (ii) or state (iii) (see Figure 142, pages 147 and 148). Then the voltage at A is equal to that at B, and:

$$y = z = -\frac{R_0}{R_i} x$$

If now the input x varies in such a way that output z reaches one or other of the limits set (or alternatively, when the current through the bridge reaches one or other of the current limits set), the bridge opens, i.e. will be in either state (i) or state (iv) (again see Figure 142).

151

If in state (i), the equivalent circuit is:

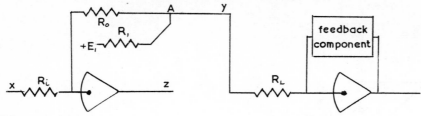

Figure 151

or, still more simply:

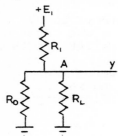

Figure 152

From Figure 151 it is evident that, at point A,

$$\frac{y}{\dfrac{R_0 R_L}{R_0 + R_L}} = \frac{E_1}{R_1 + \dfrac{R_0 R_L}{R_0 + R_L}}$$

and hence

$$y = \left(\frac{R_0 R_L}{R_0 R_L + R_0 R_1 + R_L R_1}\right) E_1 = E_{c_1} \quad \text{(say)}$$

Similarly, if the bridge opens into state (iv),

$$y = -\left(\frac{R_0 R_L}{R_0 R_L + R_0 R_2 + R_L R_2}\right) E_2 = -E_{c_2} \quad \text{(say)}$$

Thus, in either state (i) or (iv), y is maintained at a fixed value once the bridge has been driven into limit.

Referring back to Figure 151 we see that, in the limit states, the feedback loop of amplifier 1 has been broken, and in consequence the amplifier output z will increase very rapidly and lead to an overload. In order to prevent this, a soft feedback limitation on z (see Figure 148, page 150) is added.

The complete circuit is then:

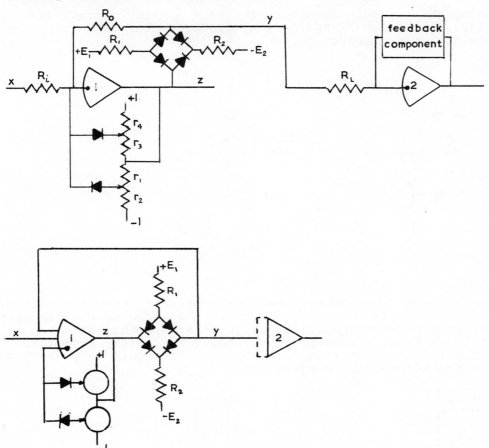

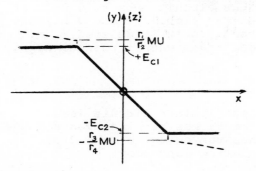

Figure 153

The pots r_1/r_2 and r_3/r_4 are set, in practice, to give soft limits
on z which are just outside (but close to) the hard y limits
afforded by the bridge - the reason for this will be discussed
later (see page 167).

Plotting the transfer characteristics of y and z against x,

Figure 154

5. FEEDBACK COMPARATOR (SOFT)

In essence, this circuit is a soft feedback limiter circuit (see Figure 148) from which R_0 has been removed, but in which there may be two or more input resistors:

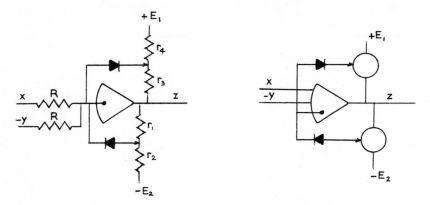

Figure 155

Since R_0 has been removed, the feedback resistance when both diodes are not conducting is very large, so that the slope of the transfer characteristic between the limits is very large; thus when $(x - y)$ passes through zero, the output z changes very rapidly from one limit value to the other (for this reason the circuit is sometimes loosely referred to as a "Bang-bang"):

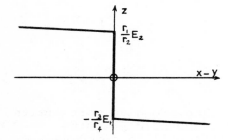

Figure 156

    In the form shown in Figure 155 the circuit acts as a *voltage* comparator since it changes state when the signals x and y balance each other. If the second input to the circuit is deleted (i.e. $y = 0$ permanently), the circuit changes state when x changes sign, i.e. it acts as a *sign* comparator.

6. INPUT COMPARATOR (HARD)

In essence, this circuit is a hard input limiter circuit (see Figure 141) in which the input resistor R_i has been removed and the feedback component is a resistor - thus the output of the diode bridge is connected directly to the summing junction:

154

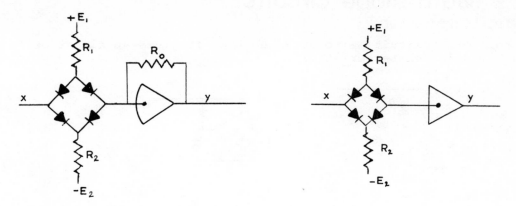

Figure 157

When x is such that the bridge is closed (either state (ii) or state (iii), Figure 142) the input resistance to the amplifier is virtually zero so that the slope of the transfer characteristic between the limits is virtually infinite:

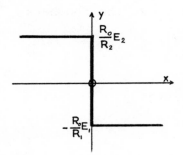

Figure 158

This circuit, having only one input, can act only as a sign comparator; if it is required to perform voltage comparison, we must add a further amplifier:

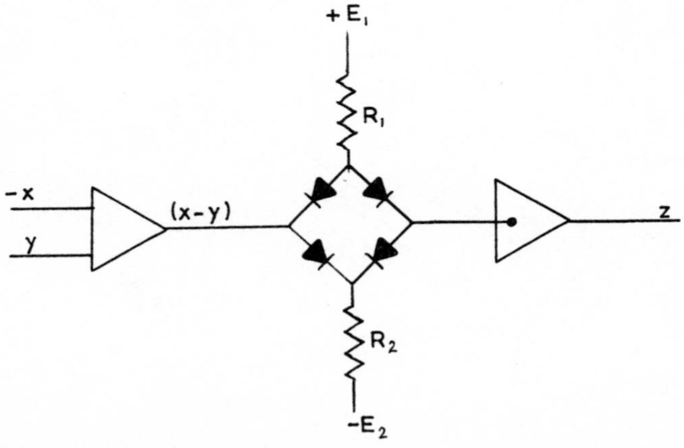

Figure 159   155

14.2 Multi-slope circuits

1. "IDEALIZED" DIODE

The following circuit is so arranged that it gives an almost perfect diode transfer characteristic:

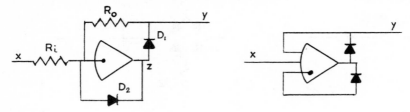

Figure 160

If the input signal x goes positive, the amplifier output z will go negative until D_2 conducts (i.e. $z \simeq -\frac{1}{2}$ volt). In this state, D_1 will be off, and hence $y = 0$.

    If, now, x goes negative, z will increase and D_2 will be cut off; the amplifier feedback loop will now be open-circuited, consequently z will increase very rapidly - but as soon as z reaches $+\frac{1}{2}$ volt, D_1 will conduct. R_0 is now brought in as the feedback loop of the amplifier, and

$$z = - \frac{R_0 + r_F}{R_i} \; x + \frac{1}{2} \quad \text{volt}$$

where r_F is the forward resistance of D_1. Evidently

$$y = - \frac{R_0}{R_i} x$$

Drawing the graphs of z and y against x, the following transfer characteristic is obtained:

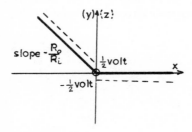

Figure 161

156

If $R_0 = R_i$, the circuit of Figure 160 is equivalent to:

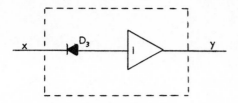

Figure 162

(in which D_3 represents a "perfect" diode).

If, in the circuit of Figure 160, both diodes are reversed in sense, the transfer characteristic becomes:

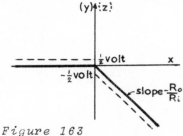

Figure 163

and, again putting $R_0 = R_i$, the equivalent circuit will be:

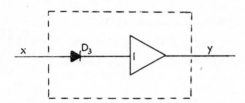

Figure 164

Note: for an ordinary single diode:

conduction (or non-conduction) is determined by the values of *both* E_1 and E_2 (more specifically, by $E_1 - E_2$); whereas, in the idealized diode circuit of Figure 160, conduction (or non-conduction) is determined *solely* by the value of x. This implies that the idealized diode circuit can be used only in cases where it replaces an ordinary diode plus an inverter, connecting the output of one amplifier to the input of another; thus it could not be used to replace any of the diodes shown in the circuits so far considered in this chapter.

2. SIGN-DEPENDENT SLOPES

The basic circuit is:

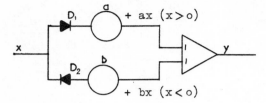

Figure 165

Evidently D_1 will conduct for positive x (D_2 off)
while D_2 will conduct for negative x (D_1 off).

Hence the transfer characteristic is:

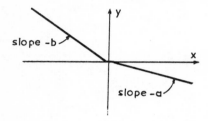

Figure 166

Note that, due to diode imperfection, a small "dead-space" (of
approximately $\pm \frac{1}{2}$ volt) results. This dead-space may be removed if
required, by replacing D_1 and D_2 by idealized diodes (suitably
arranged as to sense):

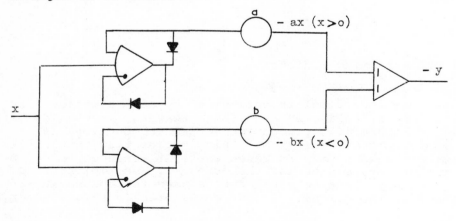

Figure 167

The flow diagram of Figure 167 can now be further improved by
merging the two separate idealized diodes into a double idealized
diode employing one amplifier only:

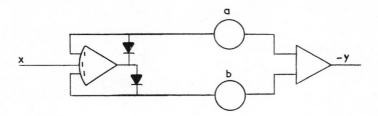

Figure 168

3. VOLTAGE-DEPENDENT BREAK-POINT, ONE SLOPE ZERO

The basic circuit is:

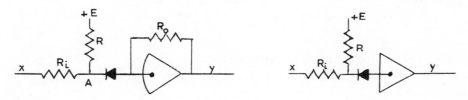

Figure 169

For all $x \geqslant - \dfrac{R_i}{R} E$ the diode will not conduct; hence $y = 0$.

For all $x < - \dfrac{R_i}{R} E$ the diode conducts and hence

$$y = - \frac{R_0}{R_i} x - \frac{R_0}{R} E$$

The transfer characteristic will be:

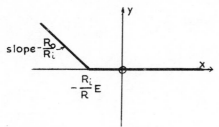

Figure 170

Changing the polarity of the control voltage E, a similar argument leads to the transfer characteristic:

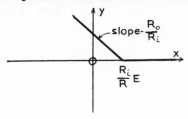

Figure 171

The sense of the diode can also be reversed, i.e.

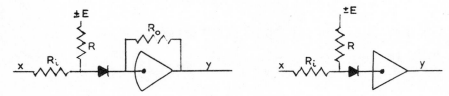

Figure 172

which gives the transfer characteristic:

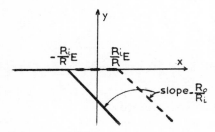

Figure 173

Note that the $\pm \frac{1}{2}$ volt needed for the diode conduction is allowed for provided that the break-point is set by measuring the *output* of the circuit.

The circuits discussed in this paragraph lead on to function generation, dealt with later (page 165).

160

14.3 Dead-space circuits

1. INPUT DEAD-SPACE

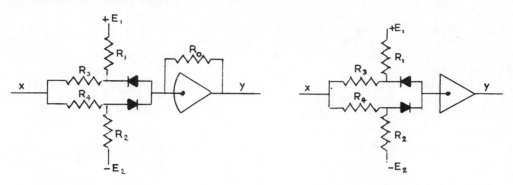

Figure 174

It can be seen that the circuit of Figure 174 is, in effect, the circuit of Figure 169 combined with that of Figure 172 (using $-E$). From this it follows that the transfer characteristic will be:

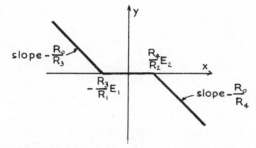

Figure 175

2. FEEDBACK DEAD-SPACE

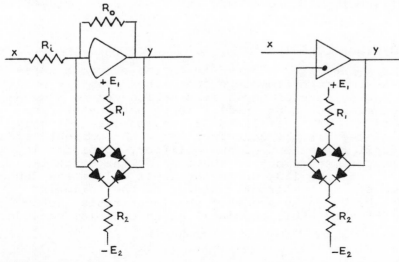

Figure 176

If x is sufficiently small to cause y to be such that the bridge is closed (in state (ii) or state (iii), see Figure 142), the feedback loop is effectively short-circuited and hence $y \simeq 0$. In this state, as x varies, the *current* flowing through the bridge will vary, until it becomes limited (at either E_1/R_1 or $-E_2/R_2$).

The bridge will then open (into either state (i) or state (iv), see Figure 142) so that the feedback loop of the amplifier will consist only of R_0, i.e. the circuit will act as a normal summer. The bridge opens when

$$\text{either } -\frac{x}{R_i} \geqslant \frac{E_1}{R_1} \quad \text{or} \quad -\frac{x}{R_i} \leqslant -\frac{E_2}{R_2}$$

In the former case we have: $\quad y = -\dfrac{R_0}{R_i}x - \dfrac{R_0}{R_1}E_1$

In the latter case we have: $\quad y = -\dfrac{R_0}{R_i}x + \dfrac{R_0}{R_2}E_2$

It follows that the transfer characteristic of the circuit will be:

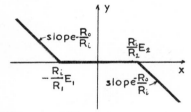

Figure 177

Note. If the input to a dead-space is the sum of several variables, the feedback circuit (Figure 176) with additional input resistors must be used; any attempt to use the input dead-space circuit (Figure 174) with duplication of the input circuits to the summing junction, would result in the sum of the group of dead-spaces, one for each individual input, instead of the required dead-space of the sum of the inputs.

NOTES ON SETTING UP DIODE CIRCUITS

The control voltages E_1 and E_2, referred to in the previous paragraphs, may be taken from potentiometers fed either from the machine references or from the outputs of amplifiers (whichever is the case, the appropriate sign must be maintained). If potentiometers are used, they are not set to pre-calculated values, but are adjusted so that the *output* of the circuit concerned takes the correct value. If the output is itself the output of an amplifier, no difficulty will arise in the measurement; but in the case of the circuits shown in Figures 133, 141 and 153, where the limit values are dependent on the load imposed by the input resistor of the following amplifier, care must be taken to see that the input resistance of the voltmeter does not alter this loading. As an example, consider the circuit:

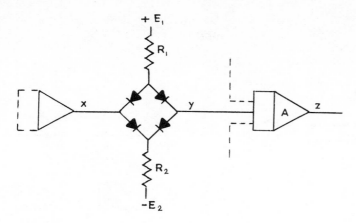

Figure 178

It is required to set E_1 and E_2 to give the desired limits on y; measuring y directly would put the voltmeter resistance in parallel with the input resistor of amplifier A, and hence would alter the load on the bridge. If y enters amplifier A through a gain of 1, A may be temporarily replaced by a summer of gain 1 (only one input used) and $-y$ measured at its output. If on the other hand the y-input gain of A is not unity, the bridge output should be transferred temporarily to another amplifier B having the same input gain as A, the feedback resistance of B being chosen to give an overall gain of unity.

14.4 Diode circuits for 10 V reference machines

The circuits discussed so far were originally produced for use on machines with a 100 V MU. Nowadays - unfortunately, in the opinion of the authors - the majority of smaller machines have a 10 V MU; on a 100 V machine, the ½ V diode error is only ⅛% of 1 MU and consequently can be ignored in many applications, but on a 10 V machine the ½ V diode error represents 5% of 1 MU and is therefore ten times as significant.

The following section shows some of the ways in which the problem of diode error can be overcome, in particular where 10 V machines are concerned.

As we have seen earlier, the input bridge limiter and the idealized diode produce no error, and therefore can be safely used without modification on 10 V machines. Also, by using the idealized diode, the following characteristics can be built up:

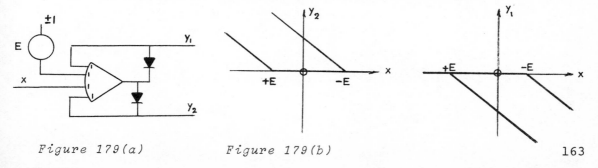

Figure 179(a)   *Figure 179(b)*   163

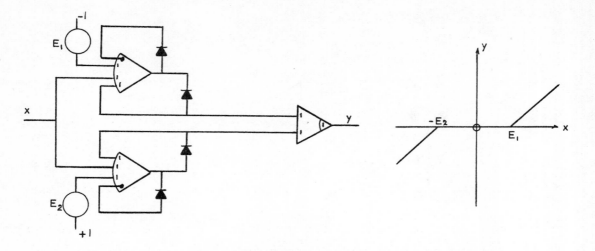

Figure 180(a)

Figure 180(b)

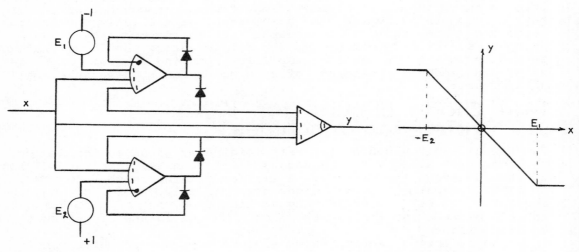

Figure 181(a)

Figure 181(b)

It will be seen that in general these circuits are expensive in computing elements; however, all their pot settings may be pre-calculated, which is an added advantage in the case of those machines which have digital set-up facilities.

14.5 General purpose diode function generators

As the name implies, these are devices which incorporate diode
circuits and are used for the generation of functions - in particular, arbitrary functions which are otherwise difficult to produce
by the simple computer set-ups previously described in this book.

In principle the general purpose diode function generator
(D.F.G.) consists of a group of multi-slope circuits (e.g. of the
type shown in Figure 172) added together, and with the provision
of a second summer which can be brought in in order to change the
sign of the output when required. Unlike the diode circuits so far
described, and which the operator patches on the computer as and
when required, the *passive* elements of a D.F.G. are usually made up
into a chassis module by the computer manufacturer; this unit will
then have to be associated with *two* of the computer amplifiers (see
Figure 183).

The effect of adding several transfer characteristics of the
type shown in Figure 173 is shown in the following diagram:

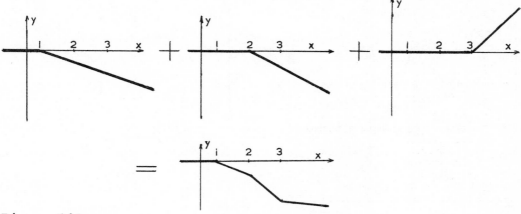

Figure 182

The resulting curve, consisting of a series of straight line segments of different slopes, may be regarded as an approximation to a
continuous curvilinear function. Conversely, if the continuous
curvilinear function has been given, it has to be replaced by a set
of straight line segments which are then simulated separately. In
practice, most D.F.G.s are provided with ten multi-slope circuits,
so that any given function which can be approximated to reasonably
well by a suitable division into ten linear segments, can be produced at the output of the unit.

D.F.G. circuits vary considerably in detail; one common
arrangement can be shown, in principle, as follows:

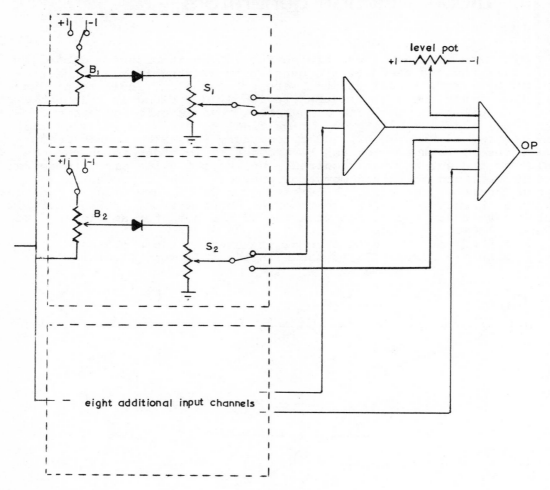

Figure 183

The pots B_i (i = 1,2,3 ... 10) and their associated switches,
determine the break-point positions; the pots S_i and their associated switches, determine the *change* of slope between one segment
and the next; the Level pot enables the whole function to be
raised or lowered relative to the origin. In practice, since the
circuits used by various manufacturers differ considerably, the
setting-up of a given D.F.G. must be done in accordance with the
particular manufacturer's instructions.

To conclude this chapter, a few words must be said concerning
the dynamic limitations of the majority of the circuits described.

A cut-off diode behaves like a small capacitor, so care must
be taken to see that circuits which incorporate diodes are not
driven by signals which change rapidly - otherwise, serious errors
may result when computing at high speeds; i.e. the accuracy of the
circuit transfer characteristic tends to fall off as frequencies
increase.

    In practice those circuits whose transfer characteristic con-
tains an (ideally) instantaneous change in voltage across a diode,
are badly affected when the current through the diode is supplied
via a resistor (since the diode capacitance has to be charged
through this resistor);   e.g., in the case of the soft feedback
comparator shown in Figure 155, the high frequency transfer characteristic becomes:

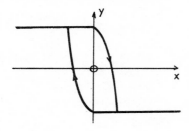

Figure 184

If the soft limits of the hard feedback limiter shown in Figure 153
are set well outside the hard limits, the high frequency transfer
characteristics for z and y become:

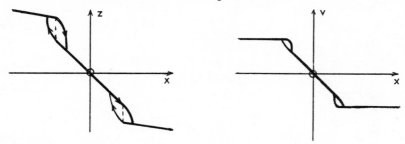

Figure 185

This defect may be mitigated by setting the soft limits very close
to the hard limits, so making the instantaneous change in level of
z very small:

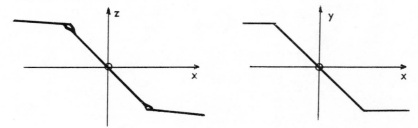

Figure 186

    On the other hand, in the case of the hard comparator shown in
Figure 157, since the output of the bridge is connected directly to
the summing junction and if the input to the bridge is taken directly
from the output of an amplifier, the circuit may be driven at
frequencies above 200 rad s^{-1} without showing any serious deformation

167

of the transfer characteristic. Similarly, the feedback dead-space circuit shown in Figure 176 may also be driven at frequencies of 200 rad s^{-1} and over.

Other circuits in which diodes draw current through a resistor will exhibit some rounding of the transfer characteristic in the neighbourhood of the break-point(s), when the circuit is driven at high frequencies - the effect usually becomes marked at frequencies above 20 rad s^{-1}.

CHAPTER 15
DIODE CIRCUIT APPLICATIONS

The following treatment is by no means exhaustive; this chapter introduces only a few ideas of the many and varied uses to which diode circuits can be put.

15.1 Approximation to curves, with error correction

(incorporating D.F.G.s - see 14.5)

As was seen in the previous chapter, the direct generation of functions can often be achieved by using a general purpose D.F.G., but the technique is sometimes inaccurate and therefore unsatisfactory, for one or more of the following reasons:

(*a*)   the inherent limitation on the number of linear segments;
(*b*)   the difficulty in setting the D.F.G. pots accurately, due to their sensitivity;
(*c*)   the inherent limitation on the amount of slope change available
        - e.g. in the case of the Solartron TR1221.2 unit, change of
        slope between segments cannot exceed 2½, consequently a greater
        change than this can be achieved only by making the segment
        concerned of zero length (i.e. by making two consecutive break-
        points coincide), thus effectively worsening condition (*a*)
        above.

LINEAR APPROXIMATION WITH ERROR CORRECTION

Consider a typical arbitrary function as shown:

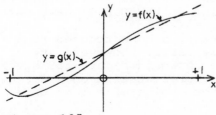

Figure 187

Let $g(x)$ be a straight line approximation to it; suppose that
$$g(x) = mx + c$$
If we now plot $z = f(x) - g(x)$ against x, we have:

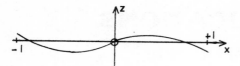

Figure 188

If $g(x)$ has been well chosen, all the ordinates of z should be small (relative to 1 MU) and z can be rescaled by a factor n (where n is some simple integer) so that $nz \leqslant 1$ MU:

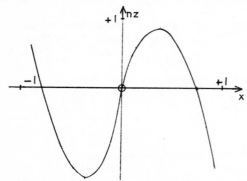

Figure 189

A D.F.G. is now set up to produce nz as output, and the flow diagram arranged as follows:

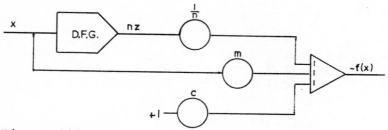

Figure 190

Evidently the output of the summer will be $- (z + mx + c)$, i.e. $- f(x)$, and the errors arising from setting up the D.F.G. have been reduced by a factor of $1/n$.

It might at first appear that the errors can be reduced to a very small amount by making n sufficiently large; however, any attempt to do so will result in the curve shown in Figure 189 having large changes of slope, hence making its representation on a D.F.G. difficult and inaccurate. In practice, the choice of n must be a sensible compromise.

170

The above technique can sometimes be further improved, by using (say) a parabolic curve, an exponential, or a sinusoid, as a first approximation to the given function $f(x)$ instead of a straight line. The best choice of first approximation curve will obviously depend on the general shape of the graph of $f(x)$, but care must be taken to see that the gain in accuracy achieved by the technique is not thrown away by inaccuracies arising from the generation of the chosen first approximation curve.

15.2 Problem discontinuities

(incorporating single diodes, or idealized diode circuits - see 14.2)

Simple discontinuities can often be simulated by the use of single diodes; if high precision is required, an idealized diode circuit can sometimes by used, provided that

    (i) the limitations on the use of that circuit are borne in mind, and

  (ii) the sign change consequent upon the use of the associated amplifier is allowed for.

15.3 Pseudo-backlash

(incorporating input dead-space circuit - see 14.3 and 14.4)

Called pseudo-backlash, since no account is taken of the impact forces involved when the simulation concerns a mechanical system. The circuit is also used to give a crude approximation to hysteresis.

    Basically, the block flow diagram is:

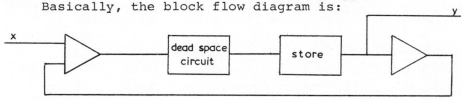

Figure 191

In circuit form, this is realized as:

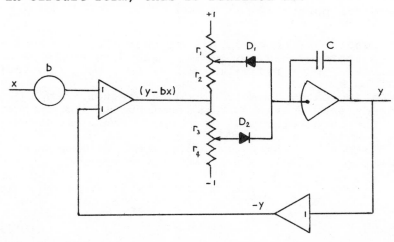

Figure 192

First, consider x as increasing from zero; the dead-space circuit gives zero input to the integrator, and will continue to do so until $(y - bx)$ becomes less than $-(r_2/r_1)$ MU. Then D_1 will conduct, and the integrator output will change at a rate

$$+ \left(\frac{bx - y - \dfrac{r_2}{r_1}}{r_2 C} \right) \ \text{MU s}^{-1} \tag{i}$$

(neglecting the forward resistance of the diode D_1).

In this state the circuit behaves as a first order lag, with an equivalent flow diagram:

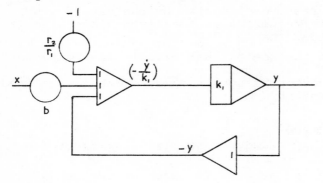

Figure 193

The gain k_1 of the integrator is $1/r_2 C$ (from (i) above) and the differential equation being solved by the flow diagram is:

$$\frac{\dot{y}}{k_1} = \left(bx - y - \frac{r_2}{r_1} \right)$$

The solution of this differential equation is evidently of the form:

$$y = A e^{-k_1 \tau} + \left(bx - \frac{r_2}{r_1} \right)$$

i.e. it has a steady state output of $\left(bx - \dfrac{r_2}{r_1} \right)$

In practice, we require k_1 to be large, so that the transient dies away rapidly; to achieve this, we make r_2 and C as small as is conveniently possible: $(r_2 + r_1)$ is usually a free pot; so that r_2 is of the order of 10 kΩ or less.

If, now, x should decrease, $(y - bx)$ becomes greater than $-(r_2/r_1)$ MU; the dead-space operates, and the input to the integrator becomes zero: the integrator will then hold y at a constant level.

If x decreases further, so that $(y - bx)$ becomes greater than $+(r_3/r_4)$, then D_2 will conduct and the integrator output will change at the rate:

$$- \left(\frac{bx - y + \dfrac{r_3}{r_4}}{r_3 C} \right) \ \text{MU s}^{-1} \tag{ii}$$

(neglecting the forward resistance of diode D_2).

In this state, the circuit once again behaves as a first order lag, in which the integrator has a gain $k_2 = 1/r_3C$ (from (ii) above), and the steady state output will now be $\left(bx + \dfrac{r_3}{r_4}\right)$. Once again, r_3 and C should be small, and $(r_3 + r_4)$ is usually made a free pot, so that r_3 is of the same order of size as r_2.

Evidently, the above procedure will produce the required result provided that x does not change too rapidly. The transfer characteristic is:

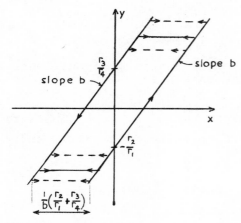

Figure 194

15.4 Motion between end-stops
(incorporating comparator, idealized diode and feedback dead-space circuits - see 14.1, 14.2, 14.3)

In many physical systems (electrical as well as mechanical), constraints are imposed on some of the variables concerned. In the case of mechanical systems, a body may be constrained to move between end-stops, and the simulation of such a constraint involves the consideration of the forces acting when the stop comes into action as well as the mere limitation of the body's displacement. Thus the simple application of a diode limiter circuit to the analogue displacement variable will not give a satisfactory simulation - the simulation must take account of the reduction of the velocity of the body to zero. If the end-stop is virtually inelastic, the velocity is reduced suddenly to zero and the displacement will be held constant at the end-stop position. If the end-stop is elastic, neither velocity nor displacement are abruptly limited at the end-stop - the latter will deform, storing the impact energy by elastic strain, and thus supply a force which will gradually reduce the velocity to zero and then reverse it.

ELASTIC END-STOPS

Consider first the case of a body of mass M moving in a straight line under the action of an external force $F(t)$, and meeting a perfectly elastic end-stop (coefficient of restitution = 1):

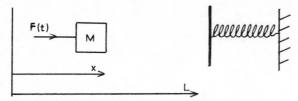

Figure 195

Suppose that the end-stop can be regarded as a spring of stiffness K; then the equations of motion for the mass are:

For $x \leqslant L$, $\quad M\ddot{x} = F(t)$ (i)

For $x > L$, $\quad M\ddot{x} = F(t) - K(x - L)$ (ii)

These imply a simple discontinuity in the problem (see 15.2), and lead to the unscaled flow diagram:

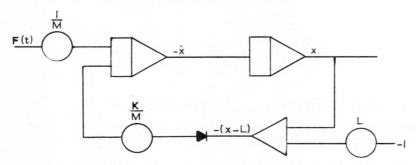

Figure 196

While $x < L$, the single diode is off, and equation (i) is simulated. While $x > L$, the diode conducts and completes the feedback loop so that equation (ii) is simulated.

The system has the merit of simplicity, but has two drawbacks:

(a) due to the imperfection of the diode, there is slight "leakage" of signal round the feedback path while the diode is nominally off,

(b) K cannot conveniently be made greater than 10 without introducing scaling difficulties.

Considerable improvement in the simulation is obtained if an idealized diode circuit is used. (Note that its use is permissible within the restrictions discussed in 14.2.) An idealized diode circuit involves the use of an amplifier, of course, but this can be made the summer of the flow diagram shown in Figure 196 (thereby saving *two* further amplifiers):

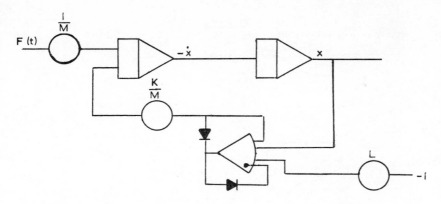

Figure 197

Note that this circuit also enables the use of input gains of 10 into the idealized diode summer (necessary if K is large), without making the summer overload while the body is not at the end-stop - indeed, accuracy is still further improved since the rapidity of "switching" of the amplifier output is thereby increased.

Suppose now that the body oscillates between two perfectly elastic end-stops; the simulation can be realized by duplicating the idealized diode circuit of Figure 197 as follows:

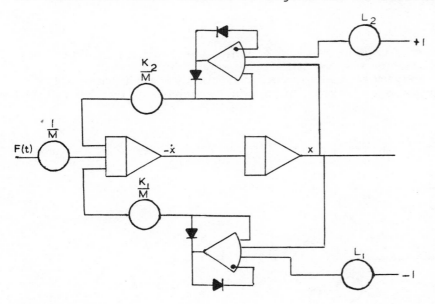

Figure 198

If the end-stop stiffnesses K_1 and K_2 are equal, we can economize on amplifiers by using, instead of the two idealized diode circuits shown in Figure 198, a single dead-space circuit:

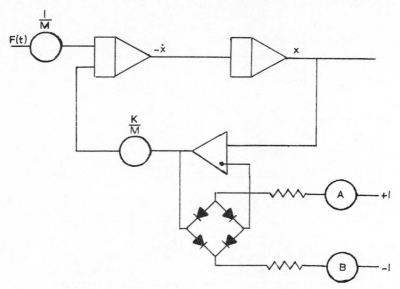

Figure 199

The pots A and B are set so that the dead-space width is

$$- L_2 \leqslant x \leqslant + L_1$$

INELASTIC END-STOPS

Consider now the other extreme - i.e. when the body is constrained by an inelastic end-stop (coefficient of restitution = 0). The *velocity* of the body must be reduced (virtually instantaneously) to zero, and must remain at zero. This can be achieved by the following circuit:

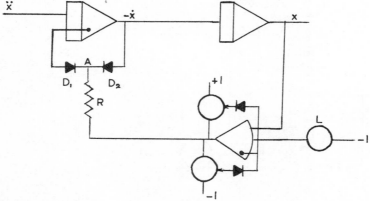

Figure 200

While $x \leqslant L$, the comparator circuit is adjusted to supply a small positive bias to point A thus keeping D_1 off; the integrator thus produces $- \dot{x}$ as output in the usual way.

176

When the body reaches the end-stop (this requires - $\dot{x}$ to be a negative voltage), and x tries to exceed L, the comparator "bangs over" and supplies a large negative bias (possibly slightly less than - 1 MU) to point A thus causing both D_1 and D_2 to conduct. The first integrator will then have virtually a short-circuit feedback path, and $\dot{x}$ decays rapidly to zero; how rapidly will depend on the size of the integrator's feedback capacitor (nose gain); the smaller the capacitor (the larger the nose gain) the faster the decay. The x output of the following integrator is then held constant, simulating the effect of the body remaining in contact with the end-stop.

Note that the resistor R (usually 1 MΩ or 100 kΩ) must NOT be omitted from the circuit when patching; otherwise, when D_1 and D_2 conduct, the output of the comparator amplifier would be connected directly to the output of the - $\dot{x}$ amplifier.

In practice, the use of the soft feedback comparator, with its measurable switching time, results in the graph of x possessing a slight overshoot:

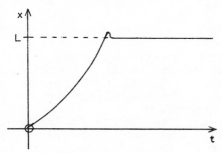

Figure 201

The width of this overshoot spike represents the comparator switching time, and its height will be a function of that time.

The use of a hard input comparator instead of the soft comparator shown in Figure 200 will significantly reduce the size of the overshoot spike, due to the much faster switching; however, two extra amplifiers will be required so that correct signs are preserved:

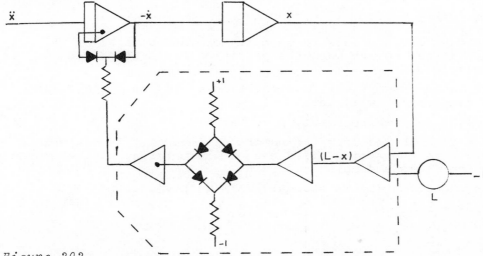

Figure 202

177

Evidently if x and $\dot{x}$ change sign during the computation (e.g., for an oscillatory motion between a pair of end-stops), the above circuit can be duplicated, giving the unscaled flow diagram:

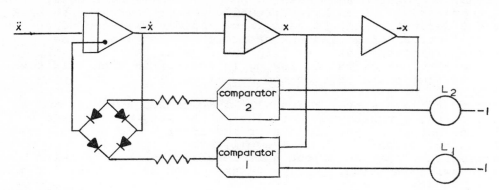

Figure 203

SEMI-ELASTIC END-STOPS

In practice, of course, end-stops are neither perfectly elastic nor perfectly inelastic. If λ is the coefficient of restitution, then $0 < \lambda < 1$, and equality signs are not viable. Before developing better simulations of collision conditions it is useful to examine a little more closely what occurs during impact.

The effect of penetration of the end-stop is partly to dissipate the energy of impact (in heat and sound) and partly to store the energy of impact (via the spring stiffness of the end-stop). In the simulations which follow, certain assumptions are made, and although the validity of these assumptions must be questioned, none of them is as sweeping as is the assumption that either $\lambda = 1$ or $\lambda = 0$.

Consider a small particle of mass M, striking freely and normally a resilient end-stop, and let us assume that

(i) deformation is confined to the material of the end-stop;
(ii) the energy dissipation is viscous in character, so that if y is the *penetration* displacement, then $y = 0$ at the moment of impact and the subsequent energy loss is of the form:

$$\oint f\dot{y}\,dy \quad \text{where } f \text{ is a constant}$$

(iii) the mass and the outward velocity of the material of the end-stop at the moment when the particle leaves it on rebound, are negligible.

With these assumptions, the equation of motion for M during end-stop penetration will be:

$$M\ddot{y} = -f\dot{y} - Ky \quad \text{where } y = 0,\ \dot{y} = V \text{ at } t = 0 \tag{i}$$

where time is measured from the moment of impact, V is the velocity of impact, K is the spring stiffness of the material of the end-stop and f is the viscous damping constant.

Re-writing equation (i) in standard form we have:

$$\ddot{y} + 2\zeta\omega_n\dot{y} + \omega_n^2 y = 0$$

where $\zeta = f/2\sqrt{(MK)}$ and $\omega_n = \sqrt{(K/M)}$ \hfill (ii)

Solving equation (ii) analytically we have the three possible solutions:

(a) $y = \frac{V}{\omega} e^{-\zeta\omega_n t} \sin\omega t$ where $\omega = \omega_n \sqrt{(1 - \zeta^2)}$ for $\zeta < 1$

(b) $y = \frac{V}{u} e^{-\zeta\omega_n t} \sinh u t$ where $u = \omega_n \sqrt{(\zeta^2 - 1)}$ for $\zeta > 1$

(c) $y = V e^{-\zeta\omega_n t} t$ for $\zeta = 1$

In the case of solution (a) and as a direct corollary of assumption (iii) above, the particle leaves the end-stop again when the $\sin\omega t$ factor has completed its first half-cycle, i.e. when $\omega t = \pi$.

Differentiating solution (a),

$$\dot{y} = \frac{V}{\omega} e^{-\zeta\omega_n t} (- \zeta\omega_n \sin\omega t + \omega\cos\omega t) \tag{iii}$$

Putting $\omega t = \pi$ in result (iii), the velocity with which the particle leaves the end-stop is

$$- V e^{-\zeta\omega_n \pi/\omega}$$

As the velocity of impact was V, it follows that the coefficient of restitution is given by

$$\lambda = e^{-\zeta\omega_n \pi/\omega}$$

i.e. $\ln\lambda = - \zeta\omega_n \pi/\omega$

Making ζ the subject of this relation and putting $\omega = \omega_n \sqrt{(1 - \zeta^2)}$, we have

$$\zeta = \frac{1}{\sqrt{[(\pi/\ln\lambda)^2 + 1]}} \tag{iv}$$

It follows that if λ and K are known for a particle and end-stop of given materials, ζ can be calculated from result (iv), and hence the appropriate value of the constant f can be found.

Note that putting $\lambda = 1$ in (iv) leads to $\zeta = 0$ (i.e. a perfectly elastic end-stop, dissipating none of the energy of impact), and putting $\lambda = 0$ in (iv) leads to $\zeta = 1$, which corresponds to solution (c) above, in which the particle takes an infinite time to return to the surface of the end-stop and can never leave the latter. We may therefore, in practice, disregard solution (c) and, similarly, solution (b).

The above results can now be applied in an analogue computer simulation of a system in which a mass M under the action of an external force $F(t)$ is constrained by a light semi-elastic end-stop with spring stiffness K and viscous damping constant f:

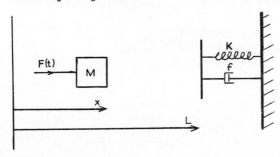

Figure 204

The equations of motion for M will be:

$$M\ddot{x} = F(t) \qquad\qquad\qquad \text{for } x \leqslant L$$
$$M\ddot{x} = F(t) - f\dot{x} - K(x - L) \quad \text{for } x > L$$

i.e.
$$\ddot{x} = \frac{F(t)}{M} \qquad\qquad\qquad\qquad \text{for } x \leqslant L$$
$$\ddot{x} = \frac{F(t)}{M} - \frac{f\dot{x}}{M} - \frac{K}{M}(x - L) \quad \text{for } x > L$$

These equations would be solved if we could realize a flow diagram of the form:

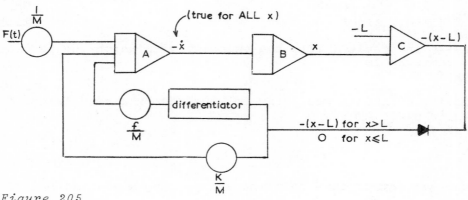

Figure 205

Such a diagram would be very troublesome to put on a computer, because of the difficulties arising from the use of a differentiating network (see A. S. Jackson, *Analog Computation*, section 4-5). However, it is evident that the output of the differentiator "box" in Figure 205 is fed into the input of integrator A and will be integrated by the latter; integrator A may therefore be by-passed and at the same time the differentiator may be dispensed with, by feeding the signal $+ \frac{f}{M}(x - L)$ into integrator B, when $x > L$:

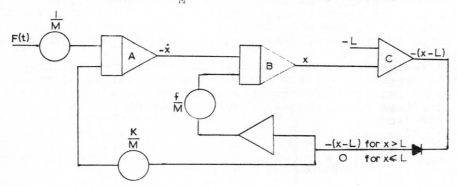

Figure 206

Note that the output of integrator A is no longer $- \dot{x}$ for all x, but is $- \dot{x}$ only while $x \leqslant L$.

180

The flow diagram also suffers from the same defects as those discussed in connection with Figure 196 (q.v.), and should be improved upon in the same way. This leads to the flow diagram:

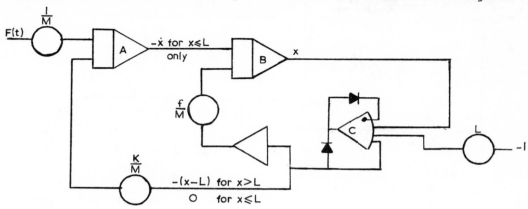

Figure 207

It may, of course, be necessary to have a simulation which will provide a true $\dot{x}$-value for all x, i.e. whether $x \leqslant L$ or $x > L$; to obtain this Figure 207 can be modified by the insertion of a summer between A and B:

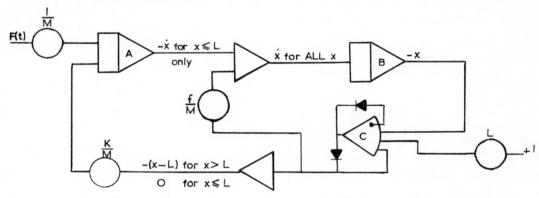

Figure 208

Whichever of the flow diagrams of Figures 207 or 208 is chosen for a given case, decomposed equations for that flow diagram must now be written out, scaled, and turned into machine equations in the usual way.

The flow diagrams of Figures 207 and 208 can be modified, to take account of oscillatory motion between two semi-elastic stops, by duplication of the idealized diode circuit. If (and only if) both stops have the same values for both f and K, we can again economize on amplifiers by using a dead-space circuit in a similar way to that shown in Figure 199:

181

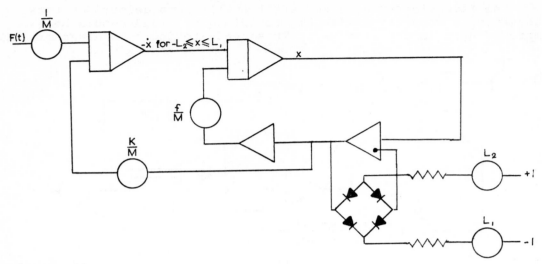

Figure 209

In practice it will be found that the simulations given in Figures 207, 208 and 209 are tolerably good for high values of the coefficient of restitution ($0.6 < \lambda < 1$), but the realism of the simulation deteriorates progressively for lower values of λ and becomes unacceptably unrealistic for $\lambda \leqslant 0.4$. For such low λ values (large ζ values) it will be found that the velocity against time graphs possess pronounced "humps" whenever the particle leaves the end-stop:

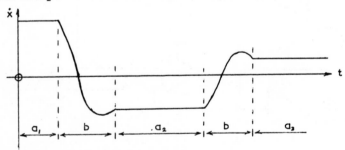

a_r : particle free from stop

b : particle in contact with stop

Figure 210

The smaller the value of λ the worse these spurious humps become. They can be interpreted as the mass sticking to the end-stop until the latter returns to its natural position ($x = L$), thus introducing a spurious negative reaction between end-stop and particle (and consequently, a spurious time-delay before the particle moves freely away from the stop).

The cause of the trouble can be discerned as lying in the third assumption made when setting up the mathematical model (see p.179), and we can significantly improve the simulation by replacing that assumption by a modified one, namely that the mass of the material of the end-stop is neglected and that the particle will leave the end-stop as soon as the total reaction force $R(t)$ between particle and end-stop $\left[R(t) = f\dot{y} + Ky\right]$ *reaches zero.*

To simulate the effect of this assumption, the flow diagram of Figure 207 for a particle moving towards a single semi-elastic end-stop, requires modification as shown in Figure 211:

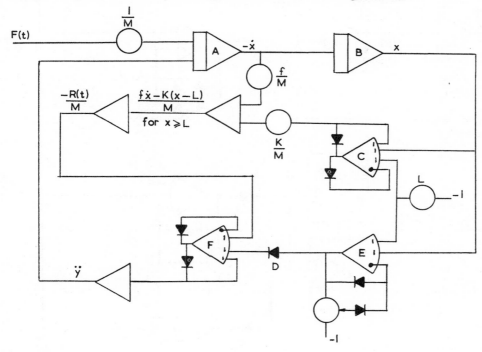

Figure 211

Amplifiers A, B and C perform the same functions as in Figure 207; the comparator (E) is arranged to produce outputs + 1 while the particle is off the stop, and 0 while penetration of the stop occurs. The + 1 signal biases off the idealized diode (F), permitting no output from F while the particle is off the stop, so that A receives as input the acceleration $\ddot{x}$ due to external forces only, while $x < L$.

When $x \geqslant L$ however, idealized diode C produces output - $(x - L)$ and comparator E produces output 0. The acceleration due to end-stop resistance - $R(t)/M$ is thereby permitted to pass through the idealized diode F, if (and only if) it remains a negative voltage. As soon as $R(t)$ becomes zero, F will cease to conduct, so A will receive no further contribution of acceleration from the end-stop, and the particle moves away under the action of the external force $F(t)$ only.

Note: The diode D is inserted between E and F to block off the ½ V signal produced by E when the latter is nominally giving zero output, thus achieving a genuine zero input to F when $x \geqslant L$.

If the particle oscillates between a pair of semi-elastic end-stops of the same material, amplifier C is made a feedback dead-space (as in Figure 209) and comparator E and idealized diode F are duplicated, so that we obtain the unscaled flow diagram:

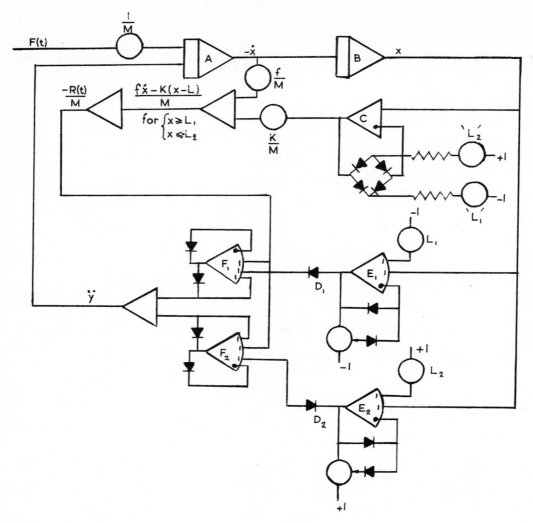

Figure 212

The flow diagram of Figure 212 can be further refined by using an *input* dead-space for C with gains of 1, thus enabling the end-stop position limits L_1 and L_2 to be set on single potentiometers (see Figure 213 opposite).

It will be seen from Figures 212 and 213 that the improved simulation is expensive in terms of computing elements, and perhaps it is worth repeating that the more crude simulations of Figures 207, 208 and 209 are reasonably satisfactory for values of $\lambda > 0.6$, and are obviously simpler to patch and to set up. However, the improved simulation should be used when $\lambda \leqslant 0.6$; and (for any value of λ) it is much superior if it is desired to compute the reaction force $R(t)$ between particle and end-stop; not only does $R(t)$ never go negative, but it will be found to commence, at each impact, with a *step* increase from zero. (Since $R(t) = f\dot{y} + Ky$, the $f\dot{y}$ term contributes this step increase at the moment of impact.)

184

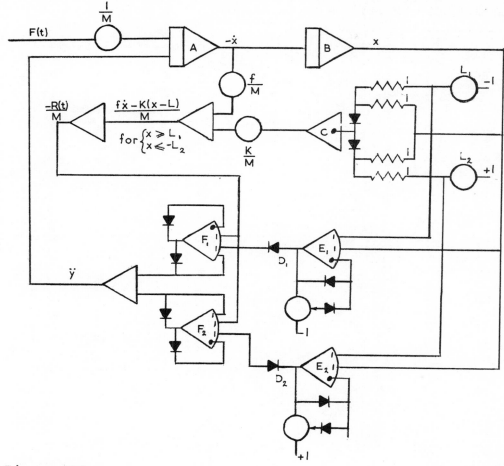

Figure 213

It is important to note that, with the improved simulations of Figures 211, 212 and 213, the formula for calculating ζ from a given value of λ (see result (iv) page 179) *no longer applies*. That formula derives from the original assumption that the particle remains in contact with the stop for a complete half-cycle of oscillation, and the assumption has now been replaced by the alternative assumption quoted on pages 182 and 183.

If we now put $f\ddot{y} + Ky = 0$, and solve to determine the duration of stop penetration and hence the velocity with which the particle leaves the end-stop, the relation between ζ $(= f/2\sqrt{(MK)})$ and λ is found to be:

$$\ln\lambda = -\frac{\zeta}{\sqrt{(1 - \zeta^2)}} \tan^{-1}\left(-\frac{2\zeta\sqrt{(1 - \zeta^2)}}{1 - 2\zeta^2}\right) \quad \text{for } \zeta < 1$$

(The verification of this result is left to the reader.)

Plotting ζ against λ gives the curve shown in Figure 214.   This curve may be used to obtain the setting for the *f*-pot needed to simulate the effect of a given value of λ when the simulations of Figures 211, 212 or 213 are employed:

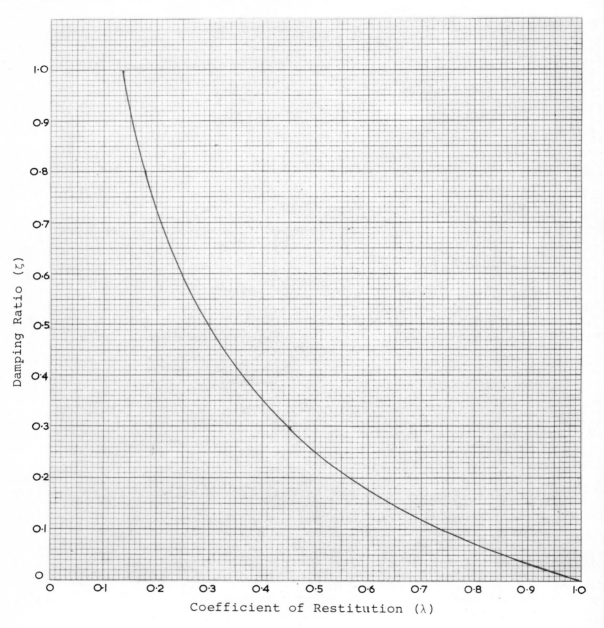

Figure 214

15.5 Damping proportional to the square of velocity

(incorporating idealized diode circuit - see 14.2)

In problems of this kind, a satisfactory analogue simulation must include a term $\dot{x}|\dot{x}|$.

The $|\dot{x}|$ term can be produced from the flow diagram:

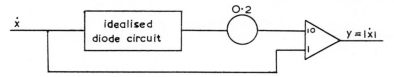

Figure 215

The transfer characteristic is evidently:

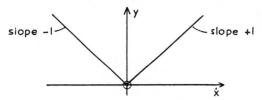

Figure 216

15.6 Coulomb and static friction

(incorporating limiter and comparator circuits - see 14.1)

Friction may be broadly regarded as falling into three categories - static friction, Coulomb friction and viscous friction. Static friction exists between two bodies in dry contact when an external force is applied tending to cause relative motion between them; the maximum value of static friction is called *limiting* friction, and until that value is reached the static friction force exactly balances the external applied force, the bodies not moving relative to one another. The value of the limiting friction depends on the materials of the bodies, and the ratio of the limiting friction to the normal reaction between the bodies is (approximately) constant, and is called the coefficient of limiting friction for the two materials concerned.

Any further increase in the external applied force will be in excess of the limiting friction, and the excess force causes relative motion between the bodies to occur. As soon as such motion takes place, the friction force ceases to be limiting and drops to a lower (approximately constant) value while motion continues; this lower value is called Coulomb or dynamic (dry) friction. This value also depends on the materials concerned and the approximately constant ratio of Coulomb friction to normal reaction is called the coefficient of Coulomb (dry) friction for the materials concerned.

If the contact surfaces of the bodies are not dry or if the bodies move within a fluid medium, the static and Coulomb friction values may be significantly reduced - but there will be an additional frictional resistance to motion, usually a function of velocity, and referred to as viscous friction; at high relative velocities, viscous friction can sometimes reach very large values.

Summarizing the above in graphical form, we might have friction force against relative velocity curves represented as follows:

(*a*) *For bodies in dry contact:*

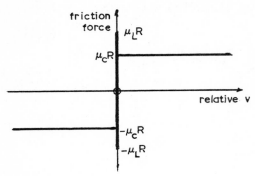

Figure 217

(*b*) *For bodies in wet contact or in a fluid medium:*

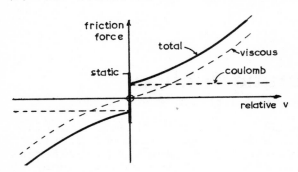

Figure 218

In the work which follows we shall confine ourselves to the simulation of static and Coulomb (dry) friction forces; viscous friction forces, regarded as a function of relative velocity, can be simulated using one of the techniques discussed previously in this book.

The general description of static and Coulomb (dry) friction given in the previous paragraphs can be rendered only approximately in mathematical terms, the more so since the laws of friction are experimental in character. With this reservation, we can proceed as follows:

For the sake of simplicity, consider the motion of a body of mass m placed on a fixed horizontal plane surface. Let R be the normal reaction between body and surface, and let μ_L and μ_c be the limiting and Coulomb coefficients of friction for the materials concerned. Let F_A be the horizontal component of a (variable) external force applied to the body. Let v be the velocity of the body and let f be the *combined* static and Coulomb friction force acting on

188

the body, at any time t. Assuming that the body is initially at rest, then

for $\mu_L R \geqslant F_A > 0$ and $v = 0$: $f = -F_A$ and $\dot{v} = 0$ (i)

for $F_A > \mu_L R > 0$ and $v = 0$: $f = -\mu_L R$ $\therefore \dot{v} = (F_A - \mu_L R)/m$

(> 0) (ii)

for $F_A > \mu_L R > 0$ and $v > 0$: $f = -\mu_c R$ $\therefore \dot{v} = (F_A - \mu_c R)/m$

(> 0) (iii)

Now suppose that the applied force is removed; then

for $F_A = 0$ and $v > 0$: $f = -\mu_c R$ and $\dot{v} = -\mu_c R/m$ (< 0) (iv)

and the body will be reduced to rest when

$F_A = 0$ and $v = 0$: we then have $f = 0$ $\therefore \dot{v} = 0$ (v)

and no further motion ensues.

A similar argument applies for $F_A < 0$.

Consider now the construction of a flow diagram which will simulate the above conditions:
If there were no friction at all, we should have

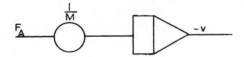

Figure 219

To incorporate the effect of introducing static dry friction up to and including the limiting value $\mu_L R$ consider:

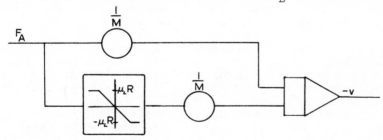

Figure 220

While $F_A < \mu_L R$, the limiter circuit merely acts as an inverter, and the sum of the inputs to the integrator (i.e. $\dot{v}$) is zero; hence $-v = 0$; this fulfils condition (i) above.

When $F_A \geqslant \mu_L R$, the limiter circuit limits at $\mu_L R$, hence the sum of the inputs to the integrator is $(F_A - \mu_L R)/m$, and condition (ii) is fulfilled. (Since $\mu_L R$ is a physical constant, the limiter shown in Figure 220 is a hard limiter.) Evidently $-v$ will no longer remain at zero, and $\dot{v}$ must take the value $(F_A - \mu_c R)/m$; this can be achieved by adding to the circuit of Figure 220 as follows:

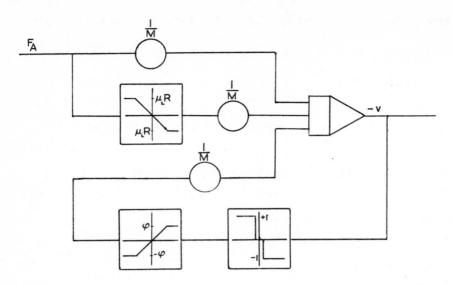

Figure 221

As soon as v departs from zero value, and provided that the dead-space is very small, the dead-space comparator will "bang over" to 1 MU and will drive the following limiter into its limit value $\phi = \mu_L R - \mu_c R$;   it follows that the sum of the inputs to the integrator is

$$\frac{1}{m} \; (F_A \; - \; \mu_L R \; + \; \mu_L R \; - \; \mu_c R)$$

and hence condition (iii) will be fulfilled. It will be seen that the above addition to the circuit does not invalidate the previous arrangements to meet conditions (i) and (ii), for while $v = 0$, the dead-space comparator gives a stable zero output, consequently the following limiter gives a zero output. Note that the limiter added in Figure 221 must also be a hard limiter, since $\mu_L R - \mu_c R$ must be held accurately.

To meet condition (iv) the $\mu_L R$ limiter must remain at its limit until $v = 0$ despite the removal of F_A;   this is so that the total input to the integrator will represent Coulomb friction only, until $v = 0$. This requirement we can achieve by a further addition to the flow diagram shown on the opposite page.

If, in the flow diagram of Figure 222, we consider $F_A = 0$ while $v \neq 0$, the output from the dead-space comparator will keep the $\mu_L R$ limiter at limit, thus fulfilling the requirements.

Finally the block flow diagram of Figure 222 must be turned into a viable computer flow diagram. It is evident that the $\mu_L R$ limiter must be of the hard feedback type, since two inputs are employed. The $\mu_L R - \mu_c R$ limiter does not involve a sign change and should therefore be a diode bridge;   the dead-space comparator should evidently have as small a dead-space as possible - a dead-space of as little as ± 0.0005 MU can be achieved by using what is basically a feedback dead-space circuit (see Figure 176) but with the feedback resistor replaced by a soft feedback limiter. The complete flow diagram will thus be as shown in Figure 223 opposite.

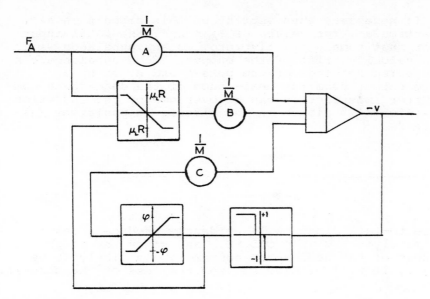

Figure 222

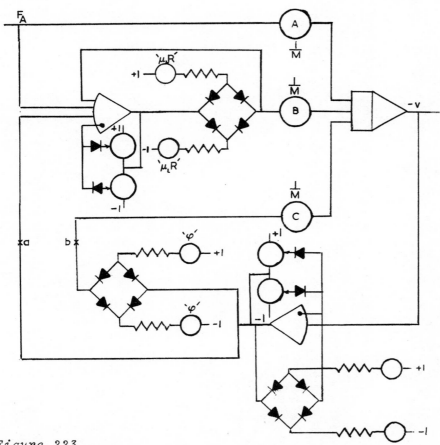

Figure 223

Great care is necessary when setting up this circuit on a computer - in particular, for values of $F_A < \mu_L R$, the total input to the integrator must remain exactly zero, as any unbalance will cause a spurious velocity drift of the output. Such unbalance can be caused by imprecise settings of the pots A and B, or by a slightly non-zero output from the dead-space of the dead-space comparator. The latter imperfection can be overcome by the insertion of pairs of "nose-to-tail" diodes in the circuit at positions (a) and (b) in Figure 223

Each pair of nose-to-tail diodes will evidently produce a dead-space of approximately ± ½ V (± 0.005 MU), and since any slight deviation from zero of the dead-space comparator is likely to be much less than ½ V, it will be blocked from the rest of the circuit.

CHAPTER 16
PROBLEM PREPARATION

In the work covered in this book so far, we have been concentrating on the techniques which enable a differential equation (or set of simultaneous differential equations) to be programmed for solution on an analogue computer. In the physical world, and particularly in the modern industrial civilization which utilizes that world, the solution to a problem usually presents a far more difficult exercise. Even when the problem itself can be clearly defined, the formation of a set of differential equations which will adequately express the problem (i.e. act as a mathematical model of it) can sometimes tax the skill and experience of the mathematician, physicist or engineer; most difficult of all may be the visualization of the problem itself in terms which are sufficiently well defined and unambiguous to enable even a start to be made on a mathematical model suitable for subsequent programming.

The ability to see a complicated problem clearly, to break it down into simpler component problems, and to translate the latter into the language of mathematics, is one which a few people are fortunate enough to possess to a high degree; however, it is demonstrable that anyone who possesses a modicum of training in the fields of mathematics, physics or engineering can acquire some facility in the art of problem modelling by the exercise of logic, patience, and the cultivation of a systematic and methodical approach to the work. This book is not a treatise on logic, nor does it presume to instruct how to acquire the virtue of patience, but the hints and the worked example which follow do demonstrate the kind of methodical approach which is desirable when solving problems which are more sophisticated than those previously discussed.

In practice, the analogue computer programmer quite often receives problems which have been formulated elsewhere, by people working in different fields and trained in disciplines other than his own. It is essential that communication between problem-poser and problem-solver should be clear, adequate and unambiguous; otherwise, misunderstandings of the problem, misinterpretation of data and/or of solution results are likely to occur, and consequential waste of expensive operator-time and even more expensive machine-time will almost certainly result. Good communication can often be greatly assisted when the problem-poser can be present during the running of the computer simulation, so that consultation on odd points that arise can be immediate; while evidently desirable this may, of course, not always be possible. In the opinion of the authors it is part of the responsibility of the analogue computer programmer to insist that the problem be properly presented; his responsibility then continues in making sure that the work which he subsequently carries out is standardized in some strictly systematic manner. Concerning this latter point, he should continually apply to his work this acid test: can the work be taken over, without delays or misunderstandings, and at any stage of the computation, by another operator?

Analogue computation services differ considerably - in size and type of computer, in the number of staff, in ancillary equipment, and in the fields of study in which the service may operate. Because of this it is not suggested that the following lay-out of work should always be rigorously adhered to; each computer team will need to evolve its own system to suit its own particular needs and problems - what will be common to all, and essential for efficient operation, is "system".

PROBLEM REQUIREMENTS (supplied by, or to be extracted from, the problem-poser):

1. An introduction to the problem; any relevant information concerning the context of the problem, and the field of study in which it occurs. Apposite book references, published papers, etc.

2. A clear statement of the problem.

3. A statement of mathematical relations, equations and boundary conditions known by the problem-poser to be relevant; to include a glossary of symbols, abbreviations, definitions, and explanation of any technical jargon associated with the problem.

4. Numerical values of constants used, stating units and dimensions where appropriate, and tolerances or nominal accuracy.

5. Range of values for each parameter to be varied, stating units and dimensions where appropriate, and quoting 'step size' of variation if appropriate.

6. Rough estimates (when possible) of expected range of values of each variable to be computed, and of expected effects on those values as a result of parameter variation.

7. Possible checks on working (e.g. analytical or numerical solutions of similar problems, if known), with appropriate references.

8. A specification of the form in which the results should be presented, and nominal accuracy requirements. (Evidently, modification of this specification may become necessary during the subsequent running of the problem.)

SOLUTION RECORDS (prepared by the problem-solver)

1. Preparation of unscaled flow diagram and decomposed equations.

2. Estimates of maxima, and amplitude scaling factors.

3. Amplitude-scaled equations.

4. Time-scale factor(s) used.

5. Machine equations and final flow diagram.

6. Static check.

7. Amplifier and pot sheets, showing static and machine check results.

8. 'Running Log': a record of all computer use during the solution; comments on method, order of treatment, machine time, faults occurring in computer elements or ancillary equipment, changes in computer set-up, etc.

9. Results: graphs, charts and tables as appropriate, all adequately and unambiguously labelled in terms of the correct *problem* units.

10. Conclusions: comments on any special features concerning the problem which have come to light during the solution process; comments on the nominal accuracy achieved (particularly important if thought to be significantly different from that asked for by the problem-poser).

An example which illustrates some of the points made above will now be given. The example originally came from an engineering research project carried out at the University of Bath in 1966, and in which all the data were expressed in imperial units. The original work, retaining these units, is reproduced here without modification.

INVESTIGATION INTO THE EFFECTIVENESS OF TWO METHODS OF EXCITATION OF A VIBRATORY CONVEYOR

PROBLEM REQUIREMENTS:

1. *Introduction*
Vibratory conveyors and hoppers are used in a number of industrial handling techniques. Their uses are of two main kinds (see ref.1): (i) conveying, (ii) screening.

(i) Conveying: vibratory conveyors are often used for the transportation of hot or abrasive materials that would be inconvenient to move by ordinary conveyors.

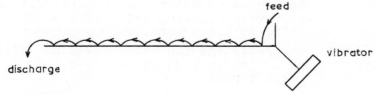

Figure 224

(ii) Screening: vibratory screens are used for grading the size of a variety of materials, ranging from fine powders to stones or solid fuels.

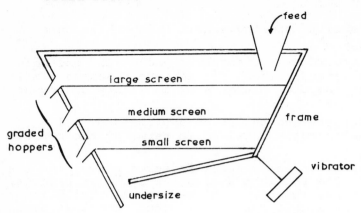

Figure 225

In both types of application the vibrating drive is applied to the conveyor surface so that the downward vertical acceleration component periodically exceeds that due to gravity. Particles on the conveyor are thus periodically in free flight, and regain contact with the conveyor at points which may or may not be the same as their points of departure. V. A. Povidaylo has shown (ref.2) that three kinds of motion are possible:

    (i) jumping and sliding backwards
   (ii) jumping without sliding
  (iii) jumping and sliding forwards

and that while cases (i) and (iii) will involve the coefficient of friction between particle and conveyor surface, under optimum working conditions no slip will occur and only case (ii) need be considered.

References

(1) Thornton, C. A. M.: The use of vibration as a means of indus-trial drive, *Proc.I.Mech.E.*, 1947, vol.157 p.20.

(2) Povidaylo, V. A.: Optimum vibratory feeder operating con-ditions, *Machines and Tooling*, 1960, 31(5)2.

(3) Povidaylo, V. A.: Design calculations and construction of vibratory hoppers, *Machines and Tooling*, 1959, 30(2)5 (Trans.).

(4) Booth, J. H. and McCallion, H.: On predicting the mean conveying velocity of a vibratory conveyor, *Proc.I.Mech.E.*, vol.178 pt.1 No.20.

2. *Statement of problem*

Consider two basic methods of excitation:

(*a*) The motion of a typical point P on the conveyor surface, executing simple harmonic motion in a plane inclined at angle α to the conveyor plane, which is always horizontal:

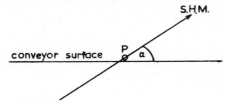

Figure 226

(*b*) The motion in which point P describes an elliptical orbit in the vertical plane, the conveyor plane again always being horizontal:

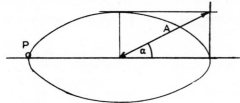

Figure 227

Investigate the motion of a particle placed on the conveyor for the two methods of excitation (*a*) and (*b*) above, for various values of the angle α and of amplitude of conveyor vibration; ignore the effect of air resistance and assume that no slip takes place, but attempt to assess whether the significance of the inclusion of friction in the simulation is great enough to warrant further investigation. Ignore the effects of elasticity of impact (see ref.2).

3. *Mathematical relations*

Symbols: x horizontal displacement.
             y vertical displacement.
   suffix p pertaining to particle.
   suffix c pertaining to conveyor.
             A amplitude of conveyor vibration.
             α angle of plane of vibration to horizontal.
             g acceleration due to gravity.
             f frequency of conveyor vibration.

For method of excitation (a): components of displacement of point P are

$$x_c = A\cos\alpha\sin\omega t \quad \text{(where } \omega = 2\pi f)$$
$$y_c = A\sin\alpha\sin\omega t$$

Therefore

$$\ddot{x}_c = -A\omega^2\cos\alpha\sin\omega t$$
$$\ddot{y}_c = -A\omega^2\sin\alpha\sin\omega t$$

Then, when the particle is in contact with the surface,

$$\ddot{x}_p = \ddot{x}_c = -A\omega^2\cos\alpha\sin\omega t$$
$$\ddot{y}_p = \ddot{y}_c = -A\omega^2\sin\alpha\sin\omega t$$

Boundary conditions:

The particle will leave the conveyor surface at time T (say), when

$$\ddot{y}_c < -g$$

and will remain off the conveyor while $y_p > y_c$.

When the particle is not in contact with the conveyor, its equations of motion will be:

$$\ddot{x}_p = 0$$
$$\dot{x}_p = \dot{x}_{pT} \quad \text{where } \dot{x}_{pT} \text{ is the value of } \dot{x}_p \text{ at time } T$$
$$\ddot{y}_p = -g$$

For method of excitation (b): components of displacement of point
P are

$$x_c = A\cos\alpha\cos\omega t$$
$$y_c = A\sin\alpha\sin\omega t$$

Therefore

$$\ddot{x}_c = -A\omega^2\cos\alpha\cos\omega t$$
$$\ddot{y}_c = -A\omega^2\sin\alpha\sin\omega t$$

When the particle is in contact with the surface,

$$\left.\begin{array}{l} \ddot{x}_p = \ddot{x}_c = -A\omega^2\cos\alpha\cos\omega t \\ \ddot{y}_p = \ddot{y}_c = -A\omega^2\sin\alpha\sin\omega t \end{array}\right\} \text{ for } \ddot{y}_c \geqslant -g$$

When the particle is not in contact with the surface,

$$\left.\begin{array}{l} \ddot{x}_p = 0 \\ \dot{x}_p = \dot{x}_{pT} \\ \ddot{y}_p = -g \end{array}\right\} \quad \text{for } y_p > y_c$$

4. *Numerical values of variables and constants used, units,
   tolerances and accuracy required*

x in inches: solutions to within ± 0.001 inch
y in inches: solutions to within ± 0.001 inch
$g = 32.2$ ft/sec^2
$f = 1\,500$ cycles/min, tolerance ± 50 cycles/min

5. *Parameters to be varied*

A in inches, in the range $0.030 < A \leqslant 0.055$ inch
                       tolerance ± 0.001 inch
α in degrees, in the range $35° < \alpha \leqslant 50°$
                       tolerance ± 1°
ω in rad s^{-1}, in the range $151.8 < \omega \leqslant 162.3$
(since f may take any value in the range $1\,450 < f \leqslant 1\,550$ cycles/min)

198

6.   *Estimates of solution variables*

x_p may be expected to grow with time - its order of size is expected to depend on the method and the magnitude of vibration (say, up to $5A$ per cycle, based on physical appreciation of the problem).

y_p may be expected to be of the same order of size as A (say, $\leqslant 2A$).

7.   *Solutions of similar problems*

None to hand.

8.   *Specification of results*

Plots of x_p, $\dot{x}_p$, y_p and $\dot{y}_p$ against time; in particular, x_p is required in terms of the period of the conveyor oscillation for different parameter values, so that average speeds of traverse of the particle may be estimated for the different conditions concerned. It is hoped that x_p and y_p may be given with a tolerance of approximately ± 0.001 inch.

SOLUTION RECORDS

Computer used: Solartron SCD-10.

1.   *Preparation*

Method of excitation (a)

The equations quoted (see pp 197 and 198) are

$$\ddot{x}_c = - \omega^2 A \cos\alpha \sin\omega t$$
$$\ddot{y}_c = - \omega^2 A \sin\alpha \sin\omega t$$

and

$$\left. \begin{aligned} \ddot{x}_p &= - \omega^2 A \cos\alpha \sin\omega t \\ \ddot{y}_p &= - \omega^2 A \sin\alpha \sin\omega t \end{aligned} \right\} \quad \text{when the particle is in contact with the conveyor}$$

or

$$\left. \begin{aligned} \ddot{x}_p &= 0 \\ \ddot{y}_p &= - g \end{aligned} \right\} \quad \begin{aligned} &\text{when the particle is not in} \\ &\text{contact with the conveyor} \end{aligned}$$

Consider first the y component: while the particle is in contact with the conveyor, we have $y_p = y_c$ (and $\dot{y}_p = \dot{y}_c$), so that the simulation is realisable by the unscaled flow diagram:

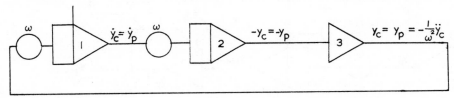

Figure 228

199

When the particle is not in contact with the conveyor, we have the same flow diagram as in Figure 228 for the conveyor, but for the particle we require the flow diagram:

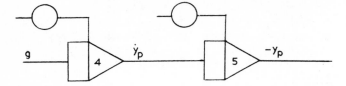

Figure 229

Suppose that the computation is run for the flow diagram of Figure 228, monitoring $-\frac{1}{\omega^2}\ddot{y}_c$ (i.e. by measuring the output of summer 3) until it reaches the value g/ω^2; then hold the computation and measure the values of $\dot{y}_p$ and $-y_p$ (at the outputs of integrators 1 and 2). These values will give the velocity and displacement of the particle at the moment when it is about to leave the conveyor surface - it follows that these values are the required I.C.s for integrators 4 and 5 in the flow diagram of Figure 229 and computation for the free flight of the particle may now be started using that flow diagram.

At the same time as the free flight computation is taking place, it must be arranged for computation using the flow diagram of Figure 228 to be resumed so that the conveyor motion is still correctly represented; the particle will come into contact with the conveyor again when y_p and y_c next have the same value, and when this occurs the computation must revert to the flow diagram of Figure 228.

The whole of the above procedure could be realized in the following way:

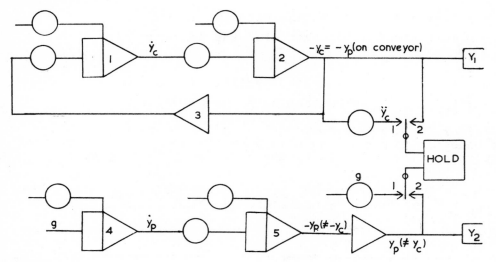

Figure 230

Using the flow diagram of Figure 230, computation would be
commenced with the double-pole switch set to contacts (1), and the
output ($- y_c = - y_p$) recorded at Y_1. The HOLD box incorporates a
comparator which changes state when $\ddot{y}_c \leqslant - g$, and is arranged to
drive the integrators into the Hold state when that occurs. At
this stage the outputs of integrators 1 and 2 are measured; the
computer is put (manually) into the Re-set mode, and the double-
pole switch thrown over to close contacts (2). The values of $\dot{y}_p$
and $- y_p$ just measured are now set as the I.C.s on integrators 4 and
5 respectively (and, of course, on integrators 1 and 2 as well).
Computing once more, gives the free flight part of the simulation,
and the output $+ y_p$ ($\neq + y_c$) may be recorded at Y_2. Meanwhile, the
output of integrator 2 will continue to provide the value of $- y_c$.

The HOLD box changes state again when $y_p - y_c$ becomes less
than zero (i.e. when $y_c \geqslant y_p$), and will then again drive the computer into the Hold state. When this occurs, the recorder input is
transferred to Y_1, the double-pole switch set to position (1), and
computation resumed until the conveyor acceleration again becomes
less than $- g$. The whole cycle of operation may then be repeated.

Having regard to the number of separate computer runs needed
to supply the required solution, the procedure just described would,
in practice, demand an inordinate amount of machine-time; we will
therefore examine ways in which the principles embodied in the flow
diagram of Figure 230 can be retained while improving on the actual
machine realization of it.

First, the manually operated double-pole switch can be eliminated as follows:

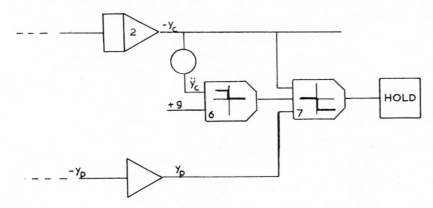

Figure 231

In this diagram, units 6 and 7 are feedback comparator circuits
(see 14.1) set to + 0.25/0 MU and 0/-0.25 MU respectively. It will
be seen that the HOLD box will be energized if *either* $\ddot{y}_c + g$ goes
negative *or* if $y_p - y_c$ goes positive. (Either will give free
flight conditions.)

It is now desirable to avoid the necessity of switching the
recording apparatus from Y_1 to Y_2 and vice versa. While the particle is on the conveyor surface, $\dot{y}_p = \dot{y}_c$, hence integrator 5 will
always produce $- y_p$ as output provided that it is arranged to have
$\dot{y}_c$ as input while particle and conveyor are in contact, replaced by
$\dot{y}_p$ as input while the particle is in the free flight state. This
can be arranged by using a relay controlled by the output of comparator 7 instead of the HOLD box:

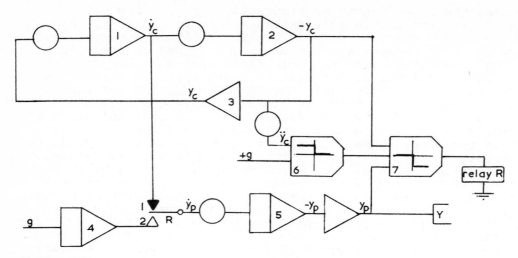

Figure 232

Consider the sequence of events in the flow diagram of Figure 232 assuming that motion commences with particle and conveyor in contact, $y_c = y_p = 0$ at $t = 0$; y_p remains equal to y_c until $\ddot{y}_c + g$ goes negative – then comparator 6 energizes the relay via comparator 7, and the relay contact then closes with ②, thus providing the free flight flow diagram. Evidently the value of the output of integrator 5 is, at the moment the relay operates, the correct initial value for the free flight state; however, there are difficulties concerning the correct I.C. for integrator 4 at the moment of change-over, and the flow diagram must be further modified to take account of this. Assuming for the moment that this can be done, y_p will then follow the correct free flight value until y_c and y_p become equal once more, and during this interval the energization of relay R is maintained by comparator 7 (irrespective of the state of comparator 6), because $y_p - y_c > 0$.

When $y_c = y_p$, the output of comparator 7 changes to zero (unless, of course, $\ddot{y}_c + g$ happens again to be < 0) and the relay R resumes normal position, thus closing contacts ① and making $\dot{y}_p = \dot{y}_c$. (It will be realized that in the event of $\ddot{y}_c + g$ being negative when y_p next equals y_c, relay R operates again at once and free flight conditions are resumed – i.e. the particle flies on through the conveyor surface – and such a contingency will have to be dealt with if it is found to arise in any of the cases under examination.)

We must now return to the problem of securing the correct I.C. value on the output of integrator 4 at the moment of change-over from in-contact conditions to free-flight conditions. One method of solving this problem is to make the output of integrator 4 follow $\dot{y}_c$; the flow diagram of Figure 232 (as far as amplifier 4 is concerned) can be modified as follows:

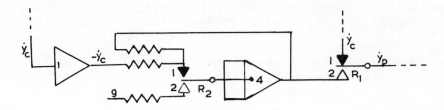

Figure 233

R_1 and R_2 are driven from the same relay; when in position ①
(i.e. the particle in contact with the conveyor) the circuit for
amplifier 4 acts as a first order lag, and will give as output

$$- \left(\frac{1}{1 + sT} \right) (- \dot{y}_c)$$

where T is the time-constant of the first order lag. It is
obviously desirable for T to be as short as possible, so that the
output of amplifier 4 $\simeq \dot{y}_c$; if the amplifier can be arranged to
have a nose-gain of 10 and both input resistors to be 0.1 MΩ, then
$T = 1/100$ sec. At a frequency of 1 rad s^{-1}, there will then be a
phase-lag of 0.001 radian between input and output. The output
from amplifier 4 will thus have an error of $\leqslant 0.1\%$ of the $\dot{y}_c$ amplitude for any frequency ω rad s^{-1} provided that the overall gain of
amplifier 4 is 100ω.

When the relay changes over, both R_1 and R_2 will move to contacts ② (at the moment of change-over from in-contact to free-
flight conditions); integrator 4 will then automatically have the
correct initial condition for the free flight period, and its input
becomes g (as before).

It is now evident that relay R_1 may be dispensed with, since
the output of amplifier 4 is (after approx. $7/100\omega$ sec computing
time) always within 0.1% of $\dot{y}_p$. Thus, for the y component of the
solution, the complete unscaled flow diagram will be:

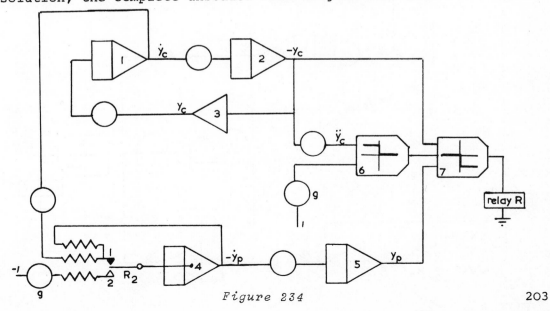

Figure 234

Consider next the x component. While the particle is in contact with the conveyor, $x_p = x_c$ (and $\dot{x}_p = \dot{x}_c$). When the particle leaves the conveyor, $x_p \neq x_c$, since $\dot{x}_p$ = constant ($\ddot{x}_p = 0$, neglecting air resistance).

These requirements may be simulated as follows:

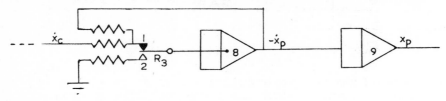

Figure 235

R_3 will, of course be operated by the same relay as operates R_2 in Figure 234; $\dot{x}_p$ will have the same accuracy limitations as does $\dot{y}_p$, provided that amplifier 8 has an overall gain of 100ω.

From the original equations for method of excitation (a), we obtain

$$\left.\begin{array}{l} \dot{x}_c = \omega A\cos\alpha\cos\omega t \\ \dot{y}_c = \omega A\sin\alpha\cos\omega t \end{array}\right\}$$

Thus both $\dot{x}_c$ and $\dot{y}_c$ are easily generated from a common sinusoid loop arranged to produce $\sin\omega t$ and $\cos\omega t$. A complete unscaled flow diagram which will generate both x and y components for method of excitation (a), may now be drawn as follows:

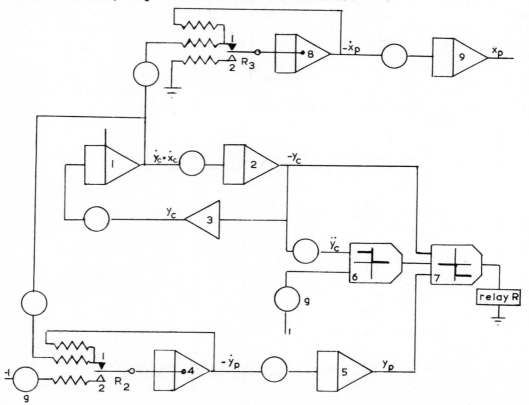

Figure 236

Decomposed equations:

(1) $\quad -\dfrac{d}{dt}(\cos\omega t) = \omega\sin\omega t$

(2) $\quad -\dfrac{d}{dt}(-\sin\omega t) = \omega\cos\omega t$

(4) $\quad -\dfrac{d}{dt}(-\dot{y}_p) = 100\omega(-\dot{y}_p + \dot{y}_c)$

$\qquad\qquad\qquad = 100\omega(-\dot{y}_p + \omega A\sin\alpha\cos\omega t)$

$\qquad\qquad$ or $= -g$

(5) $\quad -\dfrac{d}{dt}(y_p) = -\dot{y}_p$

(6) $\quad -(+\,0.25)$ when $\ddot{y}_c + g < 0$, i.e. when $-A\omega^2\sin\alpha\sin\omega t + g < 0$

(7) $\quad -(-\,0.25)$ when $y_p - y_c + $ (output of 6) > 0, i.e. when

$\qquad\qquad\qquad y_p - A\sin\alpha\sin\omega t + $ (output of 6) > 0

(8) $\quad -\dfrac{d}{dt}(-\dot{x}_p) = 100\omega(-\dot{x}_p + \dot{x}_c)$

$\qquad\qquad\qquad = 100\omega(-\dot{x}_p + \omega A\cos\alpha\cos\omega t)$

$\qquad\qquad$ or $= 0$

(9) $\quad -\dfrac{d}{dt}(x_p) = -\dot{x}_p$

2. *Scaling*

Problem equations for the conveyor in method of excitation (a) are:

$\quad x_c = A\cos\alpha\sin\omega t$

$\quad y_c = A\sin\alpha\sin\omega t$

Maximum value for $x_c = A\cos\alpha$ and maximum value for $y_c = A\sin\alpha$.

Since A and α are parameters to be varied in the problem, it would appear that a different set of maxima, and therefore of scaling factors, would need to be chosen for each individual value of A (and of α) examined. It will evidently be very much more convenient to choose scaling factors which will be independent of parameter variation; this independence may be achieved by incorporating A and α themselves within the scaling factors.

Let us scale $\left(\dfrac{x_c}{A\cos\alpha}\right) = \left(\dfrac{\sin\omega t}{1}\right)$, $\left(\dfrac{y_c}{A\sin\alpha}\right) = \left(\dfrac{\sin\omega t}{1}\right)$, and hence

$\qquad$ scale $\left(\dfrac{\dot{x}_c}{\omega A\cos\alpha}\right) = \left(\dfrac{\cos\omega t}{1}\right)$, $\left(\dfrac{\dot{y}_c}{\omega A\sin\alpha}\right) = \left(\dfrac{\cos\omega t}{1}\right)$

It follows that scaling suitable for x_p, $\dot{x}_p$, y_p and $\dot{y}_p$ will be given by:

$\left(\dfrac{x_p}{10A\cos\alpha}\right)$, $\left(\dfrac{\dot{x}_p}{\omega A\cos\alpha}\right)$, $\left(\dfrac{y_p}{2A\sin\alpha}\right)$, $\left(\dfrac{\dot{y}_p}{\omega A\sin\alpha}\right)$

3. *Scaled equations*

(1) $-\dfrac{d}{dt}\left(\dfrac{\cos\omega t}{1}\right) = \omega\left(\dfrac{\sin\omega t}{1}\right)$

(2) $-\dfrac{d}{dt}\left(-\dfrac{\sin\omega t}{1}\right) = \omega\left(\dfrac{\cos\omega t}{1}\right)$

(4) $-\dfrac{d}{dt}\left(-\dfrac{\dot{y}_p}{\omega A \sin\alpha}\right) = 100\omega\left\{\left(-\dfrac{\dot{y}_p}{\omega A \sin\alpha}\right) + \left(\dfrac{\cos\omega t}{1}\right)\right\}$ or $= -\dfrac{g}{\omega A \sin\alpha}$

(5) $-\dfrac{d}{dt}\left(\dfrac{y_p}{2A\sin\alpha}\right) = -\dfrac{\omega}{2}\left(\dfrac{\dot{y}_p}{\omega A \sin\alpha}\right)$

(6) $-(+\,0.25)$ when $-\left(\dfrac{\sin\omega t}{1}\right) + \dfrac{g}{\omega^2 A \sin\alpha} < 0$

(7) $-(-\,0.25)$ when $\left(\dfrac{y_p}{2A\sin\alpha}\right) - \dfrac{1}{2}\left(\dfrac{\sin\omega t}{1}\right) + $ (output of 6) > 0

(8) $-\dfrac{d}{dt}\left(-\dfrac{\dot{x}_p}{\omega A \cos\alpha}\right) = 100\omega\left\{\left(-\dfrac{\dot{x}_p}{\omega A \cos\alpha}\right) + \left(\dfrac{\cos\omega t}{1}\right)\right\}$

or $= 0$

(9) $-\dfrac{d}{dt}\left(\dfrac{x_p}{10A\cos\alpha}\right) = -\dfrac{\omega}{10}\left(\dfrac{\dot{x}_p}{\omega A \cos\alpha}\right)$

or $= -\dfrac{\omega}{10}\left(\dfrac{\cos\omega T}{1}\right)$

4. *Time-scaling*

Examination of the scaled equations shows that the right-hand sides
of *all* the integrator equations involve a factor of ω; the latter
is, again, one of the problem parameters to be varied, and it is
now evident that if we time-scale by a factor which incorporates ω
an omnibus set of solutions, which can be read off for various
values of ω by merely changing the time-scale of the *graphs* to suit,
will be obtained.

Let $\tau = \omega t$ (i.e. time-scale by a factor of ω).

5. *Machine equations*

(1) $-\dfrac{1}{\omega}\dfrac{d}{dt}\left(\dfrac{\cos\omega t}{1}\right) = 1\left(\dfrac{\sin\omega t}{1}\right)$

(2) $-\dfrac{1}{\omega}\dfrac{d}{dt}\left(-\dfrac{\sin\omega t}{1}\right) = 1\left(\dfrac{\cos\omega t}{1}\right)$

(4) $-\dfrac{1}{\omega}\dfrac{d}{dt}\left(-\dfrac{\dot{y}_p}{\omega A \sin\alpha}\right) = 10\left\{10\left(-\dfrac{\dot{y}_p}{\omega A \sin\alpha}\right) + 10\left(\dfrac{\cos\omega t}{1}\right)\right\}$

or $= 10\left\{\left[\dfrac{g}{10\omega^2 A \sin\alpha}\right] 1\,(-1)\right\}$

(5) $-\dfrac{1}{\omega}\dfrac{d}{dt}\left(\dfrac{y_p}{2A\sin\alpha}\right) = [0.5]1\left(-\dfrac{\dot{y}_p}{\omega A\sin\alpha}\right)$

(6) $-(+0.25)$ when $1\left(-\dfrac{\sin\omega t}{1}\right) + \left[\dfrac{g}{\omega^2 A\sin\alpha}\right]1(1) < 0$

(7) $-(-0.25)$ when $1\left(\dfrac{y_p}{2A\sin\alpha}\right) + [0.5]1\left(-\dfrac{\sin\omega t}{1}\right)$

$\qquad\qquad\qquad\qquad\qquad + 1(\text{output of } 6) > 0$

(8) $-\dfrac{1}{\omega}\dfrac{d}{dt}\left(-\dfrac{\dot{x}_p}{\omega A\cos\alpha}\right) = 10\left\{10\left(-\dfrac{\dot{x}_p}{\omega A\cos\alpha}\right) + 10\left(\dfrac{\cos\omega t}{1}\right)\right\}$

$\qquad\qquad\qquad \text{or} = 0$

(9) $-\dfrac{1}{\omega}\dfrac{d}{dt}\left(\dfrac{x_p}{10A\cos\alpha}\right) = [0.1]1\left(-\dfrac{\dot{x}_p}{\omega A\cos\alpha}\right)$

$\qquad\qquad\qquad \text{or} = [0.1]1\left(-\dfrac{\cos\omega T}{1}\right)$

These equations lead to the scaled flow diagram shown in Figure 237.
     It will be seen from the machine equations that the only pots requiring variation in order to cover all the parameter variations for the problem (A, α and ω) are PB5 and PB2.

     Let $\dfrac{\omega^2 A\sin\alpha}{g} = \xi$

(which is, incidentally, a non-dimensional vertical acceleration component).
Then PB2 is set to $\left[\dfrac{1}{\xi}\right]$ and PB5 is set to $\left[\dfrac{1}{10\xi}\right]$. By doing this, any one setting of ξ covers a whole range of related parameter settings.

     Taking $g = 32.2$ ft/sec^2 and the minimum quoted values for ω, A and α (allowing for tolerances), minimum $\xi = 0.9679$. Taking the maximum quoted values for ω, A and α (allowing for tolerances), maximum $\xi = 2.967$.
     The problem will therefore be run over the range $1 \leqslant \xi \leqslant 3$; note that the particle cannot leave the conveyor surface unless the downward vertical acceleration of the conveyor exceeds g, and this will not occur for values of $\xi < 1$.

6.   *Static check*

Choose $\xi = 4/3$, $\sin\omega t = 0.5$, $\dot{x}_p = -\omega A\cos\alpha$, $\dot{y}_p = -\omega A\sin\alpha$, and $y_p = 2A\sin\alpha$. Also, $\cos\omega t = 1$ when $t = 0$.
Substitute these values into the decomposed equations:

(1) $-\dfrac{d}{dt}(\cos\omega t) = 0.5\omega$

(2) $-\dfrac{d}{dt}(-\sin\omega t) = \omega$

(4) $-\dfrac{d}{dt}(-\dot{y}_p) = -g$ (see (6) and (7) below)

207

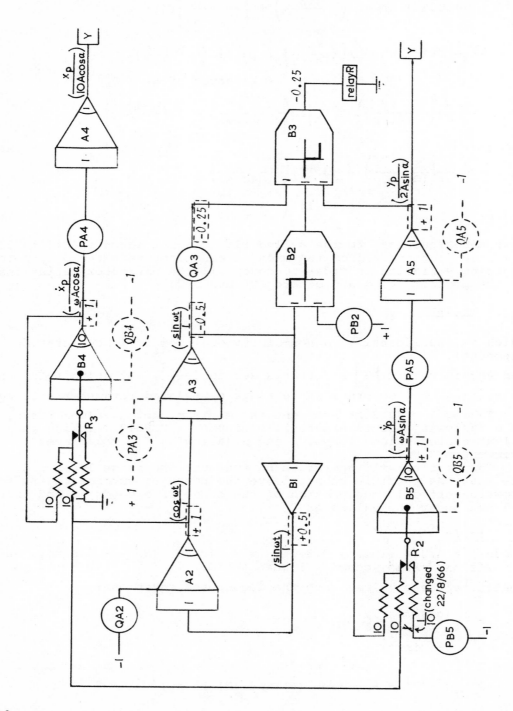

Figure 237

(5) $\quad -\dfrac{d}{dt}(y_p) = \omega A \sin\alpha$

(6) $\quad 0 \quad$ since $-\dfrac{1}{2} A\omega^2 \sin\alpha + g = -\dfrac{1}{2} A\omega^2 \sin\alpha + \dfrac{3}{4} A\omega^2 \sin\alpha \not< 0$

(7) $\quad -0.25 \quad$ since $\dfrac{3}{2} A \sin\alpha + 0 > 0$

(From (6) and (7) it follows that the particle is in the free flight state.)

(8) $\quad -\dfrac{d}{dt}(-\dot{x}_p) = 0 \quad$ (see (6) and (7) above)

(9) $\quad -\dfrac{d}{dt}(x_p) = \omega A \cos\alpha$

S.C.I.C.s: since $\xi = \dfrac{4}{3}$, $\left[\dfrac{1}{\xi}\right] = 0.75$ and $\left[\dfrac{1}{10\xi}\right] = 0.075$

$\sin\omega t = 0.5 \quad \left(-\dfrac{\sin\omega t}{1}\right) = -0.5$

$\dot{x}_p = -\omega A \cos\alpha \quad \left(-\dfrac{\dot{x}_p}{\omega A \cos\alpha}\right) = 1$

$\dot{y}_p = -\omega A \sin\alpha \quad \left(-\dfrac{\dot{y}_p}{\omega A \sin\alpha}\right) = 1$

$y_p = 2A\sin\alpha \quad \left(\dfrac{y_p}{2A\sin\alpha}\right) = 1$

From the flow diagram,

Input to A2 $= 0.5 = -\dfrac{1}{\omega}\dfrac{d}{dt}\left(\dfrac{\cos\omega t}{1}\right)$

Therefore $\dfrac{d}{dt}(\cos\omega t) = -0.5\omega \qquad$ Checks with (1) above

Input to A3 $= 1 = -\dfrac{1}{\omega}\dfrac{d}{dt}\left(-\dfrac{\sin\omega t}{1}\right)$

Therefore $\dfrac{d}{dt}(\sin\omega t) = \omega \qquad$ Checks with (2) above

Input to B5 $= [PB5]1(-1) = -0.075 = -\dfrac{1}{10\omega}\dfrac{d}{dt}\left(-\dfrac{\dot{y}_p}{\omega A \sin\alpha}\right)$

Therefore $\dfrac{d}{dt}(\dot{y}_p) = -0.75\omega^2 A \sin\alpha$

$\qquad\qquad\qquad = -0.75g\xi$

$\qquad\qquad\qquad = -g$ when $\xi = 4/3 \qquad$ Checks with (4) above

Input to A5 $= [PA5]1(1) = 0.5 = -\dfrac{1}{\omega}\dfrac{d}{dt}\left(\dfrac{y_p}{2A\sin\alpha}\right)$

Therefore $\dfrac{d}{dt}(y_p) = -\omega A \sin\alpha \qquad$ Checks with (5) above

Input to B2 $= 1(-0.5) + [PB2]1(1) = 0.25$

Therefore   Output of B2 = 0   Checks with (6) above

Input to B3 $= [QA3]1(-0.5) + 1(0) + 1(1) = 0.75$

Therefore   Output of B3 = -0.25   Checks with (7) above

Input to B4 $= 0 = \dfrac{1}{10\omega} \dfrac{d}{dt}\left(-\dfrac{\dot{x}_p}{\omega A\cos\alpha}\right)$

Therefore $\dfrac{d}{dt}(\dot{x}_p) = 0$ Checks with (8) above

Input to A4 $= [PA4]1(1) = 0.1 = -\dfrac{1}{\omega}\dfrac{d}{dt}\left(\dfrac{x_p}{10A\cos\alpha}\right)$

Therefore $\dfrac{d}{dt}(x_p) = -\omega A\cos\alpha$ Checks with (9) above

Since the above procedure checks only one combination of states for B2 and B3, further checks must be made which will take account of the other possible states. The three combinations possible are:

(i) Particle in contact with conveyor:

$\left.\begin{array}{l} \ddot{y}_c \not< -g \\ y_p = y_c \end{array}\right\}$ output of B2 = 0

output of B3 = 0

(ii) Particle in free flight

(a) $\left.\begin{array}{l} \ddot{y}_c < -g \\ y_p > y_c \end{array}\right\}$ output of B2 = 0.25

output of B3 = -0.25

(b) $\left.\begin{array}{l} \ddot{y}_c \not< -g \\ y_p > y_c \end{array}\right\}$ output of B2 = 0

output of B3 = -0.25

The static check, as so far covered, deals only with case (ii)(b); new S.C.I.C.s must be chosen so that the other two combinations may be checked.

To check case (i), let us choose $\xi = 4/3$, $\sin\omega t = 0.5$, $\dot{x}_p = -\omega A\cos\alpha$, $\dot{y}_p = -\omega A\sin\alpha$ and $y_p = \frac{1}{2}A\sin\alpha$ (so that $y_p = y_c$). From the flow diagram it will be seen that this change affects only B3, B4 and B5.

Decomposed equations concerned:

7.1: 0, since $\frac{1}{2} A\sin\alpha - \frac{1}{2} A\sin\alpha + 0 \not> 0$ which satisfies (i)

4.1: $-\frac{d}{dt}(-\dot{y}_p) = 100\omega(\omega A\sin\alpha + \omega A\sin\alpha)$
$$= 200\omega^2 A\sin\alpha$$

8.1: $-\frac{d}{dt}(-\dot{x}_p) = 100\omega(\omega A\cos\alpha + \omega A\cos\alpha)$
$$= 200\omega^2 A\cos\alpha$$

S.C.I.C.s: the only change from the first static check is
$y_p = \frac{1}{2} A\sin\alpha$

Therefore

$$\left(\frac{y_p}{2A\sin\alpha}\right) = 0.25$$

From the flow diagram,

Input to B3 $= [QA3] 1(-0.5) + 1(0) + 1(0.25) = 0$

Therefore Output of B3 = 0   Checks with 7.1 above

Input to B5 $= 10(1) + 10(1) = 20 = -\frac{1}{10\omega}\frac{d}{dt}\left(-\frac{\dot{y}_p}{\omega A\sin\alpha}\right)$

Therefore $\frac{d}{dt}(\dot{y}_p) = 200\omega^2 A\sin\alpha$ Checks with 4.1 above

Input to B4 $= 10(1) + 10(1) = 20 = -\frac{1}{10\omega}\frac{d}{dt}\left(-\frac{\dot{x}_p}{\omega A\cos\alpha}\right)$

Therefore $\frac{d}{dt}(\dot{x}_p) = 200\omega^2 A\cos\alpha$ Checks with 8.1 above

 To check case (ii)(a) we choose:
$\xi = 2.5$, $\sin\omega t = 0.5$, $\dot{x}_p = -\omega A\cos\alpha$, $\dot{y}_p = -\omega A\sin\alpha$, and
$y_p = \frac{1}{2} A\sin\alpha$.

(Note that the choice here of $y_p = y_c$ enables a check to be made on whether B3 may be correctly driven solely by the output of B2.)

 Since B4 and B5 have already been checked in both their possible states, we need now consider only B2 and B3.

Decomposed equations concerned:

6.2: $+ 0.25$ since $- 0.5\omega^2 A\sin\alpha + g$
$$= - 0.5\omega^2 A\sin\alpha + 0.4\omega^2 A\sin\alpha < 0$$

7.2: $- 0.25$ since $0.5A\sin\alpha - 0.5A\sin\alpha + 0.25 > 0$

These results satisfy the requirements for case (ii)(a).

S.C.I.C.s: the only change from the second static check is $\xi = 2.5$.

Hence $\left[\dfrac{1}{\xi}\right] = 0.4$

$\left[\dfrac{1}{10\xi}\right]$ need not be considered, since this particular check is concerned only with B2 and B3.

From the flow diagram,

Input to B2 $= 1(-0.5) + [\text{PB2}]1(1)$

$\qquad\qquad = -0.1 < 0$

Therefore Output $= +0.25$ Checks with 6.2 above

Input to B3 $= [\text{QA3}]1(-0.5) + 1(0.25) + 1(0.25)$

$\qquad\qquad = +0.25 > 0$

Therefore Output $= -0.25$ Checks with 7.2 above

Method of excitation (b)

From the equations of motion (see p. 198)

$$\dot{x}_c = -\omega A\cos\alpha\sin\omega t \left.\begin{array}{c}\\[2mm]\end{array}\right\}$$
$$\dot{y}_c = \omega A\sin\alpha\cos\omega t$$

If these equations are compared with the corresponding pair for method of excitation (*a*) (see p. 198) it will be seen that the only difference between them is in the case of $\dot{x}_c$; the substitution of $-\sin\omega t$ for $+\cos\omega t$ transforms the method (*a*) equation for $\dot{x}_c$ into the method (*b*) equation for $\dot{x}_c$. It is thus evident that only a very simple modification to the flow diagram of Figure 236 is required in order to provide a complete unscaled x and y flow diagram for the method (*b*) vibration case - namely, the input to amplifier 8 shown in Figure 236 as coming from the output of amplifier 1 must be transferred so that it comes from the output of amplifier 2 instead.

It follows that in the scaled flow diagram of Figure 237, the modification required is that the input to B4 shown as coming from the output of A2 must be transferred so that it comes from the output of A3 instead.

No other modifications will be required.

It is evident that the modification introduced will affect only the input to amplifier B4, case (i), as far as the static check is concerned.

Hence, choosing $\xi = 4/3$, $\sin\omega t = +0.5$, $\dot{x}_p = -\omega A\cos\alpha$

$$\dot{y}_p = -\omega A\sin\alpha \quad \text{and} \quad y_p = \tfrac{1}{2}A\sin\alpha$$

we have:

Decomposed equation 8.3:

$$-\frac{d}{dt}(-\dot{x}_p) = 100\omega(-\dot{x}_p + \dot{x}_c)$$

$$= 100\omega(-\dot{x}_p - \omega A\cos\alpha\sin\omega t)$$

$$= 100\omega\left(\omega A\cos\alpha - \frac{1}{2}\omega A\cos\alpha\right)$$

$$= 50\omega^2 A\cos\alpha$$

From the flow diagram,

Input to B4 $= 10(1) + 10(-0.5)$

$$= 5 = -\frac{1}{10\omega}\frac{d}{dt}\left(-\frac{\ddot{x}_p}{\omega A\cos\alpha}\right)$$

Therefore $\dfrac{d}{dt}(-\ddot{x}_p) = -50\omega^2 A\cos\alpha$ \qquad Checks with 8.3 above

7. *Amplifier and pot sheets*

University of Bath
School of Mathematics

AMPLIFIER SHEET

Sheet number 2 of 2 sheets

Name ASC
Problem Vibrating Conveyor
Computer No. SCD 10 \qquad Date 19-8-66
Time scale β = ω \qquad (β computer secs = 1 problem sec)

	Function	O/P Variable	P.C.	STATIC CHECK Calculated O/P	Calculated $\frac{1}{10}\frac{d}{dt}$	Measured O/P	Measured $\frac{1}{10}\frac{d}{dt}$
A1							
A2	$\int \times 1$	$\left(\frac{\cos\omega t}{1}\right)$	-1.000		-0.050		-0.050
A3	$\int \times 1$	$\left(-\frac{\sin\omega t}{1}\right)$	0		0.100		0.100
A4	$\int \times 1$	$\left(\frac{x_p}{10A\cos\alpha}\right)$	0		0.010		0.010
A5	$\int \times 1$	$\left(-\frac{\dot{y}_p}{2A\sin\alpha}\right)$	0		0.050		0.0498
A6							
B1	$\Sigma \times 1$	$\left(\frac{\sin\omega t}{1}\right)$	0	0.500		0.501	
B2	Comp	0.25/0	0	0 0.250	0.025 -0.010	0 0.250	0.0249 -0.0100
B3	Comp	0/0.25	0	-0.250 0 0.250	0.0750 0 0.0250	-0.250 0 0.250	0.0747 0 0.0250
B4	$\int \times 10$	$\left(-\frac{\ddot{x}_p}{\omega A\cos\alpha}\right)$	0		0 2.000		0 1.000 × 2
B5	$\int \times 10$	$\left(-\frac{\ddot{y}_p}{\omega A\sin\alpha}\right)$	0		-0.0075 2.000		-0.0077 1.000 × 2
B6							
C1							
C2							
C3							
C4							
C5							
C6							

University of Bath
School of Mathematics

POTENTIOMETER SHEET

Sheet number 1 of 2 sheets

Name ASC
Problem Vibrating Conveyor
Computer No. SCD 10 \qquad Date 19-8-66
Time scale β = ω \qquad (β computer secs = 1 problem sec)

POT.	Setting	Gain	S.C.	Amplifier	Remarks
PA1					
PA2					
PA3			0.500	A 3	
PA4	0.100	1 × 1			
PA5	0.500	1 × 1			
QA1					
QA2	1.000	IC		A 2	
QA3	0.500	1			
QA4					
QA5			1.000	A 5	0.250 for check 2
QA6					
PB1					
PB2	$\frac{1}{\xi}$		0.750		0.400 for check 3
PB3					
PB4					
PB5	$\frac{1}{\xi}$	$\frac{1}{10} \times 10$	0.750		
PB6					
QB1					
QB2					
QB3					
QB4			1.000	B 4	
QB5			1.000	B 5	
QB6					

Monday, 22nd August.   Solartron SCD-10 computer.

11.00   Computer patching. No difficulties.

11.30   Machine static check commenced.
The first reading of input to amplifier B5 showed an error
of more than 5%. This was attributed to the low pot setting
of PB5 $\left(\left[\frac{1}{10\xi}\right]\right.$, where ξ chosen as $\left.\frac{4}{3}\right)$.
This was improved by patching PB5 into a $\frac{1}{10}$ input, by using
a 10 MΩ external resistor to the normally open contact of
the relay, instead of the 1 MΩ resistor shown on the flow
diagram; then re-setting PB5 to $\left[\frac{1}{\xi}\right]$.

The initial rate for B4 and B5 in the check for case (i) is
20 MU. In normal circumstances we cannot use amplifier A1
to check this, since A1 provides either $\frac{d}{dt}(\ldots)$ or $\frac{1}{10}\frac{d}{dt}(\ldots)$;
this difficulty was overcome by patching a 100 kΩ external
resistor in parallel with the normal feedback component of
amplifier A1 (switched to integrate), thus providing (in
effect) $\frac{1}{20}\frac{d}{dt}(\ldots)$:

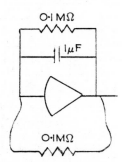

Figure 238

11.50   Machine check completed.

13.30   Test runs commenced.

Time-base for *X/Y* plotter patched, using amplifier A1:

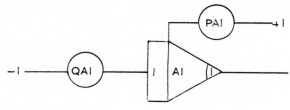

Figure 239

It was decided to plot for two cycles of conveyor vibration -
i.e., problem time t in the range $0 \leqslant t \leqslant 4\pi/\omega$ sec. Therefore computer time τ must be in the range $0 \leqslant \tau \leqslant 4\pi$ sec.

Hence QA1 set to $\left[\dfrac{1}{2\pi}\right] = 0.159$.

Traces of all outputs were observed, in turn, on the C.R.O.
No difficulties were experienced.

Trial plots using X/Y pen recorder No.5

(i) y_p against t

Plotter scales: X (for t), 2 in. per MU, plotting $\left(\dfrac{t}{4\pi/\omega}\right)$

Y (for y_p), 2 in. per MU, plotting $\left(\dfrac{y_p}{2A\sin\alpha}\right)$

Cases: $\xi = 1$, 1.25, 1.5, 2, 2.5, 3

(y_c was also plotted on the same curves, using the output of
amplifier B1, and the plotter scale change

Y (for y_c), 1 in. per MU, plotting $\left(\dfrac{y_c}{A\sin\alpha}\right)$.)

(ii) x_p against t

Plotter scales: X (for t), 2 in. per MU

Y (for x_p), 2 in. per MU, plotting $\left(\dfrac{x_p}{10A\cos\alpha}\right)$

Cases: $\xi = 1$, 1.25, 1.5, 2, 2.5, 3

(iii) $\dot{y}_p$ against t

Plotter scales: X (for t), 2 in. per MU

Y (for $\dot{y}_p$), 2 in. per MU, plotting $\left(\dfrac{\dot{y}_p}{\omega A\sin\alpha}\right)$

Cases: $\xi = 1$, 1.25, 1.5, 2, 2.5, 3

($\dot{y}_p$ taken from sign inversion of the output of B5, using an
additional inverter. $\dot{y}_c$ was also plotted on the same curves,
using the same Y scale, and taken from the output of
amplifier A2.)

(iv) $\dot{x}_p$ against t

Plotter scales: X (for t), 2 in. per MU

Y (for $\dot{x}_p$), 2 in. per MU, plotting $\left(\dfrac{\dot{x}_p}{\omega A\cos\alpha}\right)$

Cases: $\xi = 1$, 1.25, 1.5, 2, 2.5, 3

($\dot{x}_c$ was also plotted on the same curves, using the same Y
scale, and taken from the output of amplifier A2.)

It was observed that in all cases where $\xi = 1$ (i.e.
particle and conveyor permanently in contact), the curves
for a displacement or a velocity component of the particle
were in satisfactory agreement with those for the conveyor.

14.20   Trial plots completed.

It was considered that, with minor changes in plotter scales and taking more cases for ξ when plotting x_p, the final plots for method of excitation (a) could be undertaken.

14.30   Final plots for method (a) results commenced.

(i) y_p against t

Plotter scales: X (for t), 2 in. per MU

Y (for y_p), 2 in. per MU

Cases: ξ = 1, 1.25, 1.5, 2, 2.5, 3

(ii) x_p against t

Plotter scales: X (for t), 2 in. per MU

Y (for x_p), 2 in. per MU

Cases: ξ = 1, 1.25, 1.5, 2, 2.5, 3

(iii) $\dot{y}_p$ against t

Plotter scales: X (for t), 2 in. per MU

Y (for $\dot{y}_p$), 1 in. per MU

Cases: ξ = 1, 1.25, 1.5, 2, 2.5, 3

(iv) $\dot{x}_p$ against t

Plotter scales: X (for t), 2 in. per MU

Y (for $\dot{x}_p$), 1 in. per MU

Cases: ξ = 1, 1.25, 1.5, 2, 2.5, 3

(v) x_p against t

A further set of curves in addition to those in (ii) above were drawn out, using

Cases: ξ = 1, 1.1, 1.2, 1.3, 1.4, 1.5, 1.75, 2,

2.25, 2.5, 2.75, 3

Plotter scales for these were changed as follows:

X (for t), 2 in. per MU

Y (for x_p), 5 in. per MU

From this set of curves (not included here), the horizontal distance travelled by the particle in every two cycles of conveyor vibration was measured, giving the values shown in the following table:

Table 1

ξ	1.00	1.10	1.20	1.30	1.40	1.50
$\left(\dfrac{x_p \text{ per cycle}}{A\cos\alpha}\right)$	0.00	1.60	2.58	3.28	3.82	4.22

	1.75	2.00	2.25	2.50	2.75	3.00
	4.92	5.30	5.52	5.61	5.70	5.75

15.30   Final plots for method (*a*) results completed.

Computer left patched up.

Tuesday, 23rd August

10.00   Machine static check commenced for method of excitation (*b*).

10.10   Machine check completed.

It was considered that trial plots specifically for the method (*b*) solutions were not necessary.

10.15   Final plots for method (*b*) results commenced.

(i) y_p against t

Plotter scales: X (for t), 2 in. per MU

Y (for y_p), 2 in. per MU

Cases: ξ = 1, 1.25, 1.5, 2, 2.5, 3

(ii) x_p against t

Plotter scales: X (for t), 2 in. per MU

Y (for x_p), 5 in. per MU

Cases: ξ = 1, 1.25, 1.5, 2, 2.5, 3

(iii) $\dot{y}_p$ against t

Plotter scales: X (for t), 2 in. per MU

Y (for $\dot{y}_p$), 1 in. per MU

Cases: ξ = 1, 1.25, 1.5, 2, 2.5, 3

(iv) $\dot{x}_p$ against t

Plotter scales: X (for t), 2 in. per MU

Y (for $\dot{x}_p$), 1 in. per MU

(v) x_p against t

A further set of curves in addition to those in (ii) above were drawn out, using

Cases: ξ = 1, 1.1, 1.2, 1.3, 1.4, 1.5, 1.75, 2,

2.25, 2.5, 2.75, 3

Plotter scales for these were changed as follows:

X (for t), 2 in. per MU

Y (for x_p), 10 in. per MU

From this set of curves (not included here), the horizontal distance travelled by the particle for every two cycles of conveyor vibration was measured, giving the values shown in the following table:

Table 2

ξ	1.000	1.100	1.200	1.300	1.400	1.500
$\left(\dfrac{x_p \text{ per cycle}}{A\cos\alpha}\right)$	0.000	0.425	0.690	1.000	1.250	1.480

	1.750	2.000	2.250	2.500	2.750	3.000
	1.840	2.060	2.180	2.190	2.150	2.000

218

9. Results (graphs)

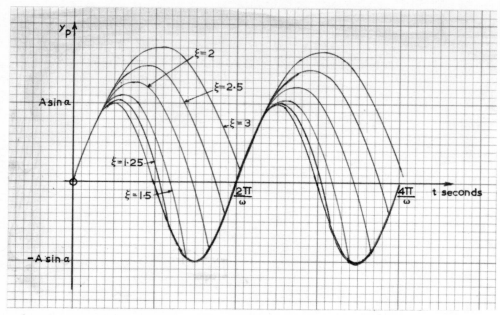

1 - Graph (a)(i)

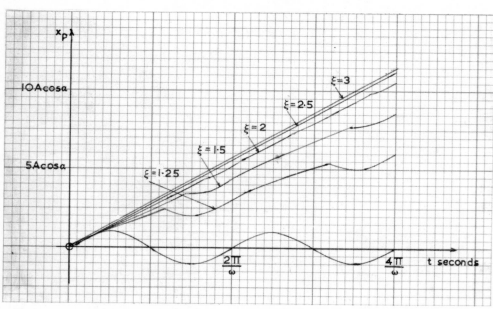

2 - Graph (a)(ii)

220

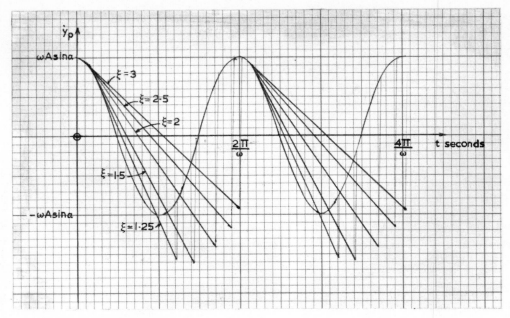

3 - Graph (a)(iii)

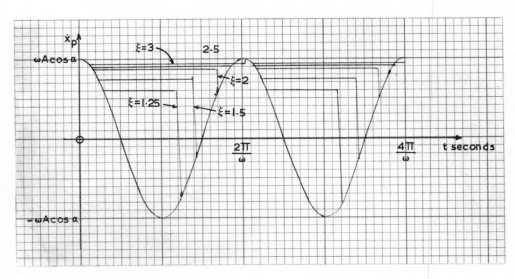

4 - Graph (a)(iv)

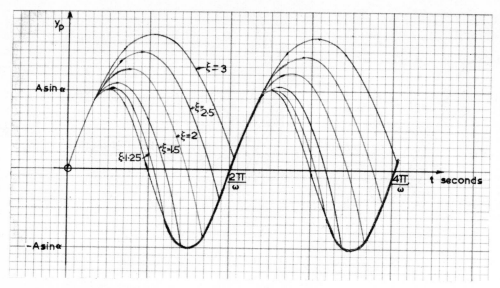

5 - Graph (b)(i)

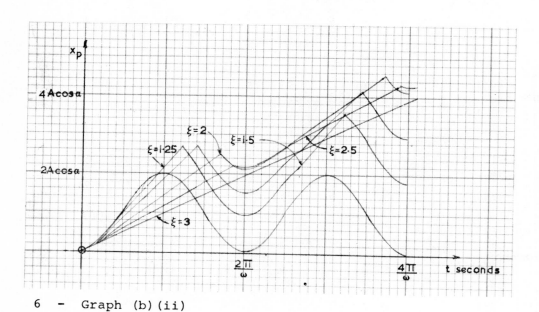

6 - Graph (b)(ii)

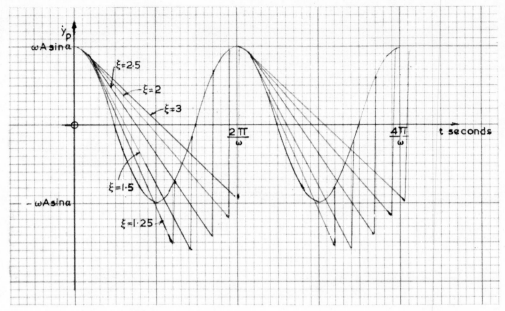

7 - Graph (b)(iii)

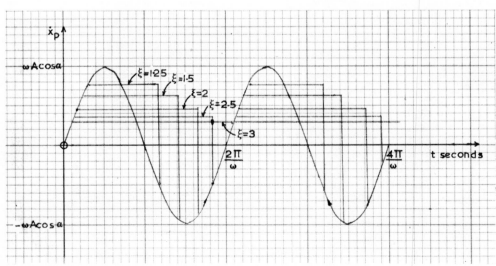

8 - Graph (b)(iv)

223

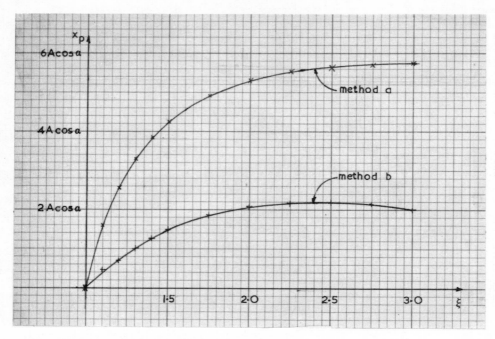

9 — Graph of x_p against ξ for
both methods of excitation

10. *Conclusions*

Within the range of values of ξ considered, it would appear that method (a) vibrations are more suitable for the conveying of particles, and method (b) vibrations are more suitable for the screening operations.

From graphs (a)(iv) and (b)(iv), for values of ξ less than about $2\frac{1}{2}$ the relative velocity between particle and conveyor at impact are high; it would appear that (for low values of ξ) the possible effects of friction could profitably be added to the simulation for further investigation.

Graphs (a)(iii) and (b)(iii) are the same (as could have been expected). From them, consideration of relative normal velocities at impact suggests that the possible effects of semi-elastic impact could profitably be added to the simulation for further investigation.

Note that additional amplifiers will be needed for the inclusion of friction and/or semi-elastic impact in the simulation; this in turn will call for a larger capacity machine than the standard SCD-10.

A point of interest which arose during the computation concerned the comparator elements B2 and B3 (see Figure 237). It might be thought that a small negative bias would be needed to hold B3 in the zero state when the particle and the conveyor are in contact (i.e., total input to B3 theoretically zero), otherwise B3 would be in an unstable condition. In practice, such a bias was not found to be necessary - probably because the output of B2 when nominally zero was in fact of the order of $-\frac{1}{2}$ V (see Chapter 14). Assuming the presence of this $-\frac{1}{2}$ V bias, B3 would be held properly at zero until $y_p - y_c$ (scaled) became less than $-\frac{1}{2}$ V.

ACCURACY OF RESULTS

The presence of the $-\frac{1}{2}$ V bias just referred to would result in a contribution to solution errors, due to the time needed for the input to B3 to reach zero after the moment when $y_p = y_c$ (this time will depend on the rate of change of $y_p - y_c$). A further contribution to error is made by the comparator and relay switching times; with the relay actually used, the total switching time was of the order of 10 msec.

The combination of these errors in time results in an error in displacement which shows up on graphs (a)(i) and (b)(i) as a spurious penetration of the conveyor surface by the particle; we have

$$\text{Total } computer \text{ time error} = 0.01 + \frac{0.005}{\dfrac{d}{d\tau}\left(\dfrac{y_p - y_c}{2A\sin\alpha}\right)} \quad \text{sec} \quad (\tau)$$

$$= 0.01 + \frac{0.005}{\dfrac{1}{\omega}\dfrac{d}{dt}\left(\dfrac{y_p - y_c}{2A\sin\alpha}\right)} \quad \text{sec}$$

$$= 0.01 + \frac{0.005\,\omega\,2A\sin\alpha}{\dot{y}_p - \dot{y}_c} \quad \text{sec}$$

$$= 0.01\left\{1 + \frac{1}{\left(\dfrac{\dot{y}_p - \dot{y}_c}{\omega A\sin\alpha}\right)}\right\} \quad \text{sec}$$

Evidently the quantity $\left(\dfrac{\dot{y}_p - \dot{y}_c}{\omega A \sin\alpha}\right)$ may be obtained, for various values of ξ, from either graph (a)(iii) or graph (b)(iii). Tabulating results,

Table 3:

ξ	$\left\|\left(\dfrac{\dot{y}_p - \dot{y}_c}{\omega A \sin\alpha}\right)\right\|$	Reciprocals of previous column	Total computer time error (τ sec)
3	1.90	0.526	0.015
$2\frac{1}{2}$	2.15	0.465	0.015
2	2.00	0.500	0.015
$1\frac{1}{2}$	1.35	0.741	0.017
$1\frac{1}{4}$	0.75	1.333	0.023

As can be seen from Figure 237, the error in the output of amplifier A5 will be the result of integrating $\left(-\dfrac{\dot{y}_p}{\omega A \sin\alpha}\right)$[PA5] over the period of the total computer time error.

Taking $\left(-\dfrac{\dot{y}_p}{\omega A \sin\alpha}\right)$ as approximately constant during this very short period, we have:

Error in $\left\|\left(\dfrac{y_p}{2A\sin\alpha}\right)\right\| \simeq \left\{\text{value of } \left\|\left(\dfrac{\dot{y}_p}{\omega A\sin\alpha}\right)\right\|\right\}$[PA5]$\{\text{computer time error}\}$

Table 4:

ξ	$\left\|\left(\dfrac{\dot{y}_p}{\omega A \sin\alpha}\right)\right\|$ (from graph (a)(iii))	Total computer time error	Final error in $\|y_p\|$ methods (a) & (b)
3	0.95	0.015	0.014$A\sin\alpha$
$2\frac{1}{2}$	1.16	0.015	0.017$A\sin\alpha$
2	1.40	0.015	0.021$A\sin\alpha$
$1\frac{1}{2}$	1.62	0.017	0.028$A\sin\alpha$
$1\frac{1}{4}$	1.58	0.023	0.036$A\sin\alpha$

Similarly,

Error in $\left\|\left(\dfrac{x_p}{10A\cos\alpha}\right)\right\| \simeq \left\{\text{value of } \left\|\left(\dfrac{\dot{x}_p}{\omega A\cos\alpha}\right)\right\|\right\}$[PA4]$\{\text{computer time error}\}$

Table 5

ξ	$\left\|\left(\dfrac{\dot{x}_p}{\omega A\cos\alpha}\right)\right\|$ (from graph (a)(iv))	Total computer time error	Final error in $\|x_p\|$ method (a)
3	0.96	0.015	$0.014A\cos\alpha$
$2\frac{1}{2}$	0.94	0.015	$0.014A\cos\alpha$
2	0.88	0.015	$0.013A\cos\alpha$
$1\frac{1}{2}$	0.76	0.017	$0.013A\cos\alpha$
$1\frac{1}{4}$	0.60	0.023	$0.014A\cos\alpha$

Table 6

ξ	$\left\|\left(\dfrac{\dot{x}_p}{\omega A\cos\alpha}\right)\right\|$ (from graph (b)(iv))	Total computer time error	Final error in $\|x_p\|$ method (b)
3	0.80	0.015	$0.012A\cos\alpha$
$2\frac{1}{2}$	0.68	0.015	$0.010A\cos\alpha$
2	0.50	0.015	$0.008A\cos\alpha$
$1\frac{1}{2}$	0.40	0.017	$0.007A\cos\alpha$
$1\frac{1}{4}$	0.32	0.023	$0.007A\cos\alpha$

It is evident from the final column of tables 4, 5 and 6 that the absolute errors in $\|y_p\|$ and $\|x_p\|$ will depend on A and α for each value of ξ quoted; however, ξ is itself a function of A, α and ω (see p.207), and it is therefore advisable to examine more closely the relationship between these factors. The field-plot of A against α for each value of ξ chosen, which allows for the possible variation in ω in each case, gives Figure 240.

The shaded areas shown in this field-plot are those within which the solution curves are applicable to the given problem. (Inter alia, this shows that the solution curves quoted for $\xi = 3$ are not significant for the ranges of parameter variation as given.)

From examination of that part of the field-plot contained by the problem parameter rectangle, it can be seen that $A\cos\alpha$ will have a maximum within each of the shaded areas when A is at its greatest and α at its least permitted value: similarly, $A\cos\alpha$ will have a minimum within each of the shaded areas when A is at its least and α at its greatest permitted value.

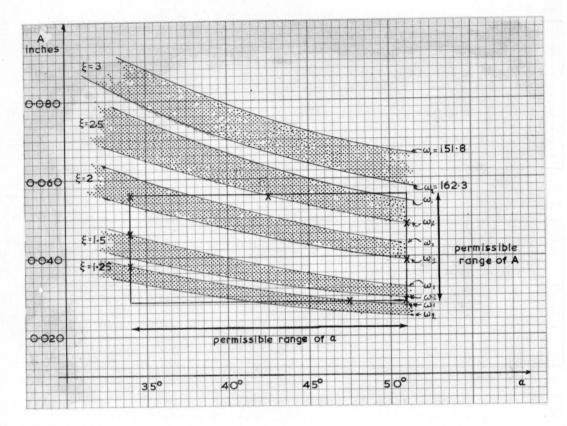

Figure 240

    Tabulating these values from the field-plot,

Table 7

ξ	max. $A\cos\alpha$	min. $A\cos\alpha$
$2\tfrac{1}{2}$	0.042	0.030
2	0.046	0.024
$1\tfrac{1}{2}$	0.038	0.018
$1\tfrac{1}{4}$	0.032	0.020

    Obviously the maximum and minimum values of $A\sin\alpha$ occur on the upper and lower boundaries of the shaded bands, and may in any case be calculated from the relation $A\sin\alpha = g\xi/\omega^2$.

228

Hence:

Table 8

ξ	max. $A\sin\alpha$	min. $A\sin\alpha$
$2\frac{1}{2}$	0.042	0.038
2	0.034	0.030
$1\frac{1}{2}$	0.026	0.022
$1\frac{1}{4}$	0.021	0.019

If the results of table 7 are combined with those of tables 5 and 6, and the results of table 8 with those of table 4, final errors in $|x_p|$ and $|y_p|$ can be tabulated:

Table 9

ξ	Maximum error, in inches		
	$|y_p|$ both methods	$|x_p|$ method (*a*)	$|x_p|$ method (*b*)
$2\frac{1}{2}$	0.0007	0.0006	0.0004
2	0.0007	0.0006	0.0003
$1\frac{1}{2}$	0.0007	0.0005	0.0003
$1\frac{1}{4}$	0.0008	0.0004	0.0002

ξ	Minimum error, in inches		
	$|y_p|$ both methods	$|x_p|$ method (*a*)	$|x_p|$ method (*b*)
$2\frac{1}{2}$	0.0006	0.0004	0.0003
2	0.0006	0.0003	0.0002
$1\frac{1}{2}$	0.0006	0.0002	0.0001
$1\frac{1}{4}$	0.0007	0.0003	0.0001

Since these errors arise from the sources likely to produce the greatest computational errors, it may be taken that the results obtained are likely to be within the nominal accuracy specified (see para 8, p.199).

The authors wish to acknowledge the assistance given by Mr. R. A. Billett, B.Sc., of the School of Engineering, University of Bath, who acted as the ideal problem-poser throughout the formulation of the example given in this chapter.

EDUCTION AND BIBLIOGRAPHY

Most modern analogue computers contain not only the analogue elements discussed in this book but also a selection of parallel logic devices (such as AND and OR gates, digital timers, etc.) together with track-hold elements and logic controlled solid state switches. With such a machine it is possible to store the result of a single point value from one computation for use in a subsequent computer run, and indeed to programme a whole sequence of computer runs with automatic parameter variation or optimization. Such methods greatly extend the power of the analogue computer in the fields of control system optimization, the solution of boundary value problems, and the location of stability boundaries of differential equations.

A hybrid computer is formed by the joining together of an analogue computer and a serial digital computer, through a suitable interface. Such an interface usually consists of a means of altering pot settings, the reading of the analogue computer element outputs, and controlling the mode of the integrators either collectively or as individual units from the digital computer. By adding to the interface analogue-to-digital and digital-to-analogue converters, problem data may also be exchanged between the two machines. In this way the human operator can almost be replaced by the digital computer, resulting in higher efficiency of analogue computer usage, albeit with a protracted programming phase.

Other aspects of analogue computing of importance to the student wishing to pursue the subject further are the stability of algebraic loops and the study of accuracy and errors. Both the accuracy of the computing equipment itself, and that of the mathematical models used, require careful appraisal in order to estimate the accuracy of a solution and its sensitivity to variation of or errors in the parameters.

Although none of the above facilities and techniques have been discussed in this book, the student who has read and worked through these pages with any thoroughness is now in a position to study these more advanced topics.

The following book list will act as a guide to the reader intent on pursuing further his analogue studies, and while by no means exhaustive, it comprises a 'short list' of books the majority of which should be found on the shelves of most University and Technical College libraries:

230

1. Ashley, R. J., *Introduction to Analog Computation*, Wiley.
2. Bekey and Karplus, *Hybrid Computation*, Wiley.
3. Eterman, I. I., *Analogue Computers*, Pergamon Press.
4. Fifer, S., *Analogue Computation (Vols.I to IV)*, McGraw-Hill.
5. Gilbert, C. P., *The Design and Use of Electronic Analog Computers*, Chapman and Hall.
6. Harris, D. J., *Analogue and Digital Computer Methods*, Temple Press.
7. Hartley, M., *An Introduction to Electronic Analogue Computers*, Methuen.
8. Howe, R., *Design Fundamentals of Analogue Computer Components*, van Nostrand.
9. Huskey, H. D. and Korn, G. A., *Computer Handbook*, McGraw-Hill.
10. Hyndman, D. E., *Analog and Hybrid Computing*, Pergamon Press.
11. Jackson, A. S., *Analog Computation*, McGraw-Hill.
12. Karplus, W. J., *Analog Simulation*, McGraw-Hill.
13. Karplus, W. J. and Soroka, W. W., *Analog Methods*, McGraw-Hill.
14. Key, K., *Analogue Computing for Beginners*, Chapman and Hall.
15. Korn, G. A. and Korn, T. M., *Analog and Hybrid Computers*, McGraw-Hill.
16. Levine, L., *Methods of Solving Engineering Problems using Analog Computers*, McGraw-Hill.
17. Mackay, D. M. and Fisher, M. E., *Analogue Computing at Ultra High Speed*, Chapman and Hall.
18. Rogers, A. E. and Connolly, T. W., *Analog Computation in Engineering Design*, McGraw-Hill.
19. Smith, G. W. and Wood, R. C., *Principles of Analog Computation*, McGraw-Hill.
20. Tomovic, R. and Karplus, W. J., *High Speed Analog Computers*, Wiley.
21. Warfield, J. N., *Introduction to Electronic Analog Computers*, Prentice-Hall.
22. Williams, R. W., *Analogue Computation Techniques and Components*, Heywood.
23. Jean-Jacques Gleitz, *Le Calcul Analogique*, Presses Universitaires de France.

In writing this book the authors have set out, with deliberate intent, to lay only the foundations of a systematic approach to analogue computing programming; they have proved from their own experience (and to their own satisfaction, at any rate!) that the use of a systematic approach of the kind which has been emphasized throughout this book, pays handsome dividends when the good computing habits so engendered are maintained in the more advanced topics - dividends in terms of confidence in one's ability to foresee and to obviate trouble, dividends in terms of time saved, and last but not least, dividends in terms of reliable and meaningful solutions to the problems being studied.

MISCELLANEOUS EXAMPLES FOR PROGRAMMING

(a) Linear problems

(1)   Solve $\ddot{y} + 50\ddot{y} + 1400\dot{y} + 10000y = 20000$

     given (i) $\ddot{y} = \dot{y} = 0,\ y = 2$ when $t = 0$
         (ii) $\ddot{y} = \dot{y} = y = 0$ when $t = 0$

(2)   A certain second-order system was set up for computation using the flow diagram shown:

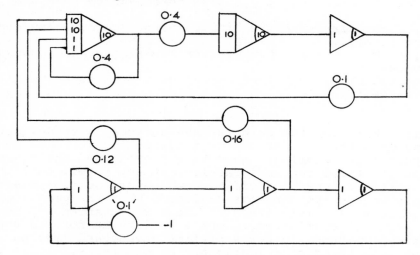

When the computer is run, an overload is observed. Assuming that unity time-scale ($\beta = 1$) is used, write down the differential equation for the system; give reasons for the overload referred to, and produce more suitable pot settings for the same flow diagram. Run the correctly scaled version on the machine, and hence solve the equation.

232

(3) For the mass/spring system shown, in which λ_1, λ_2 are the spring stiffnesses, show that the equations of motion are

$$M_1\ddot{x} = \lambda_2(y - x) - \lambda_1 x \Big\}$$
$$M_2\ddot{y} = -\lambda_2(y - x) \Big\}$$

where x, y are the vertical displacements of M_1, M_2 from their equilibrium positions.

Solve the equations for the case in which $M_1 = \lambda_2 = \frac{1}{3}\lambda_1$ and $M_2 = \frac{1}{4}\lambda_2$, given that initially $x = 0.1$ m, $y = 0.2$ m, $\dot{x} = 0.2$ ms^{-1} and $\dot{y} = 0.4$ ms^{-1}. Show that each mass will move with pure s.h.m. at any time $t > 0$; estimate the period of oscillation and demonstrate that $y = 2x$.

(4) Solve $\ddot{x} = n\dot{y}$ $\Big\}$ where a, n are positive constants, and
        $\ddot{y} = a - n\dot{x}$ $\Big\}$ given that $x = y = \dot{x} = \dot{y} = 0$ when $t = 0$

Plot y against x, over at least two cycles of the wave-form.

(5) Plot the envelope of the straight line $y = mx + \frac{a}{m}$ as m varies.

(6) By generating suitable parametric forms on an analogue computer, plot the asteroid

$$x^{2/3} + y^{2/3} = a^2$$

for (i) $a = 1/\sqrt{2}$ (ii) $a = 1$ (iii) $a = \sqrt{2}$.

(7) A system of concentric ellipses is such that the axes of symmetry of the ellipses lie along the co-ordinate axes, and for every ellipse of the system the sum of the lengths of the major and minor axes is constant. Use an analogue computer to plot the envelope of such a system in the case when this constant is 2.

(8)   A servo-mechanism has the characteristic equation

$$(D^3 + kD^2 + 25D + 100)[\theta_0] = \theta_i$$

Using a step input $\theta_i = 50.H(t)$ investigate the stability of the system for different values of k.

(9)   Simulate the transfer function

$$\frac{(1 + 6s)}{(s^2 + 4s + 25)}$$

and find the resonant frequency and the magnitude of maximum gain of the system.

(10) Simulate the system whose transfer functions are:

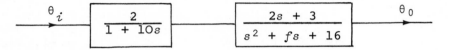

Programme so that the design parameter f can be varied over the range $2 \leqslant f \leqslant 8$ without any re-patching, and such that the arithmetic transformation relating the value of f to the relevant pot setting is a simple one.

(11) Simulate $\dfrac{s(1 + 5s)}{(1 + 3s)(1 + 10s)}$ and use the computer to obtain the gain/frequency curve for $0.05 < \omega < 5$ rad s^{-1}.

(12) Simulate the transfer function

$$\frac{2s^2 + 4s + 20}{(1 + sT)(s^2 + 12\zeta s + 36)}$$

and arrange the simulation so that the design parameters ζ and T may each be varied by a single potentiometer. Plot step response curves for the system for various combinations of ζ and T, in the ranges $0 < \zeta < 1$ and $0.2 < T < 0.5$.

(13) A certain type of microphone consists basically of two parallel discs, one fixed and one moving, with a small air gap between them. In one example the moving disc is of mass 10 g and the air gap is 1.4 mm wide; motion of the moving disc towards or away from the fixed disc is resisted by the mounting, which provides a restoring force of 5×10^4 Nm^{-1}, and there is also inherent velocity damping of 20 Nm^{-1}s. It is found that the microphone gives a distorted output when the deflection of the moving disc from its equilibrium position exceeds 1.2 mm (in either direction).
The microphone is subjected to a "test" sound wave which applies a force $50\cos\omega t$ newton, normal to the moving disc. It is required to find the values of ω (input frequency) which the microphone will accept without producing a distorted output.

Show that the equation of motion for the moving disc, when all units have been made consistent, reduces to the form

$$\ddot{x} + 2000\dot{x} + 5\,000\,000x = 5000\cos\omega t$$

Programme this problem for analogue computer solution.

(14) A mass-spring system is arranged as shown:

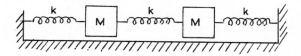

Each mass (M) is 1 kg; spring stiffness $K = 1250$ Nm^{-1} in each case and each spring is of natural length 0.25 m. Velocity damping is applied to both masses, the left-hand mass being damped by a force $\lambda_1 \times$ (velocity) and the right-hand mass by a force $\lambda_2 \times$ (velocity). In the equilibrium position all the springs are at their natural length. Investigate the motion of each mass in the following cases:

(a) $\lambda_1 = \lambda_2 = 30$ Nm^{-1}s, and the left-hand mass initially displaced 100 mm to the left.

(b) As case (a), except that $\lambda_2 = 15$ Nm^{-1}s.

(c) As case (a), except that $\lambda_2 = 60$ Nm^{-1}s.

(d) As case (a), except that both masses are initially displaced 100 mm to the left.

(15) A mass of 1 kg is suspended from a fixed support by a spring of stiffness 2000 Nm^{-1}. A second mass of 5 kg is suspended from the 1 kg mass by a spring of stiffness 5000 Nm^{-1}. The system is set in motion from the equilibrium position by giving the 5 kg mass an initial vertical velocity of 3.6 ms^{-1}. Use an analogue computer to examine the subsequent motion of the system.
A single viscous damper is available, with damping coefficient 100 Nm^{-1}s; examine the effect on the motion, and on the force transmitted to the fixed support, in the cases where this damper is connected between

(a) the 1 kg mass and the fixed support,
(b) the 5 kg mass and the fixed support,
(c) the two masses.

(16) A uniform light shaft of torsional rigidity 0.6 Nm^{2}rad^{-1} is mounted in ball-bearings offering negligible frictional resistance, and has three flywheels keyed to it. The flywheels are uniform discs each of diameter 0.25 m; the outer wheels are each of mass 0.45 kg, the centre wheel is of mass 0.90 kg, and the distance between the centre wheel and each outer wheel is 0.5 m.

If θ, ϕ, and ψ are the angular displacements of the wheels from their mean positions, show that the equations of motion are

$$I_1\ddot{\theta} = - 1.2(\theta - \phi)$$
$$I_2\ddot{\phi} = - 1.2(\phi - \theta) - 1.2(\phi - \psi)$$
$$I_1\ddot{\psi} = - 1.2(\psi - \phi)$$

where I_1 is the moment of inertia of each outer wheel and I_2 that of the centre wheel, about the shaft axis.
Plot the angular displacements of each wheel against time in the cases when

(a) the centre wheel is initially displaced and then released,
(b) one outer wheel is initially displaced and then released.

Investigate the effect in case (a) of keeping one of the outer wheels clamped, and in case (b) of keeping clamped the outer wheel with no initial displacement.

(17) A motor-alternator weighs 4 cwt, and when running "light" produces an out of balance oscillatory force in a vertical direction, of $12\sin 20\pi t$ lbf. Use an analogue computer to obtain a recommendation for the spring rate to be used in a spring suspension system (with negligible damping), so that the vibration forces transmitted to the floor shall be only one-tenth of those encountered when the machine is bolted directly to the floor.

(18) One of the electronic instruments formerly used in a certain type of naval M.T.B. was of mass 9 kg, and was mounted at a point in the hull liable to vibration of up to 2.5 mm amplitude and of frequency 45 Hz when the vessel was under way and at cruising speed. The instrument was attached to its frame by suspension springs whose total stiffness was 1.05×10^5 Nm^{-1}, damping being negligible.
After the vessel had been in service for some time, the instrument was replaced by a new transistorized unit of only 2.25 kg mass; this was hurriedly fitted to the old frame, using the original suspension springs. In service, the new unit immediately gave trouble, caused by undue vibration.
Use an analogue computer to

(a) find the amplitudes of vibration of the old and the new units;
(b) obtain a recommendation for new suspension springs with a stiffness such that the new unit experiences no worse a vibration amplitude than did the old unit;
(c) obtain a recommendation, if possible, for retaining the old suspension springs but incorporating velocity damping, such that the new unit experiences no worse a vibration amplitude than did the old unit.

236

(19) Two masses, one of 1 kg and the other of 2 kg, are connected by a light spring of stiffness 64 Nm^{-1}. The system is placed on a horizontal table so that the 2 kg mass touches a fixed barrier, with the line of the spring perpendicular to the barrier. The 1 kg mass is then moved along the table towards the 2 kg mass, thus compressing the spring to a length 10 cm less than its natural length; the system is then released and allowed to move freely. The 1 kg mass is mounted on low-friction wheels offering negligible resistance to motion, but the 2 kg mass is subject to viscous damping of 5 $Nm^{-1}s$. Taking $t = 0$ as the moment at which the spring first regains its natural length, and displacements x and y of the 1 kg and 2 kg masses respectively as being both zero at that moment, show that the mathematical model of the system for $t \geqslant 0$ reduces to the equations

$$\left. \begin{array}{l} \ddot{x} = -64(x - y) \\[2mm] \ddot{y} = 32(x - y) - \dfrac{5}{2}\dot{y} \end{array} \right\} \qquad \begin{array}{l} \text{with } x_0 = y_0 = \dot{y}_0 = 0, \text{ and} \\[2mm] \dot{x}_0 = +0.8 \text{ ms}^{-1} \end{array}$$

Programme the problem for analogue computation, assuming that

(a) $|x_{max}| < 0.2$ m   and $|y_{max}| < 0.2$ m

(b) read-out of results will be done using an X/Y plotter, and

(c) not more than five amplifiers are to be committed (apart from a time-base).

(20) An internal combustion engine of mass M_1 rests at the centre of a test bed which may be considered as a beam of span d, simply supported at the ends, and with flexural rigidity EI. The equation of motion for small vertical displacements of the engine is

$$M_1\ddot{y} + \frac{48EI}{d^3}y = f(t)$$

where $f(t)$ is vertical disturbing force.
If the engine has stroke $2a$, and the mass of the reciprocating parts is M_2, and if it may be assumed that these parts move with approximate s.h.m., show that when the engine is running at n rev/min it will be subjected to a disturbing force

$$f(t) = \frac{\pi^2 n^2 a M_2}{900} \sin \frac{\pi n}{30} t$$

Put this problem on an analogue computer for the case of an engine of mass 220.5 kg, with a stroke of 150 mm, and whose reciprocating parts are of mass 14.5 kg. The test bed is 1.83 m long and has a beam constant of 1.24×10^6 Nm^2.

(a) Find the range of rev/min over which it would be dangerous to run the engine on this rig, considering vertical deflections of amplitude $\geqslant 75$ mm as dangerous.

(b) If the test bed has 1 m clearance between engine sump and test shop floor, and a large spring balance of stiffness 1.46×10^5 Nm^{-1} and 0.3 m overall length is hung below the sump, find what mass should be attached to the spring to form a dynamic vibration absorber (DVA) which would allow the engine to be tested safely within the otherwise dangerous range of rev/min found in (*a*) above.

(*c*) Use the computer to experiment with the addition of viscous damping to the DVA of (*b*) above, either by adding the damper between the engine and the DVA, or between the engine and the test shop floor; use the computer to optimize the system as far as possible - i.e. to find recommendations for both DVA and damper which will allow 'safe' engine vibrations over as wide a range of rev/min as possible.

(21) The diagram represents a VTOL aircraft about to land with uniform vertical velocity (i.e. vertical thrust from motors = all-up weight of the aircraft). The three wheels and struts of the tricycle undercarriage are identical and are therefore represented in the diagram as a single unit. The total mass of the aircraft is 4100 kg, of which the whole undercarriage accounts for 150 kg. The combined spring stiffness of the struts (K_1) is 6.29×10^4 Nm^{-1} and that of the tyres (K_2) is 1.45×10^5 Nm^{-1}.

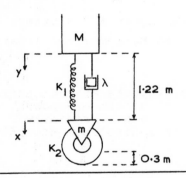

It is desired to find the optimum value of strut damping (λ Nm^{-1}s) so that the vertical landing speed of the aircraft should be as great as possible without either compressing the tyres to their rims (allow 0.3 m) or forcing the struts to "bottom" by running them to the limit of their travel (allow 1.22 m). Assume that the motors are "cut" as the aircraft first touches down, and that vertical thrust then diminishes exponentially with time, with time-constant 1 sec.
Solve the problem using an analogue computer, estimating optimum strut damping and maximum permissible landing speed. If the investigation shows that one of the design parameters has been badly chosen, use the computer to obtain a recommendation for its improvement; then find new values for optimum strut damping and maximum permissible landing speed when using the recommended design change.
By investigating chassis accelerations as well, obtain final recommendations for a general 'engineering optimum' set of parameter values which will allow reasonably high landing speeds without at the same time placing undue stresses on tyres, struts, or the occupants of the aircraft.

(22) A pendulum consists of a bob of mass M at the end of a light rod of length ℓ; the point of suspension is constrained to move horizontally under the action of two light springs, each of stiffness k, as shown in the diagram:

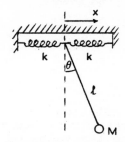

Using the method of Lagrange's equations, or otherwise, obtain the equations of motion of the system, and show that when θ is small these equations can be reduced to:

$$M\ddot{x} + M\ell\ddot{\theta} = -2kx$$
$$\ddot{x} + \ell\ddot{\theta} = -g\theta$$

Programme an analogue computer to solve these equations and at the same time to find the length of the simple equivalent pendulum of the system, in the case where

$$M = 20 \text{ g} \qquad \ell = 16 \text{ cm} \qquad \text{and} \quad k = 750 \text{ dynes cm}^{-1}$$

(23) An inductance of 0.3 henries is in series with a resistance of 100 ohms. The circuit is driven by an oscillatory 50 Hz voltage with peak value 300 volts.
Show that the current i which flows in the circuit at time t is governed by a differential equation of the form

$$\frac{di}{dt} + \frac{1000}{3}i = 1000\sin 100\pi t$$

Solve this on an analogue computer and estimate the peak value of the current flowing in the circuit in the steady state. If the 50 Hz voltage is applied to the circuit at time $t = 0$, estimate the time taken for the current to reach the steady state value.

(24) In the circuit shown, the resistance is variable ($100\Omega \leqslant R \leqslant 1 \text{ k}\Omega$). Initially the potential difference across the capacitor is 200 volts and there is no current flowing. The switch is then closed: find the charge on the capacitor at any subsequent time, taking case (i) $R = 100\Omega$, case (ii) $R = 500\Omega$, case (iii) $R = 1 \text{ k}\Omega$.

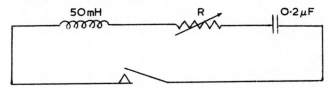

(25) An oscillatory voltage of 10 kV (peak) and frequency 1.592 kHz is applied across the terminals A and B of the circuit shown in the diagram. The variable capacitor in this circuit has capacitance which may be varied over the range 0.01 µF $\leqslant C \leqslant$ 0.1 µF.

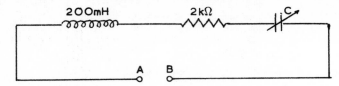

Programme the problem for analogue computer solution and hence find whether or not it is possible to tune the circuit to the applied voltage as given; if it is, estimate the value of C required.

(26) Two coils with self-inductance L_1 and L_2 are coupled as shown so that their mutual inductance is M. The capacitors in series with each one are C_1 and C_2, and at any time t the charges on the capacitors are q_1 and q_2, while the branch currents are respectively i_1 and i_2.

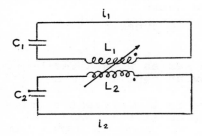

The coils are wound in the same sense so that the voltage equations for the system are

$$L_1 \frac{di_1}{dt} + M \frac{di_2}{dt} + \frac{q_1}{C_1} = 0$$

$$L_2 \frac{di_2}{dt} + M \frac{di_1}{dt} + \frac{q_2}{C_2} = 0$$

Derive the corresponding equations in terms of charge q_1 and q_2 and solve on an analogue computer for the following case:

$L_1 = M = 5$ mH $\qquad L_2 = 15$ mH

$C_1 = 0.05$ µF $\qquad C_2 = 0.1$ µF

$i_1 = i_2 = q_1 = 0$ and $q_2 = 10^{-5}$ coulombs, when $t = 0$.

(27) A sample of polluted water contains three different types of
bacteria, which show different degrees of resistance to the
germicidal action of a certain disinfectant. In laboratory
tests at a uniform temperature of 15 K, 50% of type I bacteria,
30% of type II and 20% of type III are destroyed by the end of
one hour of treatment; 75% of type I, 51% of type II and 36%
of type III are destroyed by the end of two hours of treatment.
The initial populations of the bacteria in the sample of water
are:

   Type I 6.8×10^{11} per litre

   Type II 2.9×10^{11} per litre

   Type III 9.3×10^{10} per litre

Find the population of each type as a function of time; plot
all three on the same pair of graph axes (a) as absolute values
(i.e. same population scale for all three types); (b) as %
values (i.e. each population commencing at 100%).
Find the total number of surviving bacteria at any time (a) as
an absolute value, (b) as a percentage. Determine the period
of treatment required to reduce the total number of surviving
bacteria to < 1% of the original total level.
At what time after commencement of treatment are the populations
of more than one type equal in number?

(28) A certain radio-active series of elements has three basic
members A, B and C; A decays into B with a half-life of 15
days, B decays into C with a half-life of 36 days, while the
third member C is stable. A given sample of A is manufactured
and initially contains 6.8×10^{12} atoms, the number of atoms
of B and C present being negligibly small.
Use an analogue computer to plot the number of atoms of the
three kinds of member present at any subsequent time, and find
at what time the number of B atoms reaches a maximum.

   Note: "half-life" refers to the time taken by a quantity of
radio-active substance to decay exponentially to half the
number of atoms originally present.

(b)   Examples requiring non-linear computing methods

(1)   Solve the equation $\ddot{\phi} + k\dot{\phi} + 3\sin\phi = 1$, given that $\phi = \pi/3$ and $\dot{\phi} = 0$ at $t = 0$, for values of k in the range $0.1 \leqslant k \leqslant 0.5$. Plot phase-plane diagrams ($\dot{\phi}$ against ϕ) for each value of k examined.

(2)   The equation of motion for a certain synchronous motor may be taken as:

$$\ddot{\theta} + \dot{\theta} + 30\sin\theta = 40T$$

where θ is the rotor angle relative to an axis rotating at synchronous speed and T Nm is the external load torque. It is required to investigate the transient effect on θ of known changes of load in the range $0 \leqslant T \leqslant 1$; carry out this investigation using an analogue computer.

(3)   Mathieu's equation incorporating velocity damping can be put in the form:

$$\ddot{x} + 2\lambda\dot{x} + (p^2 - 2a\sin\omega t)x = 0$$

Solve this equation for values of λ in the range $0.2 \leqslant \lambda \leqslant 1$ in the case where $p = 3$, $a = 1.5$, $\omega = 3$, and given that $\dot{x} = 0$, $x = 8$ at $t = 0$.

(4)   Investigate the solution of the equation:

$$\ddot{x} - \varepsilon(1 - x^2 - \dot{x}^2)\dot{x} + x = 0$$

given that $\dot{x} = 0$, $x = \frac{1}{2}$ at $t = 0$.

Take various values of ε in the range $0 \leqslant \varepsilon \leqslant 5$, and examine the phase-plane plot ($\dot{x}$ against x) in each case taken.

(5)   Solve van der Pol's equation:

$$\ddot{x} - \varepsilon(1 - x^2)\dot{x} + x = 0 \qquad \text{given that } \dot{x} = x = 0 \text{ at } t = 0$$

for various values of ε in the range $0 \leqslant \varepsilon \leqslant 5$.
For the case $\varepsilon = 2$, examine the effect on the phase-plane locus of taking non-zero initial conditions on $\dot{x}$, on x, and on both $\dot{x}$ and x.

(6)   Programme an analogue computer to plot the function $\sin x/x$ over the interval $1 \geqslant x > 0$, avoiding the use of division circuits and taking care to provide a stable computer set-up.

242

(7)   To find $y = \int_a^b \ln x \; dx$, we could solve the equation

$$\frac{dy}{dx} = \ln x \qquad\qquad\qquad\qquad\qquad \text{(i)}$$

with boundary conditions related to the limits of integration. Now, as $x \to 0$ from above, the function $\ln x$ is unbounded, but the function $x\ln x$ is bounded. This suggests that equation (i) might be rewritten in the form

$$\frac{dy}{dx} = \frac{x\ln x}{x} \qquad\qquad\qquad\qquad \text{(ii)}$$

Using variable time-scaling, reduce equation (ii) to a set of linear first-order differential equations, avoiding the use of division circuits, and hence use an analogue computer to plot the function

$$\int_0^1 \ln x \; dx$$

(8)   A circle in the (complex) z-plane, with centre in the first quadrant at (h,k), passes through the point $(-1,0)$. The conformal transform

$$w = az + \frac{b}{z}$$

will transform this circle into a Joukowski aerofoil in the complex w-plane. Programme an analogue computer to plot the aerofoil for the parameter values $a = b = 1$, $h = 0.4$, and $k = 0.25$; and investigate the effects on the shape of the aerofoil of making small changes in the values of each parameter in turn.

(9)   Solve the equations:

$$\left.\begin{array}{l} \dot{x} + y + z = 1 \\[2mm] x + \dot{y} + z = e^t\{H(t) - H(t - 1)\} \\[2mm] x + y + \dot{z} = 0 \end{array}\right\}$$

given that $x = y = z = 0$ at $t = 0$.
$\dot{x}$, $\dot{y}$, and $\dot{z}$ are not required as outputs, and x, y, z should be plotted against t over the interval $0 \leqslant t \leqslant 3$.

(10) A certain system has the instrument equation:

$$\{D^3 + (1 + 10\lambda)D^2 + (100 + 10\lambda)D + 400\} \; \theta_0 = 200\theta_i$$

where λ is a design parameter. Use an analogue computer to find what restriction(s) must be placed on the value of λ to ensure the stability of the system.
Taking the case $\lambda = 1$, plot the response of the system (θ_0) to an input signal (θ_i) consisting of a unit rectangular pulse starting at $t = 0$ and ending at time $t = 1$.

(11) The motion of a simple pendulum swinging freely in one plane through large amplitudes, and subject to viscous damping, can be represented by the equation

$$Mr\ddot{\theta} + f\dot{\theta} + Mg\sin\theta = 0$$

where θ is the angle of displacement from the stable equilibrium position.
In a given case, $M = 0.2$ kg, $r = 0.2$ m, and $f = 0.006$ Nm^{-1}s. Initially the pendulum is held stationary and such that $\theta = 50^{\circ}$, and the bob is then released. Use an analogue computer to obtain plots of θ against t and θ against $\dot{\theta}$.

(12) The Lane-Emden equation of order 2, occurring in astronomical physics, can be normalized in the form

$$\frac{d^2y}{dx^2} + \frac{2}{x}\frac{dy}{dx} + y^2 = 0$$

where $y = 1$ and $dy/dx = 0$ when $x = 0$.
Solve this equation over the interval $0 \leqslant x \leqslant 5$ using an analogue computer, taking particular care that the computation will commence with the correct initial values.

(13) A long uniform chain lies coiled on a shelf which is 4 m above ground level. One end of the chain is led up to and over a small pulley 1 m above the edge of the shelf, so that a length of 2 m of chain hangs freely on the other side of the pulley. The chain is then released from rest, and is subject to the equation of motion

$$(x + 1)\ddot{x} + (\dot{x})^2 = (x - 1)g$$

where x is the distance of the free end of the chain below the pulley at time t.
Use an analogue computer to examine the motion of the chain up to the time at which the free end first strikes the ground. Use a programme which permits acceleration, as well as velocity and displacement, to be available as an output.

(14) The equations of motion in the (x,y) plane for an electron under the action of an electric field in the plane and a magnetic field perpendicular to the plane may be taken as

$$M\ddot{x} = e(E_x + B\dot{y})$$
$$M\ddot{y} = e(E_y - B\dot{x})$$

where M is the mass of the electron, e the charge on it, E_x and E_y the x and y components of the electric field, and B the magnetic flux density of the magnetic field; e/M may be taken as 1.76×10^{11} Ckg^{-1}.
Use an analogue computer to plot the electron trajectories in the (x,y) plane in the following cases:

(a) $E_x = E_y = 0$, $B = 4 \times 10^7$ tesla ($1\ T = 1\ Vsm^{-2}$) and initial electron velocity is $10^8\ ms^{-1}$ in the x-direction only;

(b) as in (a) except that $E_x = 6 \times 10^7\ Vm^{-1}$;

(c) as in (a) except that $E_y = 6 \times 10^7\ Vm^{-1}$;

(d) as in (a) except that $E_x = 6 \times 10^7 \sin\omega t$, $E_y = 6 \times 10^7 \cos\omega t$

(i.e., a rotating electric field), taking frequencies 2000, 5000 and 8000 MHz in turn;

(e) as in (a) except that $E_x = 6 \times 10^7 (0.1 - 0.04y^2)$,

$$E_y = 6 \times 10^7 (0.1 - 0.04x^2)$$

(15) The system shown in the diagram lies in a horizontal plane and is initially at rest with the piston (mass M_1) at the mid-point of the closed dash-pot cylinder D. The internal length of D is 170 mm, the length of the piston is 50 mm, and the ends of the dash-pot cylinder are of virtually inelastic material. The stiffness of the spring (K) is such that $\sqrt{(K/M_1)} = 10\ rad\ s^{-1}$ and the mass of the dash-pot cylinder (M_2) can be varied. The dash-pot is filled with fluid so that relative velocity between piston and cylinder is damped by an amount $2M_1\ Nm^{-1}s$.

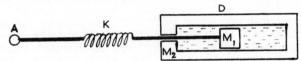

The free end of the spring (A) is then forced to oscillate along the longitudinal axis of the system, with displacement $0.1\sin\omega t$ m. Use an analogue computer to investigate the motions of M_1 and M_2 for various values of M_2 in the range $\frac{1}{2}M_1 \leqslant M_2 \leqslant 2M_1$; in each case examined, taking ω as varying over the range $5 \leqslant \omega \leqslant 15\ rad\ s^{-1}$.

(16) Investigate the responses of the following mass/spring/damper systems to a selection of step inputs $C.H(t)$ in the range $-200\ N \leqslant C \leqslant +200\ N$. In all cases assume that the system is initially at rest in the equilibrium position.

(a) Mass 12 kg, viscous damping 24 $Nm^{-1}s$, spring virtually linear and of stiffness 300 Nm^{-1}.

(b) System as in (a) except that the linear spring is replaced by a *soft* spring which gives a restoring force $(400x - 1600x^3)$ N for a deflection of x m from the equilibrium position.

(c) System as in (a) except that the linear spring is replaced by a *compound* spring which gives a restoring force $(400x - 1600|x|x^2)$ N for a deflection of x m from the equilibrium position.

(d) System as in (a) except that the linear spring is replaced by a compound spring which gives a restoring force $300\sinh x$ N for a deflection of x m from the equilibrium position.

245

(e) System as in (b), but with the addition of inelastic end-stops placed at distances ± 0.2 m from the equilibrium position.

(f) System as in (c), but with the addition of elastic end-stops placed at distances ± 0.2 m from the equilibrium position, and each of spring stiffness 1200 Nm^{-1}.

(g) System as in (d), but with the addition of semi-elastic end-stops placed at distances ± 0.2 m from the equilibrium position, and each of spring stiffness 750 Nm^{-1} and coefficient of restitution 0.4.

Some of the systems described above might be impossible to envisage as models of practical systems; comment on and account for these cases by interpreting the computer results in physical terms.

(17) A mass of 10 kg moves horizontally between a pair of end-stops, the distance between which is 0.4 m. The mass rides on an air bearing so that frictional resistance to motion is negligible. The end-stops are light blocks with coefficient of restitution 0.5 and of spring stiffness 1000 Nm^{-1}. Initially the mass is mid-way between the two end-stops, and is given a velocity $\dot{x}_0$ towards one of them. Simulate the system on an analogue computer and hence find the maximum permissible value of $\dot{x}_0$ such that the displacement x of the mass from its initial position never exceeds ± 275 mm. Using this maximum value of $\dot{x}_0$, obtain plots of x, $\dot{x}$, and force acting on the mass, against time.
Repeat the whole investigation for the case when the supply of air to the air bearing is cut off, taking the coefficient of static friction between the mass and its slide bed as 0.6, and the coefficient of Coulomb friction as 0.4; using the new maximum permissible value of $\dot{x}_0$ for these circumstances, find when and in what position the mass eventually comes to rest.

(18) In a small island community of 850 people, an epidemic is discovered by the resident medical officer. At the time of discovery, 19 people have the disease, 88 are immune, and the remaining 743 are susceptible to catching the disease. Assume that each victim of the disease can infect, on average, one per 500 of the susceptible population each day that he has the disease himself; assume further that after 3½ days (on average) each victim recovers, becomes immune to re-infection, and ceases to be a carrier of the disease.
Use an analogue computer to plot, as functions of time,

(a) the number of susceptible persons (S)
(b) the number of infected victims (V)
(c) the number of recovered, and therefore immune, persons (R)
(d) the rate at which new cases may be expected to occur
$\left(- \dfrac{dS}{dt}, \text{ where } t \text{ is in days}\right).$

Hence estimate (i) the total time, from the discovery, that the epidemic can be expected to last

(ii) the total loss of man-days of work during the epidemic, assuming that the infected victims can work at only approximately one-third of normal efficiency.

For the purposes of this problem, consider the system equations as being

$$\frac{dS}{dt} = -\frac{1}{500} SV$$

$$\frac{dV}{dt} = \frac{1}{500} SV - \frac{V}{3.5}$$

$$\frac{dR}{dt} = \frac{V}{3.5}$$

Reference: Kermack and McKendrick, A contribution to the mathematical theory of epidemics, *Proc. Royal Soc.* (1927) A115, 700.

Also see: Hammond and Tyrrell, A mathematical model of common-cold epidemics on Tristan da Cunha, *J. Hyg., Camb.* (1971) 69, 423;   in which is suggested the better model:

$$\frac{dS}{dt} = -I(SV)$$

$$\frac{dV}{dt} = I(SV) - I\big[V(t-D).S(t-D).H(t-D)\big]$$

$$\frac{dR}{dt} = I\big[V(t-D).S(t-D).H(t-D)\big]$$

where I = infectivity constant, D = average duration of individual infection, and H is the Heaviside (unit step) function.

INDEX